Reconstructing
a Chicano/a Literary Heritage

Reconstructing a Chicano/a Literary Heritage

Hispanic Colonial Literature of the Southwest

Edited by

María Herrera-Sobek

THE UNIVERSITY OF ARIZONA PRESS

Tucson & London

The University of Arizona Press
Copyright © 1993
The Arizona Board of Regents
All Rights Reserved

∞ This book is printed on acid-free, archival-quality paper.
Manufactured in the United States of America

97 96 95 94 93   5 4 3 2 1
Library of Congress Cataloging-in-Publication Data

Reconstructing a Chicano/a literary heritage : Hispanic colonial
    literature of the Southwest / edited by María Herrera-Sobek.
        p.   cm.
    Includes bibliographical references and index.
    ISBN 0-8165-1350-3 (alk. paper)
    1. Spanish American literature—To 1800—History and
criticism.
    2. American literature—Southwest, New—History and criticism.
    I. Herrera-Sobek, María.
    PQ7081.A1R315   1993
    860.9'868—dc20   92-45616
                                                                        CIP

British Cataloguing-in-Publication Data
A catalogue record for this book is available from the British Library.

For Erik Jason Sobek and Joseph George Sobek, Jr.

Contents

Contributors

JUAN BRUCE-NOVOA is Professor of Spanish at the University of California, Irvine. His published works include a book of poetry titled *Inocencia perversa/Perverse Innocence,* a collection of interviews titled *Chicano Authors: Inquiry by Interview,* and the critical works *Chicano Poetry: A Response to Chaos,* and *RetroSpace: Collected Essays on Chicano Literature Theory and History.* He has edited a number of scholarly anthologies. Bruce-Novoa has taught in Germany and at Harvard University, Yale University, Trinity University, and the University of California, Santa Barbara.

RAMÓN GUTIÉRREZ is Professor of History and is the founding chair of the new Ethnic Studies Department at the University of California, San Diego. He is the author of *When Jesus Came, the Corn Mothers Went Away: Marriage, Sexuality, and Power in New Mexico, 1500–1846* (1991) and has published numerous articles in journals. He has lectured extensively in the United States and in Europe.

MARÍA HERRERA-SOBEK is Professor of Spanish at the University of California, Irvine. Her publications include *The Bracero Experience: Elitelore Versus Folklore* (1979), *The Mexican Corrido: A Feminist Analysis* (1990), and *Northward Bound: The Mexican Immigrant Experience in Ballad and Song* (forthcoming); she has edited four critical anthologies: *Beyond Stereotypes: The Critical Analysis of Chicana Literature*

(1985), *Gender and Print Culture: New Perspectives on International Ballad Studies* (1991), *Chicana Creativity and Criticism: Charting New Frontiers in American Literature* (with Helena María Viramontes; 1988), and *Chicana Writes: On Word and Film* (with Viramontes; forthcoming); she has also edited one textbook, with Seymour Menton, *Saga de Mexico* (1992). She is one of three women featured in the poetry collection *Three Times a Woman*. Herrera-Sobek is currently working on a book on *pastorelas*.

ENRIQUE R. LAMADRID is Associate Professor of Spanish at the University of New Mexico in Albuquerque. He is also the director of the Conexiones Institute based in Morelia, Michoacán, Mexico. Lamadrid has published numerous articles on Hispanic folklore. In addition to scholarly articles he has edited *Un ojo en el muro: Mexican Poetry 1970–1985* and *En breve: Minimalism in Mexican Poetry 1900–1985*. He has also produced a three-hour sound track, "Tesoros del Espíritu," for the New Mexican folk culture exhibit at the Museum of International Folk Art in Santa Fe.

LUIS LEAL is Professor Emeritus (University of Illinois), now at the University of California, Santa Barbara, and Visiting Professor of Spanish at Stanford University. Professor Leal is a highly respected scholar honored in both Mexico and the United States. Among his numerous publications are *Mariano Azuela, vida y obra* (1961), *Historia del cuento hispanoamericano* (1966), *Juan Rulfo* (1983), *Aztlán y México* (1985). Professor Leal's extensive published works have been compiled in *Luis Leal: A Bibliography with Interpretative and Critical Essays* (1988). He was honored in 1987 by the National Association of Chicano Studies with the Distinguished Scholar Award, and in 1991 he received the Aztec Eagle, the highest decoration offered by the Mexican government "for outstanding contributions."

FRANCISCO A. LOMELÍ is Professor of Spanish and Chicano Studies at the University of California, Santa Barbara. His publications include *Chicano Perspectives in Literature* (1976) and *La novelística de Carlos Droguett* (1983). He has coedited several anthologies, including *A Decade of Chicano Literature (1970–1979)* (1982), *Chicano Literature:*

A Reference Guide (1985), *Aztlán: Essays on the Chicano Homeland* (1989), and *Dictionary of Literary Biography* (1989).

GENARO PADILLA is Associate Professor of English at the University of California, Berkeley. He edited *The Stories of Fray Angélico Chávez* and has written numerous articles; he is currently finishing a book on the formation of Chicano autobiography.

TEY DIANA REBOLLEDO is Associate Professor of Spanish at the University of New Mexico, Albuquerque. She is a specialist in Chicana literature and has written numerous articles. She coedited the anthologies *Las mujeres hablan* (1988) and *Infinite Divisions: An Anthology of Chicana Literature* (1993).

TINO VILLANUEVA is a Preceptor in the Department of Modern Foreign Languages and Literatures at Boston University. He has published numerous scholarly articles in national and international journals. His poetry collections include *Hay otra voz poems* (1972), *Shaking off the Dark* (1984), and *Crónica de mis años peores* (1987). He is the editor of *Chicanos: Antología histórica y literaria* (1980, 1985) and publisher of *Imagine: International Chicano Poetry Journal*.

Preface

The first sprouts of this anthology surfaced at the Modern Language Association Annual Conference held in San Francisco on December 27–30, 1987, when poet and critic Tino Villanueva invited several scholars, including myself, to participate in a panel on colonial literature titled "Las crónicas españolas y la literatura chicana" ("The Spanish Chronicles and Chicano/a Literature"). As its name indicates, the panel focused its scholarly optic on the analysis of Spanish colonial literature of the American Southwest. The participants of that panel, aside from Tino Villanueva and myself, included Professor Luis Leal, who spoke on "Armas y letras en la *Historia de la Nueva México,*" and Armando Miguélez, who read "Conceptos de la Ilustración en las crónicas del siglo dieciocho en Aztlán" ("The Concepts of the Enlightenment and the Eighteenth-Century Chronicles from Aztlán").

My interest in the colonial period stems principally from my work on *pastorelas* (shepherds' plays). Most books on the history and literature of the Southwest point to the *autos sacramentales* (mystery plays) and *pastorelas* as some of the oldest examples of European theater; they were brought over by the Spanish conquistadores in the sixteenth and seventeenth centuries. Given that these two genres are still represented in the Southwest, I began to see a direct connection between colonial literary writings and contemporary Chicano literature. It seemed to me that this literary tradition dates back to the period of settlement and colonization. This was not necessarily a new idea.

The Chicano critic Philip Ortego initially posed the notion in 1971 in his article "The Chicano Renaissance," published in *La Causa Chicana: The Movement for Justice* (1971, p. 43) in which he comments that

> the literary period from the founding of the first permanent British settlement in Jamestown, Virginia, in 1607, to the formation of the American union represents only the British period of American literature. So, too, the literary period from the first permanent Spanish settlement at Saint Augustine, Florida, in 1565, to the dates of acquisition of these Spanish and Mexican lands by the United States should, in fact, represent the Hispanic period of American literature. More appropriately, the British and Spanish periods should both be listed under the rubric "Colonial American Literature." The Mexican period of the Southwest should simply be labeled "The Mexican Period."

Villanueva reasserted this position in his presentation at the Modern Language Association meeting in San Francisco when he said that "the task at hand is to initiate our familiarity with this body of literature [i.e., Hispanic colonial literature] and to commence to give theoretical order to whatever significance it might have in the light of contemporary Chicano literature, and, in a broader consideration, to throw open to inquiry its place in American literary history." Furthermore, he added, "if the past informs the present, then the Spanish colonial period of the Southwest is a crucial phase in the development of a Chicano ethos and culture" (Villanueva, unpublished introductory remarks).

The excitement and intellectual ferment generated by the scholarly presentations on Hispanic colonial literature of the Southwest indicated to me that the time is ripe for a book on the subject. I therefore began recruiting other scholars to write essays on the topic for an anthology. The group that participated in the Modern Language Association panel in 1987 became the core of the project, except for Armando Miguélez. I augmented this original group with Professors Francisco Lomelí, Ramón Gutiérrez, Genaro Padilla, Enrique Lamadrid, Juan Bruce-Novoa, and Diana Rebolledo. On February 24, 1989, we all met at the University of California, Irvine, to discuss our work in progress under the auspices of a conference I coordinated, "Hispanic/Chicano Literature of the Southwest." The papers presented at the conference were further expanded and refined and form the contents of this anthology.

I believe each contributor to this volume offers original perspectives on the Hispanic colonial literature of the Southwest. The essays are innovative as well as provocative and will make a lasting and significant contribution to the study of both Hispanic and Chicano/a literature as well as to American literature in general.

The essays by Professors Bruce-Novoa, Leal, and Villanueva were written in Spanish. I translated these three articles into their present English versions.

Acknowledgments

The production of an anthology requires effort, cooperation, good-will, and *funding* from various individuals and institutions. I am grateful to Dean of Humanities Terence Parsons for partially funding the conference on "Hispanic/Chicano Colonial Literature of the Southwest" held at the University of California, Irvine, on February 24, 1989. I also express my heartfelt thanks to Jane Newman, director of the Women's Studies Program; the Spanish and Portuguese Department; Professor Jaime Rodríguez, director of the Mexico/Chicano Program; and to the University of California, Irvine, Campus Lectures for their funding. My special thanks and appreciation for their assistance go to the various departmental secretaries: Karen Lowe from the Mexico/Chicano Program, Lois Mosgrove from the Spanish and Portuguese Department, Debbie Thyssen from the Latin American/Chicano Studies minor, and Alice Parsons from Campus Lectures, University of California, Irvine.

I also thank Professors Jaime Rodríguez and Alejandro Morales for chairing the panels at the conference on "Hispanic/Chicano Colonial Literature of the Southwest."

I express my sincere appreciation to the scholars who contributed their research findings to this anthology. Without their thoughtful and incisive articles this book would not have been possible.

A note of thanks is due to University of Arizona Press editor Joanne O'Hare, whose support I greatly appreciate.

Lastly, I thank my son, Erik Jason Sobek, and my husband, Joseph, for the patience, love, and understanding they gave me while I worked on this project.

Introduction

Reconstructing a Chicano/a Literary Heritage

Tradition tells us that Socrates once exhorted: "Know thyself." His maxim rings as true today as it did more than two millennia ago. It is particularly important for a minority group struggling with questions of identity, legitimacy, and ethnic pride to investigate its past as well as its present no matter what the consequences may be. Thus we are engaged in this volume with questions of national literatures and literary production, consumption, traditions, historiographies, antecedents, and precursors.

In what must be one of the greatest ironies in history, the sons and daughters of the Spanish-Mexican conquerors living in the American Southwest suffered the same fate the Aztecs and other Amerindian populations suffered at the hands of their fathers. Imperial Spain conquered and claimed most of the American continent through an ideology based on a supposed inferiority of the native population. The Spaniards negated the basic humanity of the Amerindian by suppressing, obviating, dismissing, ignoring, obfuscating, burning, and otherwise destroying most signs of their cultural tradition.

In fact, the explorers in the late fifteenth and early sixteenth centuries negated even the innate universal human capacity for speech. In his diary from his first voyage Christopher Columbus notes that he is taking some Indians back to Spain "para que desprendan fablar" ("so that they may learn to speak")! He seemed oblivious to the fact that Amerindians had languages of their own. Indeed, one of the first things he did was to rename the newly found lands. He systematically ignored the names given to them by the origi-

nal Amerindian inhabitants, thus beginning the process of Hispanicizing and
Christianizing the New World in the European image. Tzvetan Todorov perceives the naming of the islands, for example, as proceeding in a "chrono-
logical order . . . [corresponding] to the order of importance of the objects
associated with the names. These will be, successively God, the Virgin Mary,
the King of Spain, the Queen, the royal Princess" (Todorov 1984:27). The
islands were baptized in the following manner: "To the first one I came upon,
I gave the name of San Salvador, in homage of his Heavenly Majesty who has
wondrously given us all this. The Indians call this island Guanahani. I named
the second island Santa María de Concepción, the third Fernandina, the
fourth Isabella, the fifth Juana, and so to each of them I give a new name"
("Letter to Santangel," February–March 1493; cited in Todorov, 27). Obviously Columbus was fully aware that the islands already had Indian names,
but he sought to suppress them because he realized that in renaming the land
he was in effect taking possession of it.

From the very inception of the "discovery," Columbus, as Beatriz Pastor
writes, "did not apply himself to learning and recognizing the concrete reality
of the New World; instead he chose to select and interpret each one of its
elements in such a way that he was able to identify the newly discovered lands
with the imaginary model he had proposed to discover" (1988:22; my translation). Columbus was, in fact, "fictionalizing."

The act of renaming and thus taking possession was not limited to land
and inanimate objects; it extended to the Indians themselves. The two Amerindians captured and sent to Spain were baptized Don Juan de Castilla and
Don Fernando de Aragón (Todorov 1984:28). Pastor underscores the tremendous significance of this act: "The implications of this method of 'verifying'
the Indians' languages by means of falsifying, correcting them, inventing
them, and ultimately questioning their very existence are considerable. By
denying the Indians their language, the Admiral appropriates for himself a
monopoly on speech, and with this appropriation the monopoly of representing the new reality" (43). Through this process of silencing the native population, Columbus appropriated the Word and through it conferred upon himself the authority to create the New World in the preconceived image he had
constructed from his European sociohistorical and literary tradition (Pastor,
44). Further, by obliterating the native tongue, Columbus obliterated the
possibility of a pluralistic society (Pastor, 44).

Analogous to Christopher Columbus's silencing of the native populations by appropriating language, later Spanish colonizers denied writing to the New World. As René Jara and Nicholas Spadaccini state in the perceptive introduction to their book *1492–1992: Re/Discovering Colonial Writing,* "What is clear is that the domination of the New World was ultimately achieved through writing which was the primary vehicle for the establishment, rationalization, and control of the overseas institutions of the Empire" (1989:10). Language in its written and oral forms became an essential weapon in the process of achieving hegemony in the Americas.

> Within the framework of an early Modern State that seeks to exercise its hegemony over new territories, language becomes doubly important since it serves both purposes of inclusion and exclusion. Instructions, laws, geographic descriptions, territorial limits and, indeed, the very possession of land will be inscribed in the dominant language. Through the tyranny of the alphabet . . . the native Amerindians are deprived of their basic natural rights and are subjected to enslavement. Through exclusive use of the official language, the native cultures were forced to surrender to the conqueror. (Jara and Spadaccini 1989:12)

Denying the Amerindians their own writing system and imposing the European system gave the Spaniards a powerful weapon in their colonization. In their hands was the task of ordering, naming, identifying, and constructing an image of America that served their particular needs, goals, and ideology at the expense of the native populations. It is at this juncture—that is, when the Spanish writing and speaking systems were imposed on the Amerindians— that the construction of the Other takes an ominous turn, because it was through the written word that the Spaniards described the New World to Europe. Europeans received a monofocal view of the New World rendered solely by the Spaniards. Amerindians, without the power of the word—oral or written—were at the mercy of the Spanish writers. The repression (indeed, the burning) of their manuscripts further relegated them to a world of silence and negated their ability to represent themselves.

Since Spain sought to legitimize its project of conquest, the New World populations were represented in terms that negated their humanity, their right to own land, and their right of self-determination. The conceptualization of the Indians as "inferior beings," "brutes," or "barbarians" (no languages, no system of writing comparable to the European) allowed the Spaniards to rationalize their right to dominate the native populations—to be their masters—in the name of "civilizing" them.

In a comparable manner Chicanos suffered the same fate in 1848 when the onslaught of Anglo colonizers arrived in the Southwest. Journalists, politicians, housewives, and others wrote to those who had remained back on the East Coast regarding the "primitive" and inferior race of Mexicans living in the Southwest. The inhabitants of the Southwest were generally viewed as cultureless, not much more advanced than chimpanzees. Later on, bilingual Chicano students were to be characterized as alingual and mentally retarded. The conquered Mexican-American population became a voiceless entity, frequently described by the terms *invisible* and *silent minority*. Denied their history, their literature, their language, and their culture, Mexican Americans' artistic expressions were marginalized and ignored by the mainstream Euroamerican community. And although Chicanos resisted colonization and oppression, as is evident in court records throughout the Southwest and as narrated in resistance *corridos,* or ballads, such as the "Ballad of Gregorio Cortez," it was not until the 1960s that this ethnic group began to reassert itself into the national consciousness.

I have selected Juan Bruce-Novoa's essay, "Shipwrecked in the Seas of Signification: Cabeza de Vaca's *La Relación* and Chicano Literature," as the lead article in this anthology because it not only focuses on one of the oldest extant writings of the Southwest, it also orients us to the significance, interrelationship, and fundamental ties of colonial writings with contemporary Chicano literature and culture. Bruce-Novoa attacks head-on the difficult question of how a sixteenth-century text is relevant to today's Chicano culture. He is right in asserting that it is not enough for Chicanos to claim *La Relación* as the cornerstone text on which the foundations of Chicano literature rest; it is imperative that we also provide empirical proof refocusing on previous analyses of colonial texts and "demonstrating how the text exerts a creative force on Chicano letters." The task before Chicano critics, as Bruce-Novoa envisions it, is to pinpoint the "defining characteristics of a colonial text and discover how these defining characteristics are our own." He asserts that we should expect contemporary Chicano works to manifest aspects of the characteristics found in colonial writings, and that a Chicano-oriented analysis will "exert a definite influence on future critical analysis of the works" in question.

In adhering to the above exhortations, Bruce-Novoa has undertaken a re-reading of the Spanish conquistador Alvar Núñez Cabeza de Vaca, who roamed the Southwest in the sixteenth century and bequeathed to us a detailed account of his wanderings in *La Relación* (1542). Bruce-Novoa points out how the name of the author and the title of the book have suffered from the same ambiguity and "alterability" that has characterized Chicano names, status, and nationality. The title of Cabeza de Vaca's narrative account of his adventures, for example, was altered from *La Relación* (its original title) to *Naufragios*. His own life was likewise marked by an alterability reminiscent of present-day Chicanos. After he was shipwrecked in the Gulf of Mexico he wandered through the South and Southwest, was captured by Indians, and became a slave. Later, out of the sheer necessity to survive, he transformed himself into a folk healer much admired by the native populations. Critics have seen this metamorphosis and adaptability in both positive and negative terms, according to Bruce-Novoa. Sylvia Molloy, for instance, calls Cabeza de Vaca an "incongruent hybrid, Indianized but not an Indian," while Todorov perceives him as a "blurring of identity," and Frederick Turner more sensitively names him a "white Indian." These European-oriented critics are unable to name precisely the new entity Cabeza de Vaca has become in America because, Bruce-Novoa tells us, their optic is bipolar—one can either be this or that, but nothing in between. The space between *this* and *that* is a mystery to the European mind, which tends to think in binary polarities. And, Bruce-Novoa points out, the undefined space is even more threatening to the Mexican mind because it hits closer to home; thus the pejorative labels *pocho, descastado, agringado, pachuco,* and so on, which seek to distance the Chicano from the Mexican. According to Bruce-Novoa, the Chicano represents a threat to the Mexican because he sees in the Chicano his future.

Bruce-Novoa perfectly delineates the important parameters that define Chicano literature and does it in a most admirable manner. After reading his article there can be no doubt that Alvar Núñez Cabeza de Vaca's texts relate to contemporary Chicano culture in numerous ways, for Cabeza de Vaca's experience in the Southwest is the Chicano experience of cultural and linguistic adaptation, of suffering as well as the joy of experiencing other cultures and other unique modes of existence; it is the experience of losing oneself in the Other and transforming oneself into a new being, a truly New World, American being. Alvar Núñez Cabeza de Vaca charted the way for future Spanish immigrants and Mexicanos, who form the basis of the Chicano culture.

Genaro Padilla's essay, "Discontinuous Continuities: Remapping the Terrain of Spanish Colonial Narrative," challenges us to face painful questions regarding our colonial literary heritage. This *herencia literaria* is tainted by being inscribed in a discourse that can only be characterized as a dialogue of domination, of subjugation: it is the discourse of an expanding Spain bent on conquering the Americas and their inhabitants and stamping its imperial seal on the face of the new continents. It is nevertheless the task of succeeding generations to discover or uncover the past and face the music, however discordant its notes may prove to be. For if we neglect to do this, we will suffer the consequences of Santayana's edict that those who forget the past are condemned to repeat it.

Padilla detects a certain logic in the paradoxical phrase *discontinuous continuities*. His position is that it isn't necessary to insist that Chicano literary tradition has continued uninterrupted, but rather that it has "presence enough to recover itself discontinuously through a form of discursive memory, the intracultural collective memory and transmission of textual narrative without actual material presence."

Padilla believes this presence manifests itself in the fact that a culture may be thoroughly impregnated with a literary tradition without every individual having read it. Its existence is apprehended through oral tradition, in bits and pieces from literary writing, and from its inscription in other contexts such as historical monuments. Our Spanish and Mexican forefathers and foremothers left their imprint inscribed in place names like "California." Indeed, the American Southwest's topography is decorated with Spanish names and cultural artifacts.

Thus Padilla argues a strong case for examining our colonial literary heritage in spite of some ideological misgivings. He insists it is important for us to see how our literary discourse "branches and imbricates, sustains itself but also exhausts certain practices at one historical juncture only to recover some approximate practice at other junctures, crosscuts, jumps between genres, or borrows forms and infiltrates historically dissonant articulation through them, disappears, and then arches from one necessary discursive moment to another." Padilla perceives the task before us as a search for epistemological origins, trying to know who we are and where we came from, for in this search we can find ourselves and gain the empowerment to take charge of our own destinies.

Tino Villanueva's essay, "A Franciscan Mission Manual: The Discourse of Power and Social Organization," on the other hand, affords a specific instance of the "discourse of power" as manifested in the colonial writings of an anonymous Franciscan friar from the Purísima Concepción mission in San Antonio, Texas. This unknown friar wrote a manual titled *Instrucción para el Ministro de la Misión de la Purissima Concepción de la Provincia de Texas,* which carries the significant subtitle *Methodo de Govierno que se observa en esta Misión de la Purissima Concepción, assi en lo espiritual, como en lo temporal.* The manual is twenty-two pages long and was written in 1760 with the expressed purpose of guiding the new ministers appointed to the mission of the Purísima Concepción in the rituals, duties, and functions of the church.

Villanueva's overriding premise is that there is no such thing as an "innocent" text; all texts are ideological. A manual written by a member of the ruling elite for purposes of instructing another member of the ruling elite on how to perform the functions of the established church means that it is ideologically tainted in favor of promoting the power of the ruling class to the detriment of the subjugated class. Villanueva analyzes the text behind the text by scrutinizing the linguistic strategies in the presentation and preservation of power. He notes, for example, the predominance of the impersonal reflexive form of the verbs used, which "carries more forcefully the imprint of an order." Both grammatical structure and the obsession for minute detail in describing church rituals and functions denote an imperative, as Villanueva asserts, "to promote order in the empire," order in the conqueror's life as well as in the conquered's daily existence, and thus to continue the affirmation and promulgation of the status quo; in this case the hegemony of Spanish Crown and Catholic church.

Villanueva's contribution provides us with a clear example of a particular type of colonial literature written by the clergy (in the tradition of medieval Europe) with an expressed ideological purpose. It is a perspective useful in examining the strategy of gaining power through literature that was common in past centuries; but our understanding of this past also provides us with a better grasp of the present.

Ramón A. Gutiérrez's illuminating essay, "The Politics of Theater in Colonial New Mexico: Drama and the Rhetoric of Conquest," examines the political function of theater in colonial New Mexico. He asserts that the plays and religious dramas enacted in the Southwest during the period of Spanish colonization were intended to inculcate the spirit of submission and obedience to Spanish rule. Colonial dramas, Gutiérrez says, were far from the innocent, "folkloric," literary entertainment most scholars in the past have projected them to be; they were instead political instruments of domination employed by the Spanish hegemonic forces who wanted to instill in the native Indian population a recognition of the power, sovereignty, and superiority of Spanish rule and European civilization. The fantasies and fabricated historical "myths" (in the sense of falsehoods) presented in these dramas were designed to hammer in the inevitability of Spanish victory. Political plays (such as *Los Moros y Cristianos*) as well as religious dramas (such as the *autos sacramentales*) were carefully thought out and choreographed by the state, as represented by the conquistador Juan de Oñate, and by the church, represented by the Franciscan missionaries.

It is significant that a political play was immediately enacted upon crossing the Río Grande in the El Paso area on April 20, 1598, and that a second political drama, *Los Moros y Cristianos,* was presented in San Juan de los Caballeros soon afterward. Both plays explicitly carried the message to the Indians of past Spanish conquests, projecting in the minds of the startled Indians future conquests to be undertaken in their own New Mexican lands.

Gutiérrez has isolated three thematic structures in the plays: greetings (i.e., ritual greetings between Indians and Spaniards), symbolic battles, and submission. However, the desired end result is evident, for in all the plays the ending is the same: the defeat of the Indians and their acceptance of the Christian faith.

Gutiérrez does not present the Indians as passive recipients of Spanish ideological brainwashing. Indeed, numerous Indian revolts routed the Spanish settlers and sent them packing or to their graves. In addition, as the Indians eventually began to participate in the plays both as actors and as choreographers, they inserted subversive elements such as humor, sexual innuendoes, comic gestures, burlesque behavior, verbal plays on words, and erotic imagery. In fact, in Mexico the *autos sacramentales,* particularly the *pastorelas,* were banned and forced to go underground by the Inquisition and church and crown officials because of their subversiveness and raunchiness— *indecentes y de mal gusto.*

My essay, "The *Comedia de Adán y Eva* and Language Acquisition: A Lacanian Hermeneutics of a New Mexican Shepherds' Play," applies contemporary critical theories to a colonial-period text. In my study I utilize some of the critical theories posited by the French philosopher Paul Ricoeur and the French psychoanalyst Jacques Lacan and propose a radically different interpretation of this New Mexican version of the ancient story. My central thesis is that the play *Comedia de Adán y Eva,* which is based on the biblical story of the creation of Adam and Eve, their expulsion from Paradise, and their eventual redemption through the birth of Jesus Christ, allegorizes the acquisition of language; that is to say, it allegorizes humanity's "fall" into language. This is a new conceptualization, in that traditional exegesis of the biblical narrative posits "carnal knowledge" (the fall into sexuality) or the acquisition of knowledge per se (eating the forbidden fruit from the Tree of Good and Evil). The essay demonstrates that contemporary critical theories can yield new and innovative results.

Although prose is the most common genre found in the literature of the colonial Southwest, poetry and theater also form part of the literary heritage still extant in the area. In his essay "Poetic Discourse in Pérez de Villagrá's *Historia de la Nueva México*," Luis Leal examines Pérez de Villagrá's poetic discourse in his epic poem *Historia de la Nueva México* and views it as a work prototypical of Chicano literature because it originated in the crucible of conflict between two cultures: the Spaniards-Mexicans and the New Mexican Indians. Leal perceives the work as a harbinger of things to come and therefore considers it a cornerstone of Chicano literature. He analyzes the poetic structures of the work, refuting those critics who have categorized it as a mere historical document devoid of poetic imagination and artistic merit.

However, Don Luis goes beyond merely inscribing Villagrá's work under the rubric of an epic poem. He carefully examines the structures that make the epic a distinctively poetic work of art. Among the structures he considers particularly imbued with poetic nuances are the mythic elements found in the story of the Aztec migration, the theme of arms and letters so popular during the Renaissance and particularly explored by Cervantes in *Don Quijote*, and the literary descriptions rendered of the Southwest and the activities commonly undertaken in that particular region at the time (e.g., the descriptions of the American buffalo, the Indian "cowboys," etc.). Leal points out that Villagrá can be appreciated at several levels: as a poet, as a chronicler who documented the conquest of a territory that was to become part of the United States, and as the founder of a national literature—Chicano literature.

Francisco Lomelí's contribution, "Fray Gerónimo Boscana's *Chinigchinich*: An Early California Text in Search of a Context," focuses on the difficult-to-categorize text *Chinigchinich*, written by Boscana during his sojourn at the San Juan Capistrano mission. Fray Boscana's manuscript attempts to "reconstruct a people's history and mythology" and offers a compendium of information regarding the Juaneño Indians living in the area surrounding the mission, including their concept of matrimony, rituals, religious practices, various beliefs about the supernatural, child rearing practices, and concepts of time.

Like Juan Bruce-Novoa, Lomelí has discovered a colonial Hispanic writer who at first held fast to his ethnocentric European views but gradually came to understand and even to respect the Southwest Indians' systems of religious, political, and social beliefs, although, of course, never completely; he always viewed European civilization as superior. Both Alvar Núñez Cabeza de Vaca and Fray Boscana shared similar experiences in their acculturation and exposure to a radically different culture. Through their writings both authors became intermediaries between the two cultures: the Native American and the European.

Tey Diana Rebolledo's excellent "'¿Y Dónde Estaban las Mujeres?': In Pursuit of an *Hispana* Literary and Historical Heritage in Colonial New Mexico, 1580–1840" undertakes the difficult task of identifying women's literary endeavors. Although women were an integral part of the colonization and settlement process of the Southwest (Juan de Oñate's expedition included forty-seven wives), they are often ignored in the annals of history. Indeed, as Rebolledo points out, oftentimes the careful counting and description of utensils and equipment such as horses, carts, wagons, armor, and even reams of paper superseded the inclusion of women in the men's journals. To complicate matters further, many women did not have the means (or the time or education) to sit down and pen their memoirs. Rebolledo is correct in postulating an alternate focus in reading women's historical and literary experiences during the colonial period.

If official literary expressions are few, then other means by which we can study colonial women's daily lives and experiences need to be identified. Rebolledo has discovered that there were indeed unofficial avenues for recording women's daily lives. These stories can be found in *dichos, cuentos* (folktales), *memorates,* rituals, religious ceremonies, and other types of folklore. In addition, the careful scrutiny of official records of marriages, baptisms, court proceedings, and other archival documents yields information regarding women's involvement in the colonization process.

Of particular interest here is the creative role New Mexican women played in composing a large body of oral literature. The Federal Writers' Project in the 1930s and 1940s was of paramount importance in recording the oral literature of the Hispanas handed down from generation to generation, dating back to the colonial period. The oral literature recorded by the project details a literature rich in expression indicative of the fertile imaginations of these women. Rebolledo correctly informs us that women were there both physically and spiritually in the early period of New Mexican colonization and settlement, and through their stories and other sources—the "underside" of history—we can piece together the great mosaic that will yield a true picture of the Hispanas' historical and literary experience in the Southwest.

Enrique Lamadrid, in his study *"Entre Cíbolos Criado*: Images of Native Americans in the Popular Culture of Colonial New Mexico," posits a different view from that expressed by Gutiérrez with regard to the dramas and rituals that emerged from the Spanish colonization. Lamadrid focuses more on the *mestizaje,* or syncretism, that emerged as a result of the conquest and on the interrelationships that developed as a result of the cultural pluralism in the New Mexico area. In contrast to Gutiérrez, Lamadrid views the literary folklore extant in the Southwest and originating in the colonial period as a *mestizo* (racially mixed, mostly Indian and Spanish) type of folklore, and not as peninsular Spanish, as most folklore scholars from the early twentieth century have characterized it. This folklore represents the views of the *mestizo* population, seen by Lamadrid as cultural mediators in the emerging pluralistic frontier society. He perceives the *coyotes* (racially mixed offspring, Indian and Hispanic or Indian and Anglo) and the *genízaros* (the emerging class of captives, slaves, orphans, and other "detribalized" individuals) as major contributors to the cultural landscape of New Mexico and to folk Catholicism. The folklore that emerged from *mestizo* New Mexico could not be harsh and inordinately cruel to the Other because those in control of it identified with or had some ties to the Other's culture. Therefore the dialectic of the noble versus the ignoble savage in New Mexican folklore could not function for long. This elitist view can be found mostly in the writings of the Franciscan missionaries and was more a projection of their European-imbued imagination than actual reality.

Instead, what we actually encounter in Hispanic literary folklore is what Lamadrid terms the "popular culture of warfare"; in particular he cites the origins of the folk genre *indita* ballads, which deal with the relationships between Hispanics and Indians in both love and war. The *inditas,* also called *cautivas* (captives), generally describe the travails of women captured by Indian warriors during the period of internecine warfare (thus the name *cauti-*

vas). The stories of these women have been passed down through the generations ever since.

In spite of the bloody warfare, the resultant folklore is not venomous; the
cultural conflict between the different peoples is defused through humor.
Lamadrid describes this as the stage in which the ignoble savage became the
funny Indian, or the comedy of cultural conflict. Popular culture in the colonial period after the Comanches were more or less subjugated produced
texts in which the comic portrayal of the Indian is common. Many *inditas*
lampoon the Comanches either in their attempts to become Hispanicized
(which was viewed by the general *mestizo* population as almost impossible) or
in the intersexual relations between Indians and Hispanics. Some examples
include "Indita de Cochití" and "Los cañuteros."

Hispanic syncretism with native Indian cultures is perceived by Lamadrid
as the result of the need for survival. In a hostile environment such as the
New Mexico desert, people cease to be enemies when the natural elements
are against all. A drought is the great equalizer and has the power to make
people realize their basic humanity. Hispanics, when weather conditions
spelled disaster for their crops, were not too proud to ask Indian elders to
pray for rain. Concomitantly, Indian peoples prayed to Catholic San Isidro for
rain. Ritual dances such as *Los Matachines* became, in Lamadrid's perspective,
"spiritual bonds between the cultures" and expressed a definite syncretism
after centuries of living and fighting together. Thus, like the city of Jerusalem, which is a religious center for three of the world's most renowned religions, the Shrine of Chimayó in New Mexico reflects a syncretism between
the native Pueblo Indians and Catholic Hispanics.

The motive force propelling Hispanic writers in earlier centuries was a deep
pride in Hispanic culture, a pride that to a certain extent can be viewed as
ethnocentric, but nevertheless a primary force impelling them to disseminate
their culture throughout the Americas. This pride in Hispanic culture is the
legacy left to contemporary Chicanos/as, who continue to nurture it even
today. And this tenacity in adhering to Hispanic culture has been successful
to a certain extent, for it continues to flower in spite of the hostile environment it frequently encounters.

The essays in this volume are irrefutable evidence of the rich heritage of
Hispanic literary culture. Unfortunately, this literary wealth has been ignored
for too long. Only recently have American literature anthologies begun in-

corporating some of these texts. For example, the editors of the 1990 edition of the *Heath Anthology of American Literature* decided to include an unprecedented number of women and minorities (*Los Angeles Times,* Orange County section, August 27, 1990, p. A1). According to the *Los Angeles Times* the new anthology features

> nearly 200 pages of works by Native Americans, Spanish explorers and French settlers before getting to John Smith and William Bradford. Slave spirituals, the *corridos* folk ballads of Mexican-Americans and early feminist manifestos are presented alongside the Federalist Papers, Henry David Thoreau's essays and short stories by Stephen Crane. Nathaniel Hawthorne and Walt Whitman are among the 275 authors represented, but so are Mourning Dove, the first Native American woman novelist, and contemporary Puerto Rican poet Victor Hernández Cruz.

This caused a tremendous backlash from conservative, traditional English professors such as Peter Shaw, vice president of the National Association of Scholars (an association characterized by the above newspaper as a "Princeton-based group of conservative academics"), who is quoted in the *Los Angeles Times* as saying that his group opposes "the affirmative action link," believing that the inclusion of literature written by women and ethnic groups is "not judgments of literature on merit, but for political reasons and . . . part of a larger politicization of both curricula and college teaching that we were formed to oppose" (August 27, 1990).

The sad truth is that exclusion of writers from American ethnic groups (and of women) has led to a distortion of what American literature is as well as misinformation (politically motivated) of historical facts. The present anthology seeks to redress that omission in American literature and thus to enrich it with a new color taken from America's ever-expanding ethnic rainbow.

REFERENCES

Colón, Cristobal. 1954. *Diario del primer viaje.* In *Colección de relaciones para la historia de los viajes y descubrimientos.* Martín Fernández de Navarrete edition. Madrid: Instituto Histórico de Marina.

Jara, René, and Nicholas Spadaccini. 1989. "Allegorizing the New World." In *1492–1992: Re/Discovering Colonial Writing.* Ed. Jara and Spadaccini. Minneapolis: Prisma Institute.

Los Angeles Times, Orange County section. 1990. "Literary Anthology Rattles Traditionalists." August 27.

Pastor, Beatriz. 1988. *Discursos narrativos de la conquista: Mitificación y emergencia.* Hanover, N.H.: Ediciones Norte.

Todorov, Tzvetan. 1984. *The Conquest of America: The Question of the Other.* Trans. Richard Howard. New York: Harper and Row.

Part I Critical Reconstruction

Shipwrecked in the Seas of Signification

Cabeza de Vaca's *Relación* and Chicano Literature

JUAN BRUCE-NOVOA

For Dolores Novoa Bruce, whose *naufragio* lasted many more years
and who taught me the vitality of alterity.

In memoriam.

In the most influential article on periodization of Chicano literature,
Don Luis Leal suggested extending its range toward the very origins of European incursions in what is today the United States. In "Mexican American
Literature: A Historical Perspective" (1973), Leal proposed that works "dating before 1821 and written by the inhabitants of this region with a Spanish
background . . . belong to an early state of Chicano literature" (22). Since
the proposal emanated from a well-respected intellectual as well as a nationally and internationally respected specialist of Mexican literature, it acquired
the aura of de facto authorization. For others, however, it has raised the spec-
ter of an intellectual fifth column.

Since then, those of us who toil in the malleable field of Chicano criticism
have utilized Leal's position to our advantage because it provides us with a
historical base for what many consider to be a phenomenon too recent to be
taken seriously at the level of national literature, or even established regional
literatures. Nevertheless, one of the strategies that literary criticism incor-
porates to privilege certain canons is the theory of genealogical origins—the
tracing of literary heritages to a remote antiquarian lineage. In the United
States, where it is customary to judge groups according to the number of
generations their ancestors have been in this country, this tactic is highly
valued. In general, those who arrived first (e.g., on the *Mayflower*) are deemed
the best. This excludes American Indians, of course, whose ancestry in
America makes newcomers of all Europeans. The positing of a colonial period

for Chicano literature afforded Chicanos dignity in the politics of literature. To the question "When did Chicano literature begin?" (a question that barely covers the a priori denial of our having any status among the established canons) we respond that it began about four centuries ago; that is to say, *before* the English founded their first permanent colony on the Atlantic Coast. It was a useful and comforting thought.

I do not belittle the strategies for surviving our academic battles. The creation of a literary genealogy is a legitimate goal of any group. But it is time now to fully develop the processes that will aid us in responding to the questions this self-designated literary tradition poses. The mere affirmation of such a position is not enough. We need to undertake Chicano readings of the various texts Leal enumerated; for example, Alvar Núñez Cabeza de Vaca's *La Relación* (a narrative account which details his eight years of adventurous roaming through the southern part of what is now United States territory between 1528 and 1536). Now, in order for us to continue to affirm that Alvar Núñez's *Relación* marks the beginning of Chicano literature, we need to fully explain what it means to us as Chicanos as well as what it means in general. This requires a dual analysis. First, regarding its contextual analysis, we must refocus the traditional critical analyses. Second, since we have se-lected it as a fundamental text cementing the origins of our literary history, we have to demonstrate how the text exerts a creative force on Chicano letters. Furthermore, it is necessary for us to illustrate how the defining characteris-tics we discover in the work are, in one way or another, our very own. We can legitimately expect contemporary Chicano works to manifest aspects of characteristics found in colonial writings. This new perspective will exert a definite influence on future critical analyses of Chicano literature.

In this essay I adhere to the following strategy: I will reread *La Relación* of Alvar Núñez Cabeza de Vaca (from this point designated as ANCdV) as a founding as well as a fundamental text of Chicano literature and culture.

From *La Relación* to *Naufragios,* or the Shipwreck of the Relation

The quality that surfaces immediately and characterizes ANCdV's text through-out is the ambiguity produced by the alteration inside the code's signification. This process of continuous displacements commences at the first encounter with the text: the title itself. What ANCdV called *La Relación* in 1542 has come to be known as *Naufragios,* the title Andrés González Barcia conferred on the work when he renamed it in 1749 and included it in his series *Histo-riadores primitivos de las Indias Occidentales*. It has been conjectured that Gon-zález Barcia was inspired by the table of contents from the 1555 edition, which features a reference to "la presente Relación y naufragios" (this account and shipwrecks; Favata and Fernández 1986:xiv); or perhaps the editor al-lowed himself to be influenced by the success of Daniel Defoe's *Robinson Crusoe* (1715). Furthermore, it is not difficult to comprehend that the title *Naufra-gios* functions better to provoke readers' interest, and, even more important for the editor, increases their desire to buy the text. Between a faithful ren-dering of the text and greater sales potential, who can doubt which one an editor will select? Whatever the reason for the change, it documents the history of the metamorphosis inside the sign itself that the text represents. We encounter not only the predicted variation in meaning that the different historical contexts bring about in its reception, but also an alteration of the same signifier as a result of readers' perception over time inside the dialogic field, at the level of both intra- and intertextuality.

A similar process occurs with Cabeza de Vaca's own name. Our author at times may be found cataloged under *N* and at other instances under *C*. "Alvar Núñez" is altered to "Cabeza de Vaca," or vice versa, according to the whims or needs of the writers and editors involved. It may be advantageous to be able to fluctuate between surnames; certainly it avoids the boredom of repe-tition. Editors prefer Alvar Núñez because it occupies less space, but writers and the general public prefer the more emotive Cabeza de Vaca. Nevertheless, almost no one follows the author himself, who, in spite of the almost ridicu-lous clash at the expressive level that the juxtaposition of *Núñez* and *Cabeza de Vaca* poses, utilized all five names together. Editors and librarians always amputate one or two lines of his heritage. And one need not even mention the confusion between *B*aca and *V*aca: only someone with a name like Novoa can appreciate the extent of the problem.

Librarians have found it impossible to resolve the confusion. Following their professional guidelines, they underline the *N* of Núñez, indicating that the determining surname begins with that letter and that our author will vary eighteen degrees from the *A* and seven from the *Z* in the reality of the library stacks. Nevertheless, at times card catalogs or electronic indexes place him under *C,* a reorientation that alters his position sixteen degrees on the level of the ideal and textual plane. But while at an ideal plane this fluctuation does not represent a grave problem, at the level of scholarship it can cause an *aficionado* or a neophyte student to leave the library convinced that nothing exists either by or about the author in question. ANCdV is continuously shipwrecked in one or another of his surnames' initials, which, ironically, were meant to provide him with a coherent and solid identity and grounding to his genealogy as well as to his own personal experience.

The life of ANCdV was itself a series of displacements, both spatially and existentially speaking, and these displacements have helped to transform him into an enigma for Western thought. As Thomas W. Field stated in 1871, "Everything in the life of Alvar Núñez Cabeza de Vaca seemed destined to occur out of the ordinary course; and to be either clouded by the perversity of fortune, or obscured by a mystery impossible to penetrate" (Smith 1966:30). At thirty-seven years of age, this young nobleman with a promising military career received from the Emperor Charles V of Spain the official commission of "King's Treasurer" in the expedition headed by Pánfilo de Narváez for the conquest of Florida. Thus, with his destiny almost assured within what was then the center of European power, ANCdV veered off course and headed for America. We do not know if this action was due to personal whim or imperial edict. He embarked on the voyage in 1527, shortly after the conquest of Mexico by Hernán Cortés. Perhaps he was dreaming of repeating Cortés's marvelous adventure; whatever his purpose, from the very beginning things went wrong for him.

Even before the expedition began, Narváez had been discredited as a commander, having been defeated and jailed by Cortés in Veracruz when he tried to reinstate Diego Velásquez's authority as governor of Cuba. When the emperor supported Cortés, Narváez and Velásquez attempted to carry on the struggle, petitioning for a monopoly on the conquest of the territory north of what Cortés controlled in central Mexico. Charles V granted Narváez his petition, but in order to ensure imperial control he assigned the expedition a "treasurer of the king": a young man loyal to the emperor, ANCdV. Our author commenced his career as a conqueror under a most ambiguous sign: he traveled under Narváez's command but as the emperor's official, loyal to the central power. Thus he represented interests alien to Narváez. "You will inform yourself," Charles V ordered, "of the diligence used in the collection of our revenues, of the five percentum and duties appertaining to us, and of the persons appointed to take charge thereof, from whom you will receive account of what they have, and collect it of them and out of their goods . . . according to the instructions we have . . . sent to our Governor and officers in that country" (Smith 1966:218). The imperial *we* resonated menacingly, descending as a heavy mist over the command of the expedition. And ANCdV was part and parcel of that all-encompassing mist.

In chapter 38 of *La Relación,* the author narrates how a woman traveling with the expedition predicted that disaster would befall all who joined Narváez, as though she was sealing their destiny. This most likely was a simple literary motif invented to make the story more interesting. It was the historically real imperial seal of Charles V that determined ANCdV's fate. The emperor wrote:

> You will have a *separate book,* wherein shall be entered the account kept by our Comptroller in those lands . . . informing us extensively and particularly of every matter, especially of how our commands are obeyed and executed in those lands and provinces, of how the natives are treated, our instructions observed, and other of the things respecting their liberties that we have commanded, especially the matters touching the service of the Indians and the Holy Faith, and many other things of our service, as well as *all the rest you see,* and I should be informed of. (Smith 1966:218–21; emphasis mine)

ANCdV journeyed to America as the emperor's eyes and ears, entrusted to observe everything and to inscribe it all in a journal written from the perspective of someone belonging to the expedition but at the same time from an exterior, analytical position. The book was to relate even the most dispersed elements under the all-encompassing rubric of official authority and order. The imperial edict dictated that ANCdV's function was to alternate between treasurer and chronicler, diplomat and policeman—and perhaps even official of the Holy Inquisition. It is important to note also that the book envisioned by Charles V was a hybrid at various levels: as a semiotic system it encompassed numbers and words; at the level of genres it included narration, essay, and exposition; and as semantic codes there were the deeds that could be analyzed through a juxtaposition of the interpretations of the conquerors and the representatives of the emperor.

From the Imperial Court, the most powerful in Europe in the sixteenth century, ANCdV was transported to a group of people traveling to the outer ends of the empire, and simultaneously to the margins of history as well when the expedition failed because of the ineptness of its members. ANCdV's ambivalence and differences of opinion with Narváez eventually solidified and crystallized in the desperate and irresponsible "save your own skins!" cry from

the commander, who bid ANCdV and the text farewell and disappeared in
the Gulf of Mexico (Favata and Fernández, 44). The shipwrecked ANCdV
was enslaved by Indians, but incredibly, as time passed, his status with the
natives, as well as that of the three other survivors, changed from slave to
a type of traveling guru (anticipating, perhaps, the televangelists of our
time). He attracted the sick and the curious, who then fell into the hands of
ANCdV's unscrupulous guides and assistants; the latter, in turn, cheated
them out of their goods and possessions but left them, in spite of the thefts,
happy and healthy. As a healer, ANCdV situated himself at the center of an
imperial parody: surrounding him were hundreds of Indians who lived off his
activities; he in turn was elevated to power by divine intervention. The difference between Charles V's Imperial Court and this imperial parody is that
ANCdV now occupied the center.

When he finally returned to Spain, ANCdV found himself far from both
centers of power, and he struggled with the task of recuperating the goodwill
of the emperor. After a few years of petitions and self-vindications, he managed to acquire another commission, more prestigious than the last. But he
failed again, receiving first official censure and later a sentence of exile from
court and official service. The life of our author consisted of such a series of
continuous ups and downs.

Silvia Molloy comments about the manipulation of rhetoric that ANCdV
exerted in various situations: "This oscillation—at times inside the group, at
other instances outside it—is symptomatic not only of nutritional adjust-
ments but indicative of the whole process which constitutes the indoctrination of the Other" (Molloy 1986:21). Molloy is certainly correct in focusing
on the alterity of the narrator. However, she limits her own horizon in comprehending ANCdV, because in reality this constant oscillation is more than
a simple index of the process of apprehension inside the text; it is a sign
representing the text and, as I hope to explicate here, the American culture
the text represents.

What Molloy names alterity is in turn the most recent avatar of what
critics have long observed regarding the changes ANCdV experienced during
his trip. He lived among the native inhabitants and shared even their nudity,
their exotic foods—dogs, roots, cactus—their cannibalism, and their beliefs
in folk healing. The critics have progressively increased the profound significance of these changes. In 1936 Haniel Long formulated the change as a

personal crisis of the ego: ANCdV felt wounded, psychologically speaking, upon realizing that the indignation he felt with respect to the sufferings caused by the evil deeds of the Spaniards was in reality the result of having to "face the Spanish gentleman [he himself] had been eight years before . . . [and] what . . . is so melancholic as to confront one's former unthinking and unfeeling self?" (Long 1936:36–37). In 1944 Justo García Morales redirected the focus of the analysis to the interpersonal sphere, thus allowing ANCdV an extremely positive experience with the indigenous populations: "During his nine years of co-habitating with the Indians he got to know them and learned to love them." ANCdV deserves the title of the Indians' "most faithful protector and friend; a new lay Father Las Casas" (García Morales 1960:22). From loving them to identifying himself with them seems but a short step. It was not until 1978, however, that David Lagmanovich spoke about "a progressive identification on the author's part with the world of the Indians which he had initially sought to dominate." The *Naufragios,* he says, "are a narrative of conversion" (Lagmanovich 1978:32).

This trajectory appears, first, to identify the same phenomenon and then, according to the orientation of the critic, to interpret it either from a negative perspective of alienation or from a positive one of association. Some critics affirm the experience from a romantic point of view—that is, the reintegration of civilized man with nature—while others underscore the conflict the imputed conversion caused for ANCdV when he returned to civilization. From both perspectives, the fact that the Spanish conqueror occupied a space within both the Indian world and the Spanish one is the critical point. Silvia Molloy summarizes this issue with acerbic severity: "Nudity has integrated his ego into a particular system and expelled it from another, metamorphosing him into an incongruent hybrid—Indianized but not an Indian; Spanish speaking but not a Spaniard—who disconcerts us because of his peculiarity" (31). Molloy imposes on ANCdV, as well as on her own judgment and on her essay itself, the structural mark of a binary polarity: one is this or that; the space in between the two poles becomes forbidden, condemned in its "incongruity" and "peculiarity," at least from the perspective of European logic that her criticism assumes in this significant, self-revealing, and key moment in her essay.

Tzvetan Todorov seems to be in agreement with Molloy, although his change in focus results in his being more sensitive and understanding. Ironically, while Molloy, an Argentine, judges ANCdV from an outsider's perspective, Todorov places the crisis of revelation within the narrator by displacing the focus to another moment later in the narration when he has reencountered Spanish colonists in Mexico. ANCdV believed he could guarantee the freedom of the hundreds of Indians who accompanied him, but the Spaniards proceeded to enslave them. Todorov cites the following passage from *La Relación*: "We sought to ensure the freedom of the Indians, and at the moment when we believed we had achieved it, the contrary occurred. They [the Christians] had in fact determined to attack the Indians whom we had sent away reassured as to their peaceful intentions. They took us through forest and wastes so we would not communicate with the natives and would neither see nor learn of their crafty scheme. Thus we often misjudge the motives of men; we thought we had effected the Indians' liberty where the Christians were but poising to pounce" (Todorov 1984: 199). Then he adds: "Here Cabeza de Vaca's mental universe seems to vacillate, his uncertainty as to the referents of his personal pronouns contributing to the effect; there are no longer two parties, we (the Christians) and they (the Indians), but indeed three: the Christians, the Indians, and 'we.' But who is this 'we,' external to both worlds, though having experienced them both from within?" (199). Todorov does not respond to his own query, perhaps because he lacks an ideology capable of serving as a basis from which he could explain it; that is, in spite of his sensibility and good intentions, he is essentially on the side of the Christians, which is synonymous with "Europeans."

For what Todorov denominates a "blurring of identity" and Molloy calls "incongruent hybrid"—both pejorative characterizations—historian Frederick Turner has a term with more positive connotations. Turner's sobriquet is derived from ANCdV's years of captivity with the Indians. He deduces the term after postulating a complete psychological transformation on the part of ANCdV and his fellow Spaniards after they had practiced their *curanderismo* (folk healing). Turner suggests that in spite of the prejudices they were imbued with, the Spaniards were granted "a brief but vivid glimpse of that spiritual bond between humans that always lies awaiting acknowledgment. By themselves they could not change the course of their civilization, and we have noted the inappropriate uses to which Soto and Coronado put Vaca's story. . . . But in this narrative we may follow a trail that leads to a more genuine treasure than those so tragically sought in so many places under so many names" (Turner 1980: 254). And thus after naming this genuine treasure that the Old World found in the New, Turner likewise responds to the question Todorov posits and the pejorative formulations of Molloy. That treasure, according to Turner, is "White Indians, these . . ." (254).

It is imperative to reiterate that Turner closes the chapter with this suspended sentence; or more precisely stated, he leaves the chapter perpetually open-ended in the midst of a silence that once again underscores an incapacity to identify what critics have found impossible to express: the identity of the white Indian. Who is he? A similar immense silence reverberates in ANCdV's *Relación* when he again encounters Spaniards after eight years among the Indians. "Y otro dia de mañana alcance quatro christianos de cavallo que rescibieron gran alteracion de verme tan estrañamente vestido y en compañia de indios. Estuvieron mirando mucho espacio de tiempo, tan atonitos que ni me hablavan ni acertavan a preguntarme nada" (Favata and Fernández, 127; "And next day in the morning I caught up with four Christians [i.e., white men] on horseback who were greatly disturbed upon seeing me so strangely clad and in the company of Indians. They stared at me for a long period of time and so astounded were they upon seeing me that they were left speechless and did not speak to me nor thought of asking me any questions"). The reality ANCdV *presents* negates all possible reaction from his fellow humans, who resemble him but little, just as ANCdV's image *represented* in the text has left the critics in a suspended state precisely before final enunciation. The reason is that the new being ANCdV presents and represents is the apparition of the ineffable. How do we formulate a name for a being who does not belong on one side or the other of the binary oppositions of "we" and "the other?" Our only recourse is to situate him on the line that divides the two; that space from which, on the basis of his imposing presence and his insistent autotextualization, he threatens to create his own center—the ambiguous *we* that both fascinates and perturbs Todorov. For this kind of being there was no name, at least not yet.

In the text the suspension is resolved in a very significant manner, because it reveals for the first time what ANCdV will be from that point onward. All that was anterior to this revelation was mere learning, initiatory rites for becoming a knight, a *pícaro* (rogue), an Indian, and, how can we deny it, even a sacred Being. But on closing the circle and initiating his return to the society whence he originated, ANCdV is already the protagonist of his fabulous adventure, and he becomes trapped in his own being; a being whose essence is alterability. ANCdV speaks with the captain, who explains that "estava muy perdido alli, porque avia muchos dias que no avia podido tomar indios, y que avia por donde yr, porque entre ellos comencava a aver necessidad y hambre" (Favata and Fernández, 127; "he was quite lost there because a few days had passed and he had not been able to capture any Indians and it was apparent they had to leave because amongst them hunger and need were becoming apparent"). ANCdV, who has been lost for eight years and is in search of his cultural reintegration, becomes a guide for those he had been looking to for personal reorientation. He directs them to his fellow Spaniards, who are accompanied by their faithful Indian friends. In return for this practical orientation, which ANCdV garnered as a result of his exposure to the natural environment and from the indigenous peoples, he receives from the Spaniards what he has desired the most: "testimonio [d]el año y el mes y dia que alli avia llegado, y la manera en que venia, y ansi lo hizieron. Deste rio hasta el pueblo de los christianos que se llama San Miguel, que es de la governacion de la provincia que dizen la Nueva Galizia, ay treynta leguas" (Favata and Fernández, 128; "testimony as to the day and year he had arrived there and the manner in which he had appeared to them. And that is how they did it. From this river to the Christians' town which is called San Miguel belonging to the province called New Galicia there are thirty leagues"). ANCdV exchanges the concrete and real for the abstract and ideal.

The above exchange deserves careful analysis. The Spaniards are not lost because of their lack of geographic knowledge—they know exactly where they are—but because they have been unable to "capture Indians" to serve and feed them. Even though he will not realize it until later, ANCdV has already betrayed the Indians; he has surrendered them to the Spaniards without knowing it. In exchange for this betrayal he is granted a reorientation within the dual semantic system—religious and civil—of European power. However, in the chapter that follows, the Spaniards are not able to convince the Indians that ANCdV and his companions are Spanish and Christian like themselves. While ANCdV has already demonstrated his desire to reintegrate himself into the Spanish system, the Indians still perceive him in terms of his recent past while in their company. In a manner analogous to two maps of the world whose topography is identical but whose contours do not interface with each other, the two groups interpret ANCdV from two distinct codes which are impossible to translate due to lack of contact; in the idiom of the day, they lack a common tongue. What they do have in common is ANCdV. Even though they see him from different vantage points, he can relate to all of them through his own being. ANCdV becomes a marked man because of his alterity, the alterity that permits him to be the intermediary between two exclusive codes. He incarnates two key tropes of the relation: metonymy and synecdoche—mutable enough to convey movement in both directions.

This alterity originated from an intercultural and interlinguistic ability developed during his captivity. Shipwrecked—that is to say, deprived of the base that sustained him and maintained him afloat in the ocean (the ship is a metaphor for the culture)—he had to survive his status of being unanchored in the high seas as well as lost among the Indians. Once again the elements are new metaphors seeking a new relation between his Being and the surrounding context, which in the final analysis redefines him by first imprinting the sign of adaptability and then becoming a permanent alterability. During his apprenticeship with the Indians he acquired expertise in the proper modes of serving his masters, first as a merchant who traveled between various tribes: "procure de usar el oficio lo mejor que supe. Y por esto me davan de comer y me hazian buen tratamiento, y rogavanme que fuese de unas partes a otras por cosas que ellos avian menester, porque por razon de la guerra que contino traen, la tierra no se anda ni se contrat tanto" (Favata and Fernández, 61; "I tried to make use of my occupation as best as I could. And for this they fed me and treated me well and would beg me to go from one place to another for things that they needed because due to their constant warring it is difficult for them to travel or to find anything"). That is to say, he became a border merchant who crossed back and forth across the dangerous demarcations that marked the various exclusive territories, alternating between one group and another until he was transformed into a connecting link between them. Later, when he assumed the profession of folk healer, he was able to interconnect the spiritual with the physical. If we examine this relationship from a geometric point of view, he first formed a horizontal net, and to this he later added a vertical plane; in the movable center where the two planes converged, he practiced the ritual healing prayer, the sacred rite of orienting the individual to his society and to the universe. ANCdV thus came to incarnate a hierophantic *axis mundi,* a classic response to the problem of chaos—through the process of cosmicization (Eliade, 328–45; Bruce-Novoa, 3–13). In this priestly role, which he began by imitating the native folk healers—"Dan cauterios de fuego, que es cosa entre ellos tenida por muy provechosa, y yo lo he experimentado y me suscedio bien dello. Y despues soplan aquel lugar que les duele" (Favata and Fernández, 57–58; "They suture with fire which they view as very beneficial. I have used it too and have had good results. And later they blow on the spot that hurts them")—he was able to correlate two semiotic codes: the Christian and the indigenous. "La manera con que nosotros curamos era santiguandolos, y soplarlos, y rezar un peternoster y un avemaria, y rogar lo mejor que podiamós a Dios" (Favata and Fernández, 58; "The manner in which we cured them was by passing the sign of the cross on them, blowing on them, saying the Lord's Prayer and a Hail Mary and praying as best as we could to God").

The success of the above syncretism, religious as well as semiotic, increased his mobility as well as his authority. This success was confirmed through the gourds given to him by the other Indian folk healer as proof of acceptance and as a sign of rank within the Indian system. "Y entre otras cosas dos fisicos dellos nos dieron dos calabacas. Y de aqui comencamos a llevar calabacas con nosotros, y añadimos a nuestra autoridad esta ceremonia, que para ellos es muy grande" (Favata and Fernández, 107; "And among other things two of their healers gave us two gourds. And from then on we proceeded to carry gourds with us and we added to our healing repertoire this ceremony which to them means a great deal"). Under this sign Cabeza de Vaca began to introduce Christian doctrine, but at the same time, as I stated earlier, the Indians who accompanied him progressively increased the abuse they inflicted on their own kind. Even among the Indians, ANCdV "alternated" between good and evil.

The mere presence of ANCdV facilitated the exchange between tribes. They utilized him as an intermediary among themselves and as a goodwill ambassador, while he in turn used them as intermediaries between himself and other indigenous peoples. This initial mobility granted him by those in power was used to advantage when he encountered Spaniards later on and served as an intermediary between them and the Indians. He utilized his status as a respected folk healer to convince the Indians to return to the cultivation of the land. That is to say, he aided the Spaniards in repopulating the zones that had been abandoned by the Indians who fled from the Spanish abuse. ANCdV combined the promise of healing the body with the assurance of booty. But after deceiving the Indians—and perhaps sincerely deceiving himself—he bequeathed them the talisman he always carried with him, even though unseen: the holy cross as a sign of protection within the Christian belief system.

Mandamosles que baxassen de las sierras y viniessen seguros y en paz poblassen toda la tierra e hiziessen sus casas, y que entre ellas hiziessen una para dios y pusiessen a la entrada un cruz, como la que alli teniamos, y que cuando viniessen alli los Christianos, los saliessen a rescebir con las cruzes en las manos, sin los arcos y sin armas, y los llevassen a sus casas y les dieseen de comer de lo que tenian, y por esta manera no les harian mal; antes serian sus amigos. (Favata and Fernández, 135)

We ordered them to come down from the mountains and to come confident and in peace and to settle and populate the land, and to build their houses there and together to build one for God and to place at the entrance a cross, similar to the one we had there, and when the Christians came there they should go out and greet them with the crosses in their hands, without bows and arrows or weapons, and they should take them (the Christians) to their houses and give them food and whatever else they had, and in this way they would not harm them; instead they would be their friends.

That the Indians could live as friends with the Spaniards under the sign of the cross was as much a utopic illusion as Turner's "white Indian." Although ANCdV almost achieved this feat, in the end it proved impossible for the Indians to attain such a utopia. He left them the cross as representative of his own self, of his authority, and even more, of his alterability—his capacity to shift from one code to another, without ever ceasing to be one or the other. He left them the illusion that his representation could link them to the official system and simultaneously maintain them safe inside their own system: in other words, ANCdV left them the illusion of achieving the ideal of living among different cultures and enjoying the best aspects of each.

ANCdV hoped to complete his reorientation upon returning to the center of signification itself, the Court of Charles V, but he failed (*naufragó*) again. His new failure arose from the actual shipwreck and resembled yet another. Because he had failed, he was once again reduced to the status of a loser without the support of the system. From sacred *axis mundi* worshiped by multitudes, he became an isolated figure seeking imperial favor, but the Crown treated him as just one among many losers who were seeking favor from the Court. Lost in the jagged rocks of his own demeaned image of a shipwrecked loser, ANCdV fell back on his previous experience and dedicated himself to adapting and changing himself (*alterándose*) according to his new surroundings. Since he did not have anything to sell, he became a salesman of his own self, of his own life, converting it into the Word and sacred talisman with which he sanctified himself. That is to say, he adapted what he had learned to the environment of the Court: he attempted to convert his hostile hosts, first, into buyers of his "merchandise," and, second, into believers in his capacity to provide them with what they desired most; all through the magic of the Word. But once in Spain, the oral world had been left behind and he had to avail himself of the written word. His text is impressive for the hybrid quality of the combination of orality and literariness. And once again his text is interlingual and intercultural: among the Spanish lexicon he intersperses American vocabulary words; into the European semiotics he injects strange actions, images, and signs. Finally, ANCdV slips back in among the Spaniards as the possibility of otherness within sameness itself. Above all, because he failed to achieve the goal most highly prized by the Christians—the conquest of wealth—he made a virtue of his failure, of his talent for alterability, of his ability to relate different terms, and even of his resemblance to a saint. In this last point, which ANCdV never treats explicitly (perhaps so as not to risk attracting official ire), we find the essence of his rhetoric of revindication. The adventure of being shipwrecked assumes the aspect of a religious experience. The arrogant knight finds himself deprived of everything and humiliated in a process similar to that of asceticism. He is saved from the abyss by dedicating himself to the services of his fellow men. This in turn takes him, even against his will, to become a religious practitioner. He thus achieves an almost mystic image: he represents the Divine Presence in human form and is able to perform miraculous cures and even bring a dead man back to life. It is not a coincidence that in this same epoch Ignacio de Loyola founded the Jesuit order after a religious experience which could be read as a parody of ANCdV's. From a shipwrecked failure ANCdV transformed himself into a successful narrator. The proof of this success is found in his being named *adelantado* and governor of the Río de la Plata province.

ANCdV was marked forever by his experiences. His American alterability distinguished him from other Spaniards. When he tried to exert his power in Paraguay, reassuring the Indians of their rights as members of the Spanish system, the Spaniards rebelled against him. They exiled the governor back to Spain, a chained prisoner, shipwrecked on the rocks of his own culture. From narrator to shipwrecked sailor to narrator. ANCdV composed another narrative, his *Comentarios,* in order to once again reorient himself, but his own texts defeated him: what he presents as an account (*relación*) reveals his alterability as an entity ever traveling between solid zones, adrift, ready to offer a face resembling his hosts; a malleable point of syncretism without a firm base in any solid pole; a being capable of transforming any binary order into a field of plurivalent points in continuous flux—again he was a metonymy par excellence, the trope characteristic of the narrative genre (read *relación*). In the final analysis he was a glorious castaway (*naufragio*) in a sea of signification.

Alvar Núñez Cabeza de Vaca as Chicano

Frederick Turner was correct in postulating that ANCdV incarnates the best possibilities of America, an alternative to the egocentrism and arrogance of the conqueror in his multiple manifestations, which have devastated and continue to ruin this new world, transforming it into an old and spoiled continent. ANCdV is the sign of the lost American dream, the ideal of a life forever remaking itself in the process of the adventure, never limited by national borders or monolingual territories in which anyone can be everything or even everyone desired if he or she is capable of convincing others of his or her usefulness—the dream of succeeding on the basis of hard work, adaptability, and even cultural assimilation. ANCdV also represents what is quintessentially American in the sense that he proved that once he dedicated himself to the American process, living it in his own flesh as any other American, the immigrant ceased to be a foreigner and was never able to return to his place of origin. Even when he harbored certain illusions of returning, it was no longer possible because he was forever marked with the sign of Americanness: continual alterability as neither native nor foreigner, but a mixture of the two with a synthetic interlingualism. From this language, which is always in the process of shifting from the known to the strange to the creative, this American created a literature which links him to the world, forging his own image as the narrator of a shipwreck transformed into struggle, survival, and perhaps even success. ANCdV's error was to return to Spain and to try to be what he no longer could fully be.

Within the perturbed attitude of the Spaniards or Molloy's "scandalous hybridism," Todorov's "detached we," and Turner's suspended sentence reverberates Silence in search of a name, the spirit in search of a body in which to manifest itself to the world; a silence they—from their outsider's perspective—cannot name. Nor is it their function to do so. In fact, that reticence is infinitely preferable to the names some Mexicans have coined to designate

Chicanos. The disquieting feeling he felt on confronting the alterability of his brothers in the United States impelled José Vasconcelos to utter the denigrating term *pocho:* "Palabra que se usa en California para designar al descastado que reniega de lo mexicano aunque lo tiene en la sangre y procura ajustar todos sus actos al mimetismo de los amos actuales de la región" (Vasconcelos 1957:781; "Word used in California to designate the *descastado* [one who has lost caste] who denies his Mexicanness even though he is one by blood and who tries to adjust all his mannerisms in imitation of the current rulers of that region"). A *descastado* who practices mimetism in order to survive among the masters in the Southwest brings to mind ANCdV, who made mimetism a strategy which allowed him to rise through the indigenous ranks and eventually return to Spain. Vasconcelos opposes this hybridism which the *pocho* represents and which ANCdV prefigured: "No solo lo norteamericano, también lo mexicano se volvía absurdo, bajaba de categoría en la híbrida ciudad [San Antonio, Texas] que ha hecho negocio de revolver tamales con enchiladas, frijoles con carne, todo en un mismo plato" (1957:786; "Not only that which was North American but also that which was Mexican became absurd, inferior in that hybrid city [San Antonio] which has made good business of mixing tamales with enchiladas, and beans with meat, all on the same plate"). What would Vasconcelos have to say about the delicacies described by ANCdV: from prickly pears and roots to the flesh of horses, dogs, and even humans? This binary perspective that condemns the hybrid recalls Octavio Paz, who, scandalized by the aspect of the Los Angeles youth in the 1940s, condemned the *pachuco* (zoot-suiter): "El pachuco ha perdido toda su herencia: lengua, religión, costumbres, creencias. Solo le queda un cuerpo y un alma a la intemperie, enerme ante todas las miradas" (Paz 1967:14; "The pachuco has lost all his heritage: his language, religion, customs, beliefs. He is left with only body and soul exposed to the hostile elements, oblivious to all who stare"). He could very well be referring to ANCdV himself, who apparently had lost all he had, even though he really was only disguising it by mimicking the fashion style of his hosts. But ANCdV really identified himself with the symbol of the cross—just as the pachucos did with the cross tattooed on their hands—and thus he was able to survive even with his soul and body exposed to the hostile elements surrounding him. In underscoring the ambiguous alterity of the pachuco's image and comportment (he has "lost all his heritage: his language, religion, customs, beliefs. He is left only with body and soul exposed; oblivious to all who stare") Paz seems to be describing

ANCdV the Amerindian, the castaway who transformed his failure into a triumph, not only with respect to the body, but later in the body of his text itself.

If we look once more at ANCdV, perhaps we can better understand the Mexicans' viewpoint. As I described it earlier, when Amerindian ANCdV encountered the Spanish soldiers, they took one look at him and were left speechless. The author attributes to them a "great alteration," and this is the key. ANCdV's alterity provoked such consternation in the Spaniards that they themselves were altered momentarily. They were horrified at the sudden vision of the possibility of transforming themselves not only into the Other but into the hated Other, despised and dehumanized: the Indian. Today, for the Mexicans the Chicano represents that possibility of becoming their most hated rival, the North American who inevitably is destined to be their partner in the evolution of humanity. Distant critics do not have to name the Silence because it does not affect them directly. The Mexicans, on the other hand, do have to name it because it threatens their very existence. They cover the Chicano with pejorative labels because it is a way of distancing themselves from us, so as not to see themselves reflected in an alienated object. They concretize and distance the threat from that which they seek to protect—the inviolable pole of authenticity. They do this because they are painfully aware that we are their inevitable future, just as the Spaniards knew the Mexican *mestizaje* (mixture of the races) would be their future if they remained in the New World.[1]

It is impossible for the above two groups—Mexicans and more distanced critics—to see Chicanos from our own perspective because it implies the destruction of their binary system of relations. To preserve their system they must perceive our way of being, our alterability, as schizophrenic, as a mental aberration characterized by the shifting of one identity into another. Incongruent hybridism, imperceptible identity, *pocho,* and *pachuco* (as used by Paz) are euphemisms for a phenomenon that appears to them to be an unstable essence. The same thing happened with all the other names for Americans, from the misapplied "Indian" to each hyphenated ethnic, because American reality is essentially a shifting, changing one.

The crisis of alterability nevertheless provokes disturbing vacillation even among Chicanos. Oscar Zeta Acosta, after being expelled from Mexico for not behaving like a Mexican and then accused by a border immigration officer of not "looking" American, ponders in which *we* he should locate his *I*. "My

single mistake has been to seek an identity with any one person or nation or
with any part of history . . . what is clear to me after this sojourn is that I
am neither a Mexican nor an American. I am neither a Catholic nor a Prot-
estant" (1972: 199). Acosta's autobiography seems to parody ANCdV's *Relación*. At one time Acosta also participated in a grandiose project that aimed
to conquer an uncharted zone: the War on Poverty, which began as President
John F. Kennedy's "New Frontier." Acosta, however, feels like a spy within
that project; he is a lawyer who hates the law; or, put another way, he is
simultaneously inside and outside the law. When the project fails, Acosta
is left adrift among strange people who reduce him to a state of almost complete alienation. In order to recuperate his identity he travels throughout the
Southwest searching for kindred spirits. This search leads him to explore
mind-altering drugs such as cocaine, LSD, and mescaline; or to participate in
aberrant religious rites. As an ascetic trial, Acosta's adventure reduces him to
an existence denuded of all that is superficial, thus preparing him for the
culminating revelation, which in this instance takes the form of a return to
his origins, to his native land—Mexico. It is at this point that the crisis
of the alterability of his identity provokes in him the realization of his in-
betweenness cited above. However, in contrast to ANCdV, Acosta can call on
a new ideology which provides him with a name for his essence. "I am a
Chicano by ancestry and a Brown Buffalo by choice. Is that so hard for you
to understand? Or is it that you choose not to understand for fear that I'll get
even with you?" (Acosta, 199). He could very well be ANCdV confronting
the judges who exiled him from both Spain and Latin America; or perhaps
Turner's "White Indian": the *mestizo* who chooses to reorient himself through
indigenous culture. The ideal of race mixture—the logical and biological
solution to the oxymoron "White Indian"—is reiterated throughout Chicano
literature. In the 1960s the voice that was to name the Silence emerged with
the refrain so often repeated in numerous works: I am Chicano.

Those initiated into Chicano culture will now recognize the similarity
with ANCdV. In fact, the similarities are astounding: leaving a native land
in search of riches in a territory mostly unknown except for the hyperbolic
legends surrounding it; the disillusionment felt upon facing the harsh and
humiliating truth of the reality encountered; the loss of the original cultural
context in exchange for a new one which is hostile and alienating, capable
of reducing the immigrant to slavery. Through a slow apprenticeship, great

hardships, and *mimesis,* immigrants begin to improve their social position among the native population until they are able to leave menial jobs for more respected positions which permit greater mobility. Frequently immigrants must take jobs the local citizens do not care to engage in because they are difficult, dangerous, or even illegal. Oftentimes the jobs require the workers to travel from one place to another, risking their lives and exposing themselves to the vicissitudes of weather conditions, violence, and the whims of their employers, who represent the local power structure. In addition, immigrants are forced to learn a new language so that they can communicate with the local population while still trying to maintain their own language through infrequent but much-appreciated contact with other immigrants who have survived the journey. In moments of crisis the immigrants seek refuge in the memories of their native land and in their religion, at first practiced clandestinely, but later on, as the native population begins to appreciate the immigrants' utility, it is practiced more openly—even in public among the locals. Immigrants can acquire certain privileges in the educative and political process, though always under the control of those who manipulate the system for their own benefit. At times immigrants are granted a prize by the native cultural priests, of which they tend to be overly proud, showing it off as if it were a Nobel Prize. These rewards open up new spaces through which the immigrant travels, playing the role of the marvelous newcomer never envisioned by the hosts. The hosts are fascinated by the prodigious feats the newcomers are able to accomplish. These accomplishments greatly surprise the local people, who have perceived the immigrants as ignorant and useless entities. Equally shocking is the ease with which some immigrants are able to betray their compatriots and sell them out in order to please the hosts. On the other hand, there is a desire on the part of the more established Mexicans and Chicanos to share social mobility with the less fortunate by offering them the superficial signs of success, without fully comprehending the futility of possessing the signs without having the cultural preparation acquired through assimilation, education, and, above all, fluency in the language. The immigrants awaken the interest of native scientists, who try to associate with them in order to participate in their new and exciting vitality. There is, however, vacillation among these scientists and among librarians as to the proper classification under which the immigrants fall, resulting in the placement of the immigrants under a series of multiple listings and classification systems. There is an apparent surface acceptance as long as the immigrants maintain a discreet distance and a respect for native institutions. And, of course, there is an insistence on categorizing us as a floating population— always the foreigners—while in Mexico they view us as *descastados*, too assimilated to the "American way of life"; but in spite of all this they utilize us to establish international relations when it is to their advantage both on this side of the border and on the other side; and so on, and so on.

Today the designation *Chicano*, even though it offers the possibility of encompassing all within a common liberating experience, seems to be relegated to the status of an anchorless entity drifting within the community it seeks to unite. The Chicano is left isolated between the binary poles—near one pole are the supposed Mexicans, who even though they reside in the United States insist on being what they are not; and near the other pole are the Mexican Americans, who insist that they are no longer what the binomial reminds them they are. In the face of Anglo-American society, the Mexican American is the one who shifts identities, becoming more like the Chicano while at the same time attempting nervously to move toward an illusory Mexican. When facing the Mexican national the game may seem different, though its fundamental dynamics are one and the same. In the final analysis, our essence is in the legacy of an alterability in search of its own center from which we can relate all under a stable and vital order without forgetting that at any moment our ship can sink, leaving us once again shipwrecked in the seas of signification. In that sense we represent the true American dream. That is to say, the most disturbing thing about Alvar Núñez Cabeza de Vaca and his descendants is that they reveal in their alterity the inherent instability of any identity system, and they make out of it a virtue and a source of great pride.

NOTES

This essay was awarded the Premio Plural for best essay written in 1989. It was translated from the Spanish by María Herrera-Sobek.

1. For more information on the attitudes of Mexican writers toward Chicanos see Bruce-Novoa, "Chicanos in Mexican Literature," in *Missions in Conflict: Essays on U.S.-Mexican Relations and Chicano Culture*, ed. Renate Von Bardeleen, Dietrich Briesemeister, and Juan Bruce-Novoa (Tübingen: Gunter Narr Verlag, 1989), 55–64.

REFERENCES

Acosta, Oscar Zeta. 1972. *The Autobiography of a Brown Buffalo*. San Francisco: Straight Arrow Books.

Bruce-Novoa, Juan. 1982. *Chicano Poetry, a Response to Chaos*. Austin: University of Texas Press.

Eliade, Mircea. 1972. *Tratado de historia de las religiones*. Mexico City: Ediciones ERA, 1972.

Favata, Martín A., and José B. Fernández, eds. 1986. *La "Relación" o "Naufragios" de Alvar Núñez Cabeza de Vaca*. Potomac, Md.: Scripta Humanística.

García Morales, Justo. 1960. "Prólogo" to *Naufragios*. 2d ed. Madrid: Aguilar. González Barcia Carballido y Zúñiga, Andrés. 1749. *Naufragios De Alvar Núñez Cabeza de Vaca, y Relación De La Jornada que hizo a la Florida con el Adelantado Pánfilo de Narváez*. Vol. 1 of *Historiadores primitivos de las Indias occidentales, que junto, traduxo en parte y sacó a luz, ilustrados con eruditas Notas y copiosos índices, el Ilustríssimo Señor D. Andrés González Barcia*. Madrid: n.p.

Lagmanovich, David. 1978. "Los *Naufragios* Alvar Núñez como construcción narrativa." *Kentucky Romance Quarterly* 25(1): 27–37.

Leal, Luis. 1979. "Mexican American Literature: A Historical Perspective." In *Modern Chicano Writers, a Collection of Critical Essays*. Ed. Joseph Sommers and Tomás Ybarra-Frausto. Englewood Cliffs, N.J.: Prentice-Hall, 18–30.

Long, Haniel. 1936. *Interlinear to Cabeza de Vaca, His Relation of the Journey from Florida to the Pacific, 1528–1536*. Santa Fe: Writer's Editions.

Molloy, Silvia. 1986. "Alteridad y reconocimiento en Los *Naufragios* de Alvar Núñez Cabeza de Vaca." In *Selected Proceedings of the Seventh Louisiana Conference on Hispanic Languages and Literatures*. Ed. Alfred Lozada. Baton Rouge: Louisiana State University Press, 13–33.

Paz, Octavio. 1967. *El laberinto de la soledad*. Mexico City: Fondo de Cultura Económica.

Smith, Buckingham, trans. 1966. *Relation of Alvar Núñez Cabeza de Vaca*. Ann Arbor: University Microfilms.

Todorov, Tzvetan. 1984. *The Conquest of America, the Question of the Other*. New York: Harper and Row.

Turner, Frederick. 1980. *Beyond Geography: The Western Spirit Against the Wilderness*. New York: Viking Press.

Vasconcelos, José. 1957. *La tormenta*. In *Obras completas*, vol. 1. Mexico City: Libreros Mexicanos Unidos.

Discontinuous Continuities

Remapping the Terrain of Spanish Colonial Narrative

GENARO PADILLA

Writing in his "Memorias"[1] of an 1870 journey of some two hundred miles to resettle his family, Rafael Chacón makes a startling imaginative recovery: "Since this trip from my old dwelling place [Peñasco, New Mexico] to a new country with my family was in all ways typical of an emigration much like that which might have been made in colonial times by our ancestors, for curiosity's sake I wanted to keep a concise diary of the journey."

In one culturally integrative moment, Chacón summons forth the experiential and discursive network of the Spanish colonial exploration and settlement period. His reverence for the *crónica*, the *diario*, and *derrotero* (navigation journal) tradition is at once an unexpected and yet entirely logical cultural reaffiliation with a set of narrative practices that preceded him by two or more centuries. Although he never names Francisco Coronado, Antonio de Espejo, Juan de Oñate, Fray Alonso de Benavides, or Padres Domínguez and Escalante, nor can we be sure that he had read any of their various narratives, he knew that his colonial ancestors kept diaries of their journeys over a terrain that in being described was being mapped, and in being mapped was undergoing transformation into colonial geographical space that would sustain a new geocultural identity and, henceforth, a home in a different but no longer unknown territory. The homeland invented in just such an imperial cartographic maneuver was sustained from the end of the sixteenth century to the middle of the nineteenth, when another imperial regridding shook that domestic space. Writing after the map of the Hispano-Mexicano homeland had

been torn apart by the North American conquest, Chacón's glimmering colonial recursion discloses a descent line that shadows forth a discursive grid
presented in its absence. It is the problematics of this discursive continuity
in discontinuity that I reflect upon in this essay.

I

My first line of questioning proceeds from my own work in recovering and
studying Chicano autobiography. In a recent essay that outlines my thinking
on the emergence of autobiography in Chicano culture I wrote:

> Reconstructing the history of autobiography discourse largely entails construct-
> ing a tradition. Constructing a tradition likewise demands making decisions
> that are likely to have socio-literary, cultural, and ideological consequences. I
> might argue, for example, that we can legitimately trace the autobiographic
> tradition to the Spanish exploration narrative. Alvar Núñez Cabeza de Vaca's
> La Relación (1542), one may say, represents the first autobiographical account
> of life in the New World, which together with Pedro de Castañeda's Relación de
> la jornada de 1540, Juan de Oñate's Proclamación (1598), Eusebio Kino's Favores
> Celestiales (ca. 1711), and scores of other military and missionary "relaciones"
> and "diarios" constitute an enormous field of narrative that may be considered
> autobiographical.[2]

I went on, however, to make the usual self-serving disconnection with the
"early" Hispanic colonial literary activity by moving quickly to an easily
conceptualizable social-political event that, as literary historians are wont to
do, I equated with a measurable discursive break: "The project to resituate
this [Spanish colonial] literature must commence," I said, "but here is of
necessity deferred in order to consider the autobiographical literature that
came into formation after the American invasion of northern Mexico in
1846."[3] I still agree with Raymund Paredes and others of us who mark the
U.S.-Mexican War as the "great divide in Chicano [literary] history" and still
affirm that "the war itself and the rapid Americanization of the West set off
social, political, economic, linguistic, and cultural shock waves that generated a rhetorical situation in which Mexicans inscribed themselves upon history as a warrant against oblivion."[4]

Yet, there is a contradiction here. On the one hand, I argue that we may
trace the autobiographic tradition to scores of colonial relaciones, diarios, crónicas, and derroteros; on the other hand, I say that there indeed was a decisive

rupture, which generated a radically distinct rhetorical situation after 1848. But perhaps such contradiction is the necessary juncture of loose ends that will reinvigorate our thinking about the precursive presence of a disrupted colonial narrative tradition. The self-competing notion of continuity in discontinuity is suggested in Luis Leal's well-known essay "Mexican American Literature: A Historical Perspective" when Don Luis refers to the "long uninterrupted literary tradition which while undergoing development of the literature of the region . . . did not interrupt the tradition."[5] And Francisco Lomelí hints at such a continuity when referring to the "literary samples" found in newspapers during the half century after the American invasion that "indicate a direct transference of the Colonial and Mexican period" in "segments of memoirs and diaries."[6]

As both of my colleagues would agree, we must set ourselves the task of recovering this long-uninterrupted, but buried, literary tradition. I shall address that portion of the project in the second part of this essay, but first I wish to ask a question or two. Something about these hopeful equations, especially my own, strikes me as inadequate explanation of what took place between the end of the late colonial period—the end of the eighteenth century—and the last quarter, say, of the nineteenth century. Although there can be no doubt that the sociopolitical rupture caused by the U.S.-Mexican War created an immediate spatial and political discontinuity—the map of Mexico had been altered forever—*other* reasons may be cited for the decline of certain discursive practices before the American conquest. And it is these intraculturally discursive gaps that we must account for more clearly. For while it may be the case that an oral poetics (*cuentos, romances, dramas, inditas, corridos*) remained in uninterrupted practice, the same cannot be said of a narrative tradition that establishes the ground of autobiographical discourse, and although I may be pushing things, the development of the novel. To pursue the other side of Leal's and Lomelí's theory of literary continuity, we might wonder what kind of *discontinuities* were appearing before and despite the American presence.

What I wish to consider here are the discursive devolutions that were already taking place by the end of the eighteenth century: the gradual decline in the practice of writing elaborate *relaciones, crónicas,* and *derroteros.* The reasons for this decline may perhaps best be understood in light of a cartographic metaphor. The cartographic narrative served as what William Boelhower calls, in referring to European mapmaking of New World territory, a "military apparatus, a means of monitoring possessions, a tool of power, an operational scheme."[7] The Spanish colonial charting of what David Weber and others refer to as "New Spain's far northern frontier"[8] was nearly complete by the end of the eighteenth century. The last great wave of narratives was composed during the establishment of settlements in northern California during the last quarter of the eighteenth century, including Juan Bautista de Anza's two major exploration and settlement expeditions: one charting the terrain between Sonora (Tubac, Arizona) and California (San Gabriel mission), and another that established the first settlement in San Francisco in 1776. The two expeditions generated thirteen diaries; examples of these include de Anza's own "Diario de la Ruta y Operaciones" (1775–76); Fray Pedro Fónt's short "Diario" (1775–76), and his "Diario Completo" (composed in 1777); Fray Francisco Garcés's "Diario" (1775); Joachín de Moraga's "Carta de la ocupación de San Francisco"; and the well-known Fray Francisco Palóu's "Noticias de Nuevo California" (1776)—a narrative several hundred pages in length. And, of course, there is the famous Domínguez-Escalante narrative (1775–76) of the unsuccessful mapping of a trail from Santa Fe to California. A handful of other *relaciones* and *diarios* were written after this period, but the aforementioned are really the classic and final articulations of the mapping colonial "I."

Hence it appears that the cartographic function had largely exhausted itself by the beginning of the nineteenth century. Topographic identity had been established with the settling of Texas, New Mexico, Arizona, and California. Numerous official reports detailing social and economic conditions in colonial territories were regularly written: for example, Miguel de Constansó's "Report of 1791"[9] on the California presidios; Governor Juan Bautista de Elguezábal's "Description of Texas in 1803,"[10] and Governor Manuel de Salcedo's "Governor's Report on Texas in 1809;"[11] and in New Mexico, Governor Fernando de Chacón's "Economic Report of 1803,"[12] Pedro Baptista Pino's "Exposición sucinta y sencilla de la provincia del Nuevo México (1812),"[13] and Antonio Barreiro's "Ojeada sobre Nuevo México que da una idea de sus producciones naturales, y de algunas otras cosas" (1832).[14] But the exploring "I" virtually disappeared once the terrain had been mapped. Or, put another way, topographic identity had been sufficiently established that narratives substantiating presence and possession were no longer required.

Once the map was complete at the end of the eighteenth century— complete in the sense that the Spanish colonial project had calcified, had marked its boundaries, and would be largely satisfied to build its home on terra cognita—further mapping was deemphasized. The cartographic colonial "I" had renamed the rivers, bays, mountains, valleys, and forests. This toponymic transformation, along with the establishment of a line of missions, presidios, and towns from California to Nuevo México, from Pimería Alta (Arizona) to Tejas, signaled Spanish colonial control of what had been indigenous domain.

Then, of course, New Spain became Mexico (1821), and most of northern Mexico became United States territory—borders were violated once again, and another cartographic transformation ensued. Sociodiscursive necessity arose. The colonial narrative enterprise was remembered as a memory of discursive practice, if not as an actual textual repository. That is to say, the conditions for inscribing themselves on history and resituating themselves on the map had been prepared for unborn Mexican Americans by a colonial discourse that was itself a warrant against oblivion, albeit an imperial warrant. The accruing volume of a cartographic discourse that quite literally marked out the colonial terrain of far northern New Spain—a discourse generated and sustained by imperial desire to possess bodies, souls, and landmass—would reappear only after the Spanish colonial and Mexican maps had been recharted. The post-1848 (1836 in Texas, of course) deposed colonial subject—now the subject in subordination in its truest political sense—would recall a disused practice to sustain itself.

After the U.S.-Mexican War, personal narrative appeared that may be read as issuing from a threatened geocultural locus of identity. Remembering a pre-American cultural landscape may be regarded as the attempt to remember one's place on the map of another world. This in part explains why there is such a compelling tendency for personal narrative to read nostalgically, and why much of this narrative mythifies the Spanish colonial enterprise. Mariano Guadalupe Vallejo's "Recuerdos históricos y personales" (1875),[15] for example, resembles the very history that would swallow it—namely, Bancroft's *History of California*[16]—but it also resembles Spanish colonial discourse in its tracings of the *crónicas* and *relaciones,* its articulation of Spanish colonial possessiveness, its ethnological descriptions, and its remapping of the California hinterland. Vallejo's is a narrative that anguishes for the substance of an absent colonial self. Indeed, most of the Californio narratives nostalgically recall a pre-American map glimmering under a Spanish flag. But it is not only in California that we discover imperial nostalgia. J. M. Rodríguez's "Memoirs of Early Texas" reestablishes noble lines of descent to supposedly pure Spaniards from the Canary Islands, among them a lieutenant "who was knighted by the King of Spain for meritorious conduct . . . November 1786" and other ancestors "born in Castille." [17]

The difference, of course—and this is the crux of my thinking on this matter—is that whereas the colonial cartographic narrative is a discourse of power, a discourse in which the Spanish subject is a figure of domination, the post-1848 narrative is a discourse in which figurations, or self-conceits, of power are cracking at the seams. The post-1848 Mexican American narrator—embittered Californios or the dispossessed Tejanos—finding themselves shoved off their property, seek to recover a legitimating relation between themselves and a remembered, or imagined, colonial presence that will sustain a narrow ground upon which to stand now that the map has been pulled out from under their feet.

Self-deluding, socially contradictory, and politically futile, these reenactments of a colonial drama of grandeur and power are narratives of resistance to the American hegemony. Of course, after reading extensive *diarios* and *relaciones* of journeys covering thousands of miles by Castañeda, Kino, de Anza, Crespi, Fónt, and Garcés, Rafael Chacón's reenactment of the colonial travel diary evinces the pathetic condition of disempowerment in which nineteenth-century Hispanos found themselves. Chacón's original diary is only a few pages covering a journey of only two hundred miles, and the same diary reconstructed in his "Memorias" is not much elaborated or lengthened; Fónt's original short diary, or *borrador,* consists of eighty pages, while the complete diary, "with some extension and clarification," is over four hundred pages long.

My rather extravagant comparison here is not meant to diminish or denigrate Chacón's achievement, because I regard his "Memorias" as a stunning example of a genealogically reempowering narrative. However, I do mean to call forceful attention once again to a paradoxic condition of continuity in discontinuity: Chacón's conscious reenactment of a colonial practice signifies continuity, but the product is obviously muted by social discontinuity—the disrupted spatiocultural grid allowing neither expansive journey nor elaborate notation. Yet, Chacón's micro-*diario* opens into the wider text of his "Memorias," which itself sustains a line of continuity for the emergence of such narratives as Fabiola Cabeza de Baca's densely topographic and toponymic *We Fed Them Cactus* (1954), which opens with an elaborate remapping of the *llano* (plains) in southeastern New Mexico explicitly traceable to Castañeda's narrative of Coronado's expedition of 1540–42.

I would venture to say that a good deal of Mexican American personal narrative has been obsessed with renegotiating cartographic identity; that is, whereas the map of pre-American identity was firm ground—in the colonial imagination if not in fact—the post-1848 map was in disarray, was resectored into estranging grids, as evidenced in Chacón's ambivalence about the re-mapped territory of southern Colorado, a vast area that was culturally continuous with northern New Mexico. For members of Chacón's generation, the Americanized map was quite simply culturally illogical. One discovers in much autobiography a *necessary* preoccupation with the formation of identity in the bound association of colonial culture and geography. Hence, the autobiographic imperative—when it did emerge after 1836–48—was motivated by a desire to reconstruct a geocultural terrain on which the "I" might once again make a permanent home.

Often, home is never found or reestablished, as in the case of Juan Seguín, who seemed doomed to wander all over the map: he crossed the border to live in Mexico in 1841, returned to San Antonio after 1848, left in disgust to Nuevo León in the 1860s, died in Mexico in 1890, but sometime later was disinterred and taken back to Texas to rest—strangely enough—in his name place, Seguín. His "Personal Memoirs" (1858)[18] does not trace this entire schizophrenic movement, but it does predict it. Following the American usurpation of Texas, which he had helped foment and by which he had been betrayed, Seguín became a ghostly presence who, to borrow from Boelhower borrowing from John Smith, in having a "*History* without *Geography wandereth* as *vagrant* without a *certain habitation*."[19]

Yet, Chacón's *diario,* however truncated, documents his intention of recombining history and geography when he moved his family to a "new country" that had been created by an act of Congress, which, he writes, took "from New Mexico all that part that lay between Ratón and the Arkansas River" (314). Although this country was peopled by numerous relatives and friends, it had been cartographically defamiliarized by the Americans. As Chacón wrote during the journey, he and his wife, Juanita, "were going . . . to test what destiny would hold in a strange country and among strange people." It is simultaneously an act of fear and faith, a gesture of continuity in discontinuity, that generates his conscious reconnection with a colonial discursive practice: he keeps a "diary of the journey" not, as he says, for "curiosity's sake" but because the diary serves the cartographic function we see in Fónt, Garcés, Crespi, and Palóu. Chacón's "concise diary of the journey" restores history and geography in a recursive cultural maneuver intended to recolonize the map, and in so doing restores a place of habitation that Chacón from 1870 to his death in 1925 would know as home; likewise, his "Memorias" reoccupies the colonial narrative habitus that had been abandoned but not forgotten.

Upon reading Chacón's reconnection with the colonial cartographic habit of tracking the journey, I knew I was witnessing the complex play of discursive practices within our own Chicano culture. It is not necessary to insist that our literary tradition has continued uninterrupted; yet it has had presence enough to recover itself discontinuously through a form of discursive memory, the intracultural collective memory and transmission of textual narrative without actual material presence. Castañeda's "Relación," Benavides's "Memorial," Palóu's "Noticias," and Pino's "Exposición" might all be widely known in the culture without being read. Rather than arguing for uninterrupted development, therefore, it might make more sense to discern how our literary discourse branches and imbricates, sustains itself but also exhausts certain practices at one historical juncture only to recover some approximate practice at other junctures, crosscuts, jumps between genres, or borrows forms and filters historically dissonant articulation through them, disappears, and then arches from one necessary discursive moment to another. Such a literary tradition complicated by multiple social, cultural, and political contingencies quiets expectations that a tradition requires an unbroken line of literary practices and gives those of us who are recovering our literary antecedents the relief of knowing that our job is not that of reconstructing a seamless line of descent.

II

Reading Hispanic colonial literary discourse back into the cultural archive, only a decade after reference to the Spanish colonial presence was regarded with suspicion by many Chicano scholars, signals another necessary revisionist turn in our thinking about Chicano literary formation. Notice how María Herrera-Sobek marked the incongruity that must guide our thinking here: the poster for the conference held in 1989 at the University of California, Irvine, advertised the title "Hispanic/Chicano Colonial Literature of the Southwest." What a provocative conflation of terms. What is our intention in undertaking this reconnective, or reconstructive, procedure? Do we wish to valorize a discourse from which a decade ago we ideologically disaffiliated ourselves? Are we proposing that the literature of the colonial period may now be incorporated entirely into that of the contemporary period? Is this a move to invent continuity between colonial Hispanic and Chicano literary discourse—the first a hegemonic discourse of possession and domination, the second a counterhegemonic discourse generated by dispossession and subordination? And do we wish to resuscitate a literary antecedence that we shall now ideologically launder before incorporating it into the current counterhegemonic project? Or do we wish to engage in a cultural analysis that unravels the contradictions, the unsettling social reversals that destabilize and enrich our analysis? Finally, what are the implications for future literary scholarship—not to mention the implications for future literary discourse itself—the novel, drama, poetry?

I believe that we must train ourselves to accept the entire discursive field of the Spanish colonial period as part of the enabling work constituting our social subjectivity. There are profound ideological stakes involved because much of this literature constitutes a discourse of domination over indigenous people: the *relaciones, diarios,* and *cartas* map the terrain of imperial exploration, describe the military strength or vulnerability of various tribes, and in a typical Eurocentric manner degrade native social and cultural practices. Spanish colonial literature is generally a discourse of power and "othering." We must recover this literature not to celebrate a vanished imperial discourse but to reestablish the lines of a socioideologic complexity that will illuminate the continuity in discontinuity that characterizes the formation of our literature before and after 1846. Hence, the recovery of this literary discourse must be attended by a critical enterprise that at the level of recovery describes diachronic formations but, not satisfied with tracing elementary lines of descent, also engages in a discussion of the systemic operations of a colonial discourse generated by the empire's exercise of power. For it was sheer colonial power that established a discursive grid of presence in scores, hundreds, of *relaciones, diarios, cartas,* and *derroteros.*

It is this discourse of presence—often conveyed in epic and heroic language—that we need to reconsider with revisionary zeal. One form of revision would examine the formation of a cultural consciousness in narratives that shift from description of movement to description of settlement; that is, narrative less and less preoccupied with mapping the trail in—so as to mark the trail back—than in fixing the quadrants of a new home. Narrative, one hopes, that is less and less a discourse of colonial power than one of *mestizaje*, or Indo-Hispano process. When, for instance, does the *diario*, the *relación*, or the *derrotero* cease being an official report on the *provincias* and become a discourse of presence and permanence for groups whose daily experience was increasingly nativized by contact with indigenous groups and unique ecological habitats? We must read for the exigencies that test the known terrain of colonial knowledge, and in the process restructure language's imperial gaze. Only when we have a full reading of such transformations can we begin to understand how the grid of colonial discourse was turned on its head after 1848 when personal narrative, *romance* and *corrido* (ballad), poetry and fiction began to combat the unraveling of a sociopolitical presence it had taken for granted during its own period of colonial domination.

We must also consider what effect the recuperation of a prior discursive configuration, in all of its manifestations, will have on future Chicano cultural production. Indeed, a general project to reconstruct a literary heritage entails precisely the kind of archaeological recovery and interpretive activity that will map out future continuities where there have been major discontinuities, gaps, broken lines of literary filiation. This requires a critical act of imagination in which the presence of the past becomes traceable in the contemporary Chicano literary culture even as material absence would interdict evidenciary intertextuality.

Reconstructing a literary genealogy with lines from the colonial period to the present is, some scholars may worry, a superficial or forced critical maneuver. One might argue that while the archaeological effort to recuperate prior literary material demonstrates that people were writing literature long before the Chicano movement, a true intertextual history cannot be established except by sleight of hand. That is, the argument continues, such an effort would recover texts that by definition could not have had much influence—if any at all—on the writers of the Chicano movement. Hence, laudable as such an archaeology may be in certain respects, it would furnish only a doubtful basis for a true intertextual history.[20]

Such a challenge relies upon what appears to be the commonsense argument that there can be little or no "influence" without direct intertextuality, especially since literary influence has traditionally been based on the presence of imbricating and dialectically interacting texts. However provocative, such reasoning is intellectually unadventurous and retrograde. The notion that discontinuous cultural production, or a lost literature, cannot establish a true intertextual history—that, by definition, lost texts cannot be thought to furnish an adequate basis for an intertextual history, impresses me as a sequence of assertions that is myopic in its insistence that influence and intertextuality are contingent on a smoothly organic incorporation of read texts into texts in production. It bears remembering, moreover, that continuous incorporation has been historically disrupted by the dominant culture. Our literary texts have been suppressed, summarily dismissed, or read/regenred as social history, ethnography, or folklore. As I have shown relative to personal narrative, scores of autobiographical materials have been archivally silenced and other literary texts ignored because they were published in Spanish or snubbed because they were self-published. I believe that further interdisciplinary exchange between historians, cultural anthropologists, ethnomusicologists, and literary scholars will gradually show just how well and pervasively our people have sustained what I call narrative knowledge, a capacity for sustaining not only our epics, our *cuentos* and *corridos*, our poetry and drama, many of which, while not circulating textually in the social realm, were, as I suggested in my opening remarks on Rafael Chacón, well enough remembered (circulated in the domain of oral narrative) to be incorporated into new narratives.

Moreover, we must not forget that literary history is always a constructed knowledge, an artificial procedure, an extraliterary enterprise with an ultimate effect on the literary. Intertextual lines are not organic or continuous, much less chronologically overlapping. Sometimes even texts that have become major literary documents are, it turns out, scholarly reincorporations. That is to say, they are strategic and usually ethnocentric interventions intended to alter not only literary history as an academic enterprise but also literary production itself—a space is wedged open, a prior text long suppressed or forgotten is interpolated, succeeding writers working within a socioliterary configuration incorporate the prior material into the domain of new cultural production.

On discovering the contradictions in the practice of Americanist literary history, Phillip Ortego was quick to point out that recovering and reinstalling lost minority texts will be nothing new to mainstream literary scholars. Of one canonic monument he writes: "The English epic *Beowulf* found no mention in English literature until an antiquary published a garbled summary in 1707; no English translation was made until 1837. Yet we do not introduce Beowulf into English histories as literature of the 18th or 19th centuries. It is discussed as the beginning, the source materials."[21] Ortego's irony here speaks to the concerns of those who want to restore Chicano literature.

In short, we must initiate a massive publishing agenda of the kind recently undertaken by Henry Lewis Gates, Jr., for African-American, and by Arnold Krupat and Brian Swann for Native American literary discourse. We are in a position to open a space for a diversity of texts that will guarantee our own presence in the long literary tradition to which Luis Leal has so long and so eloquently directed our attention. Remember, it is not a matter of resuscitating the Spanish colonial literary discourse in a move to heroize a rather ideologically problematic past; rather, we must reexplicate the formative lines of literary practice that constitute our cultural epistemology, the topology of which was broken by the dominant American hegemony and recently has been dismissed as Hispanophilic by our own Chicano scholars. Notwithstanding these breaks, the topological formation must be reconstructed if we expect to situate ourselves within a discursive tradition that is socially empowering. We must encourage proliferation, the unsilencing of archived material, as well as the republishing of politically unfashionable discourse. Multivoiced and multi-ideological literary texts must be invited into the play of our cultural poetics, where they will compete for legitimacy and intertextual significance.

NOTES

1. See Chacón's account of this journey in the recent edition of his "Memorias," in Jacqueline Dorgan Meketa, *Legacy of Honor: The Life of Rafael Chacón, a Nineteenth-Century New Mexican* (Albuquerque: University of New Mexico Press, 1986).

2. Genaro Padilla, "The Recovery of Chicano Nineteenth-Century Autobiography," *American Quarterly* 40 (September 1988): 287.

3. Ibid., 288.

4. Ibid., 288–89.

5. Luis Leal, "Mexican American Literature: A Historical Perspective," in *Modern Chicano Writers,* ed. Joseph Sommers and Tomás Ybarra-Frausto (Englewood Cliffs, N.J.: Prentice-Hall, 1979), 22.

6. Francisco Lomelí, "Eusebio Chacón: A Literary Portrait of 19th Century Mexico" (Unpublished manuscript), 14.

7. William Boelhower, *Through a Glass Darkly: Ethnic Semiosis in American Literature* (Oxford: Oxford University Press, 1987).

8. I am referring, of course, to the title of Weber's collection of essays on the Spanish colonial period in the Southwest: *New Spain's Far Northern Frontier: Essays on Spain in the American West, 1440–1821* (Albuquerque: University of New Mexico Press, 1979).

9. See Manuel Servín, "Constansó's 1791 Report on Strengthening New California's Presidios," *California Historical Society Quarterly* 49: 226.

10. Juan Bautista de Elguezábal, "A Description of Texas in 1803," ed. and trans. Odie Faulk, *Southwestern Historical Quarterly* 46.(April 1963): 513–15.

11. Manuel de Salcedo, "A Governor's Report on Texas in 1809," ed. and trans. Nettie Lee Benson, *Southern Historical Quarterly* 71 (April 1968): 611.

12. Fernando de Chacón, "Economic Report of 1803," ed. and trans. Marc Simmons, *New Mexico Historical Review* 60(1): 81–89.

13. Pedro Baptista Pino, "Exposición sucinta y sencilla de la provincia del Nuevo México (1812)," in *Three New Mexico Chronicles,* trans. H. Bailey Carroll and J. Villasana (Albuquerque: Quivira Society, 1942).

14. Antonio Barreiro, "Ojeada sobre Nuevo México que da una idea de sus producciones naturales, y de algunas otras cosas" (1832), in ibid.

15. Mariano Guadalupe Vallejo, "Recuerdos históricos y personales de alta California" (Manuscript collection, Bancroft Library, University of California, Berkeley).

16. Hubert H. Bancroft, *History of California* (San Francisco: The History Company, 1884–89).

17. J. M. Rodríguez, "Memoirs of Early Texas" (San Antonio, 1913), 44.

18. Juan Seguín, "Personal Memoirs" (San Antonio, 1858).

19. Boelhower, *Through a Glass Darkly,* 50.

20. I am here paraphrasing an argument that appeared in an unpublished essay questioning the efficacy of literary history for understanding contemporary Chicano literary production. The argument suggests that recuperative literary history is something of an antiquarian interest. Such an argument has often been mounted in discussions between Chicano scholars.

21. Phillip Ortego, "Backgrounds of Mexican American Literature" (Ph.D. diss., University of New Mexico), 22.

A Franciscan Mission Manual

The Discourse of Power and Social Organization

TINO VILLANUEVA

History tells us that the first permanent Spanish settlement in what was later to become the United States of America was established in Saint Augustine, Florida, in 1565. History likewise records that the first British colony was not established until the beginning of the seventeenth century in Jamestown, Virginia, in 1607.

It was precisely these dates and historical events that Philip Ortego used in 1971 to postulate a radically new thesis regarding the literary history of the United States: if the literature written in the thirteen colonies by British authors before 1776 forms the roots of American literature, then it should follow that the literature from the Spanish (and Mexican) colonial period in the Southwest written before 1848 should be considered the beginnings of Chicano literature. Ortego further suggested that in literary anthologies both periods of colonization, the Spanish and the British, "should appear under the heading 'North American Colonial Literature.'" [1]

Twenty years have passed since Ortego first made these statements, but his perceptive assertions have not been altogether heeded in the teaching of Chicano/a literature; the period that is almost always left out is still the Spanish colonial period, in spite of Ortego's convincing revisionist observation regarding the origins of Chicano and Anglo-American literature. Most often, works written in the twentieth century receive the most time and attention in university literature programs. Even when another literary period is included, it tends to be the second half of the nineteenth century; that is, after

1848, when the Mexicans living north of the Río Grande were suddenly transformed into North American citizens after the signing of the Treaty of Guadalupe-Hidalgo (the document that ended open warfare between the United States and Mexico).

Nevertheless, there are scholars specializing in Chicano literature who find time in their classes for texts properly belonging to the Spanish colonial period in the Southwest—texts pertaining to all types of genres: narrative accounts (*relaciones*), letters to the viceroy of New Spain, poems, memoirs, diaries, religious plays written as *autos* and shepherds' plays (*pastorelas*), and descriptions of Southwestern flora and fauna by the soldiers, explorers, friars, engineers, and Spanish urban planners and bureaucrats who for three hundred years were the main protagonists in the colonization of the American Southwest.

There is a voluminous corpus of historical and literary writings suggesting the roots of American literature, but few if any Hispanic works are included. To be sure, the Spanish writings produced in the years encompassing the sixteenth through nineteenth centuries are as essential to the interpretation and comprehension of Chicano culture and literature as the following texts written in English are significant to the understanding of North American literature and culture: the account regarding the Indians in Virginia written by Thomas Hariot (*A Briefe and True Report of the New Found Land of Virginia*, 1588); the descriptions of New England authored by Captain John Smith (*A Description of New England*, 1616); the history of the first settlement in New England, by William Bradford (*History of Plymouth Plantation*, 1646); accounts describing witchcraft and offering advice to future preachers (*The Wonders of the Invisible World*, 1693; and *Manuductio ad Ministerium*, 1726, respectively), by Cotton Mather; and the sermons of Jonathan Edwards (for example, the well-known "Sinners in the Hands of an Angry God," 1741).

The Chicano people did not emerge from a historical vacuum; all communities must go through historical and social processes in their evolution as historical entities. It is not the purpose of this essay to lament the Spanish conquest, or to denounce the not infrequent abuse the Indians experienced at the hands of the Spaniards in the colonization process. It is enough to point out that the discovery of America in general, and the presence of such a superpower as Spain was in that epoch in particular, provided the raw materials for those individuals interested in recording the events in which they were active participants. Each of them—soldiers, friars, and bureaucrats—

wrote about their own adventures and feats and defeats, describing in detail their observations of the new and the singular in those remote and fabulous lands in which they had recently arrived. As proof of this assertion we have the writings of Alvar Núñez Cabeza de Vaca (*Naufragios,* 1542) and Pedro de Castañeda de Nácera (regarding the expedition undertaken by Francisco de Coronado: *Relación de la jornada de Cíbola conpuesta por Pedro de Castañeda de Nácera . . .*, 1542); the accounts of military incursions into New Mexico led by Captain Francisco Sánchez Chamuscado (1581), Antonio de Espejo (1582), Gaspar Castaño de Sosa (1590), Juan Morlete (1591), Francisco Leyva de Bonilla (1593), and Antonio Gutiérrez de Humaña (1593); works by Gaspar de Villagrá (the epic poem *Historia de la Nueva México,* 1610) and Juan Antonio de la Peña (*Derrotero de la Expedición en la Provincia de los Texas, Nuevo Reyno de Philipinas . . .*, 1722); and the *Diario que hizo el Padre Fr. Gaspar José de Solís en la visita que fue a hacer de las misiones de la Provincia de Texas . . .* (1767). We must likewise not overlook the proto-Chicano text, if one may be permitted to call it such, of Pablo Tac, an Indian neophyte from the Misión de San Luis Rey de Francia (Oceanside, California), who published "Conversión de los San Luiseños de la Alta California" in Rome around 1835.[2]

The religious orders, in turn, finding themselves in intimate contact with the Indians and having deciphered the secrets of their language and their traditions, collected valuable data concerning the origins of these peoples and their customs, laws, and the social and physical environment in which they lived. At other times friars wrote *autos* and shepherds' plays for didactic and religious instructional purposes. Among the compilers of this vital information were Father Junípero Serra (his epistolary was edited in bilingual format by the Academy of American Franciscan History, 1955) and Friar Benito Fernández de Santa Ana (*Cartas y memoriales del Padre Presidente, Fray Benito Fernández de Santa Ana, 1736–1754*), who described the administrative and political life of the Mission Purísima Concepción. Some of the religious plays were published by Professor Arthur L. Campa in the 1930s (*Caín y Abel, Adán y Eva, Coloquio de San José, Auto de los Reyes Magos, El Niño perdido*); and the untitled shepherds' play written by Florencio Ibáñez at the beginning of the nineteenth century is included in Antonio S. Blanco's *La lengua española en la historia de California* (1971).

The following commentary focuses on a religious text because it was specifically the *mission,* side by side with the *fort* and the settlers (or the *pueblo*), that played the most important role in the Spanish colonization process. Of these three institutions, the mission undoubtedly had the greatest influence because it not only exerted religious power but was itself a political, social, and cultural organ. Herbert E. Bolton is right in observing that

> the central interest around which the mission was built was the Indian. In respect to the native, the Spanish sovereigns, from the outset, had three fundamental purposes. They desired to convert him, to civilize him, and to exploit him. To serve these three purposes, there was devised, out of experience of the early conquerors, the *encomienda* system. It was soon found that if the savage were to be converted, or disciplined, or exploited, he must be put under control. To provide such control, the land and the people were distributed among Spaniards, who held them in trust, or in *encomienda*. The trustee, or *encomendero* . . . was strictly charged by the sovereign, as a condition of his grant, to provide for the protection, the conversion, and the civilization of the aborigines. . . . To provide the spiritual instruction and to conduct schools for the natives . . . the *encomenderos* were required to support the necessary friars, by whom the instruction was given.[3]

As Bolton notes, the friars and other missionaries assumed the role of agents who served the needs of the church as well as of the Spanish state.

As a frontier institution and civilizing and Christianizing entity, the mission eventually became a center of singular importance where the autochthonous population was instructed in the Spanish language and in Catholic doctrine as well as in crafts, weaving, poetry, tanning, cattle raising, and agricultural production. The greatest responsibility that fell on the religious orders, however, was that of Christianizing the Indians and propagating among them the traditions, doctrines, and beliefs basic to the Judeo-Christian faith and, by extension, the fundamental precepts and thought of Western culture. To overlook this significant missionary task is to ignore the considerable number of accounts, diaries, and friars' correspondence in which religious and devotional fervor are manifested in each paragraph. A cursory examination of Fray Junípero Serra's correspondence from California, for example, makes vividly patent the above claim.

It is not the epistolary of the renowned California missionary that I discuss in this essay, however, but the religious instructions of a friar who is relatively unknown—a Franciscan missionary who must have lived for some period in the Mission Purísima Concepción of San Antonio, in the Texas province. The fairly long document's title is *Instrucción para el Ministro de la Misión de la Purissima Concepción de la Provincia de Texas* (trans. as *Instructions for Minister of the Mission of Purissima Concepción of the Province of Texas*); it consists of twenty-two pages of small, crowded letters (with inconsistent punctuation). It was written around 1760, at the time of the mission's thriving period. The mission was supervised from Querétaro, Mexico, the center of the Colegio Apostólico para Misiones, which had this particular mission under its charge from its founding in 1731 up until 1772.

The *Instrucción para el Ministro* comprises eighty-three sections of instructions, as the author states, "para un Ministro que no haviendo governado Mision, se halla solo, y sin saber a quien consultar el methodo que debe observar" ("for a missionary who has never been in charge of a mission, is all alone, and does not know whom to consult for advice").[4] The text is interesting, first, for the quantity of facts it provides regarding the mission's activities. These data serve rather well as a window through which the religious and social life of the mission in the mid-eighteenth century can be viewed. But as no text is "innocent" (i.e., lacking in ideology), least of all one written by an educated man who represented the interests of the colonial viceroyalty (of the state and of the church), the second most important aspect of *Instrucción para el Ministro* is the inherent implications vis-à-vis the influence and power it could itself exert. It must be kept in mind that the borderlands were indispensable in defending the already conquered territories. The founding of the Fort of San Antonio de Béxar and the San Antonio Mission de Valero in 1718, plus four other missions founded thereafter, established in the western part of New Spain a frontier serving as a defense against the most warlike Indians (the Apaches, Comanches, Wichitas, and Karankawas). These missions also served to guard against the incursions of the French, who were advancing from the east. Consequently, establishing and having knowledge related to the maintenance of the missions in the far distant colonial provinces was of extreme importance for the Spanish colonial government. It is in this political-military and religious context that we must view *Instrucción para el Ministro*, which has as its subtitle *Methodo de Govierno que se observa en esta Misión de la Purissima Concepción, assi en los espiritual, como en lo temporal* (Method of managing spiritual and temporal affairs, as followed here at the Mission of Purissima Concepción). The eighty-three sections are followed by a brief *Advertencia* (Notice), which in turn is succeeded by a *Suplemento* consisting of footnotes to nine points of the *Instrucciones*.

It is the *Instrucciones* portion, the main body of the text, that is of interest here. If we begin with the thesis that there is no such thing as a neutral text, that all texts have a stake in this world and are connected to a specific context and reality and at times seek to further that particular reality, it is not surprising that the instructions expound mainly on Catholic doctrine. This can be seen explicitly from the first section (original spelling is conserved in the quotes):

1.

(Vease el Suplemento a no. 12.)

Todos los dias de fiesta sean de dos Cruces, que obligan a los Yndios, o sean de una cruz se dice Missa, y deben concurrir todos a oyrla; con la diferencia, que la Vispera del dia de dos Cruces se repica al medio dia, a la noche, y antes de la Missa; pero el dia de una Cruz no se repica al medio dia, sino solamente de la noche, y antes de la Missa.

1.

(See Supplement to no. 12.)

On all feast days, whether of two crosses [first-class feast], which bind the Indians, or of one cross [second class], Mass is offered and all should attend. There is this difference: on the eve of a first-class feast, the bells are rung at noon, in the evening, and before Mass; but on second-class feasts, the bells are not rung at noon, but only in the evening and before Mass.

Section 2 gives further instructions: "Todos los Sabados del año se acostumbra tambien decir Missa a la qual se repica antes de que ella; y si ay comodidad de que sea cantada, quando haiga quien la oficie, debe ser Concepcion los dias no impedido" ("On all Saturdays of the year it is also customary to say Mass and the bell is rung just before it. If it can be a high Mass [sung Mass] and someone is available to officiate, it should be the Mass of the Immaculate Conception whenever possible").

And with reference to Ash Wednesday (section 3): "El dia de Ceniza tambien se les dice Missa, despues de bendecirla, y de haverles puesto la ceniza a todos; para lo qual el Ministro previene al Fiscal[5] la Vispera para que queme la Palma y la tenga dispuesta a su tiempo" ("On Ash Wednesday Mass is also said after the blessing and distribution of the ashes. In preparation for this, the missionary delegates the *fiscal* to make preparations the evening before by burning the palms and having the ashes ready on time").

In section 4, further (and lengthy) instructions are offered for the "divine services during Holy Week." Both the *ministro* (the priest in charge of the mission) and the Indians have assigned duties and roles to carry out on Holy

Thursday, Good Friday, and Holy Saturday. Of particular interest in these initial sections is not so much the information on religious activities and how to proceed in the celebration of them, but the specific manner in which these particulars are spelled out. These introductory instructions are fraught with itemization—particulars as to who shall undertake what, on which day, at what time. What Chicano colonial literature scholar Armando Miguélez once said about another colonial document of the period might well apply to the *Instrucciones para el Ministro*: the prose of the Spanish chronicles written in the eighteenth century during the apogee of the Enlightenment came from a period in which there was avid interest in classifying and quantifying reality, almost in taxonomic fashion.[6]

A most remarkable aspect of the first four sections of this Franciscan text is that at no time does the friar instruct the future missionary with direct orders; instead, he utilizes the simple present tense in conjunction with the present progressive, employing the impersonal reflexive, which, in their ag- gregate, convey more forcefully the effect of an order. Consequently, the ver- bal phrases such as "se dice missa, y deben concurrir todos" ("Mass is offered, and all should attend"), "se repica al medio dia" ("the bells are rung at noon"), "no se repica al medio dia" ("the bells are not rung at noon"), "se acostumbra también" ("it is also customary"), "debe ser de Concepcion" ("it should be the Mass of the Immaculate Conception"), "se les dice Missa" ("Mass is said to them"), "el Ministro previene al Fiscal" ("the missionary delegates the *fiscal*"), "El hacer los oficios la Semana Santa esta al arbitrio de los Ministros" ("To hold divine services during Holy Week is left up to the judgment of the mis- sionaries"), "quando se hace la Semana Santa" ("when Holy Week services are held"), "sale procesion" ("the procession takes place"), "y a la noche predica el Ministro de los Misterios del dia" ("and at night the missionary preaches on the mysteries of the day"), "El Viernes Santo sale otra vez Procesion" ("On Good Friday the procession takes place again"), "se concluye con sermon de Pasion" ("[the service] ends with a sermon on the Passion"), "deben estar dos hombres con armas junto al Presviterio" ("two men with weapons are to be in the sanctuary"), all have concrete grammatical presence and are the signs that code the writing, together marking the text as paradigmatic of the discourse of power, because what is reiterated at every utterance is how to celebrate and carry out Roman Catholic ritual. The friar continues in section 6: "On Mardi Gras Sunday, Mass is sung in honor of Jesus of Nazareth, if possible, and for this the statue is taken from its niche and placed on the high altar, where it is kept all during Lent. On Palm Sunday the palms are blessed, which the missionary in due time has ordered to be brought from the headwater area, where all of the palms come from, and the procession starts according to the Ritual." And such is what *Instrucción para el Ministro* is all about: the continuation of ceremony, the perpetuation of order and ritual, and the doctrine of power now being transferred to other religious personnel; sentiments— nay, ideology—transmitted through grammatical structures that in the final analysis form the discourse of social order running through the entire text.

Other sections that relate to the Indians also reiterate various aspects of mission life through the use of codified grammatical structures. The colonization process was, after all, an exercise of domination and doctrinal instruction of the Indian:

> To obey the precept of annual confession, the Indians must be told when they can begin to fulfill their obligation because, although they now know that Lent is the time for that, if they are not reminded annually, they may allow the time to pass because of negligence. The best way is to assign a day for a certain number to come, and another day for another group, etc., if all the Indians cannot be taken care of in one day, as is done at Mission San José.

After that warning he continues:

> The evening before the principal feast of the Most Holy Virgin, namely the Immaculate Conception, the Rosary is said in procession on the plaza and the Indians sing the mysteries. In the meantime, firecrackers are set off and lights are lit in front of the friary. If so desired, the oil lamps are used, and candles are given to the Indian women to illumine their homes. When the Rosary is ended, the missionary sings the Litany, and the services end with the usual "Salve."

Such are some of the methods considered best to Christianize, and civilize, the Indians around Mission Purísima Concepción: the Pajalache, Tacame, Sanipao, and Mano de Perro. The power of the text resides in the instructions offered for the purpose of indoctrination to which these American Indians had to be subjected. The conquering of territory by force is of no significance if the souls of those living in that territory are not conquered as well. The friar, good pastor that he is, attempts to instruct his future colleague so that he in turn will inculcate the customs and rituals of the Catholic faith. If power can be associated with "influence" and "control," as Nelson W. Polsby has observed, and can be conceived "as the capacity of one actor to do something affecting another actor,"[7] there is no better example than the above, in which power is directed to another source of power; that is, a religious and lettered member of a ruling class, belonging to the side of the victors, addresses another religious and lettered friar from the same social class and conquering elite. And all of it exercised with the firm belief that they are under the directive of a Supreme Being (the Power behind the power) and the Holy Scriptures (the Text behind the text).

The manual *Instrucción para el Ministro* brings to light many other cultural aspects of interest for those who wish to know and understand the customs of the Mission Purísima Concepción. On the one hand, its author makes manifest the various personnel related to the mission and the functions they carry out. For example, section 20 depicts the Indian church musicians: "The musicians who perform in church usually are those who specialize in this. The missionary must supply them with musical instruments and repair them when this is needed. From time to time he sees to it that a boy learns how to play, so that there is always one who can play." This is followed by instructions on the mission cooks: "The missionary can change the cook when he wants to or alternate cooks by weeks or months, always selecting a man for the job. The employment of women could lead to disorder with single men in the kitchen."

Section 22 describes the role of the *obrajero* (overseer), the "one who understands all that pertains to his work and must be a man of judgment and maturity, since he deals with women constantly, and the boys whom he directs must find him worthy of respect."

Other sections include instructions on the various duties of the tailor (section 44), the blacksmith (section 51), the barber (section 52), and yet again the *ministro,* who "should see to it also that the small children speak Spanish in order to meet the demands of various decrees, and because of the facility which it promotes both for the missionary to understand what they are saying and for the Indians to understand him. The missionary has worked so hard on this that it is a pleasure to listen to the Indian children, even the tiniest ones speaking Spanish. In general, the men and women speak it now, except the newly arrived Indians, for the missionary spares no effort in helping them learn the language" (section 79).

Power seeks out power in an act of self-perpetuation. Indeed, what is conveyed throughout these instructions to future missionary priests is the idea of order and control, of power to be exerted at the religious and social levels of mission life. The last quote makes manifest the insistence on learning Spanish, crucial to handing down and continuing power. Thus, in terms of power relations, learning Spanish does not change the order of things one iota. Learning Spanish did not set the Indians free; rather, it enhanced the dominance of a coercive, Spanish-speaking, social institution—the Roman Catholic church. To learn from a text handed down and to become literate in Spanish was to become further subjugated, for Spanish was the language of conquest.

It is an undeniable fact that at each step of the *Instrucción para el Ministro de la Misión de la Purissima Concepción* one can sense an administrative as well as an ideological tone, all motivated by power. Through the medium of specific grammatical structures—the present-tense verbs, plus reflexive constructions and conjugations rendered in the future tense—a syntagmatic structure is created that is not narrative but exhortative in nature. What was desired for the Spanish colonies, especially for the Mission Purísima Concepción, was an established order, in the life of the conquerors as well as in that of the conquered. This desire was largely determined by the influence of an imperial western European culture set in motion by a military spirit and Catholic fervor. And behind this impulse was the belief in a God perceived to be the one who orders everything and is the author of the primordial Text, which has given rise to another text: *Instrucción para el Ministro de la Misión de la Purissima Concepción*.

NOTES

This essay was translated from the Spanish by María Herrera-Sobek.

1. Philip Ortego, "The Chicano Renaissance," in *La Causa Chicana: The Movement for Justice,* ed. Margaret M. Mangold (New York: Family Service Association of America, 1971), 43.

2. See José de Onís, *Las misiones españolas en los Estados Unidos,* which includes the treatise of Pablo Tac, "Conversión de los San Luiseños de la Alta California" (Conversion of the San Luiseños of Alta California), ca. 1835, offered here in translation by Minna and Gorden Hewes (New York: n.p., 1958).

3. Herbert E. Bolton, "The Mission as a Frontier Institution in the Spanish-American Colonies," *American Historical Review* 13 (October 1917): 43–44.

4. Anonymous, *Instrucción para el Ministro de la Misión de la Purissima Concepción de la Provincia de Texas,* translated as *Instructions for Minister of the Mission of Purissima Concepción of the Province of Texas,* by Fr. Benedict Leutenegger (San Antonio: Old Spanish Missions Historical Research Library at San José Mission, 1976), 49–50. The quotation is part of an *Advertencia,* a notice, at the end of the eighty-three sections of instructions.

My deep-felt thanks go to Sister María Carolina Flores of Our Lady of the Lake College for sending me the materials, in general, on the San Antonio missions, and for the assistance she accorded me during my visit to the Spanish archives at the same college in December 1988. All English translations of quotes from the *Instrucción para el Ministro* . . . are by Fr. Benedict Leutenegger.

5. A *fiscal* was a type of Indian trustee who made sure that other Indians carried out their religious duties.

6. Armando Miguélez, "Conceptos de la ilustración en las crónicas aztlanenses del siglo dieciocho" (Talk presented in panel 408, "Las crónicas españolas y la literatura chicana," at the 1987 meeting of the Modern Language Association of America, San Francisco, December 29, 1987).

7. Nelson W. Polsby, as quoted by Steven Lukes, *Power: A Radical View* (London: Macmillan, 1977), 13.

References

Blanco, Antonio S., ed. 1971. *La lengua española en la historia de California.* Madrid: Ediciones de Cultura Hispánica.

Bolton, Herbert E. 1917. "The Mission as a Frontier Institution in the Spanish American Colonies." *American Historical Review* 13 (1): 43–44.

Ibáñez, Florencio. 1971. "Pastorela." In *La lengua española en la historia de California.* Ed. Antonio S. Blanco. Madrid: Ediciones de Cultura Hispánica.

Instrucción para el Ministro de la Misión de la Purissima Concepción de la Provincia de Texas. [1760] Translated as *Instruction for Minister of the Mission of Purissima Concepción of the Province of Texas,* by Fr. Benedict Leutenegger. San Antonio: Old Spanish Missions Historical Research Library at San José Mission, 1976.

Lukes, Steven. 1977. *Power: A Radical View.* London: Macmillan.

Onís, José de. 1958. *Las misiones españolas en los Estados Unidos.* New York: n.p.

Ortego, Philip. 1971. "The Chicano Renaissance." In *La Causa Chicana: The Movement for Justice.* Ed. Margaret M. Mangold. New York: Family Service Association of America.

Peña, Juan Antonio. 1767. *Diario que hizo el Padre Fr. Gaspar José de Solís en la visita que fue a hacer de las misiones de la provincia de Texas* . . .

————. 1722. *Derrotero de la Expedición en la Provincia de los Texas, Nuevo Reyno de Philipinas* . . .

Santa Ana, Friar Benito Fernández. n.d. *Cartas y memoriales del Padre Presidente, Fray Benito Fernández de Santa Ana, 1736—1754.*

Serra, Junípero. 1955. *Epistolary.* Washington, D.C.: Academy of American Franciscan History.

Tac, Pablo. [1835] 1958. "Conversión de los San Luiseños de la Alta California." In *Las misiones españolas en los Estados Unidos.* Ed. José de Onís. New York: n.p.

Villagrá, Gaspar de. 1610. *Historia de la Nueva México.* Alcalá de Henares.

The Politics of Theater in Colonial New Mexico

Drama and the Rhetoric of Conquest

RAMÓN GUTIÉRREZ

This essay focuses on one small facet of the Spanish ideological enterprise in America—how the Spaniards inculcated into the Pueblo Indians a historical consciousness of their own defeat through theater. The evidence I present here comes from the Kingdom of New Mexico, an area that at the end of the sixteenth century encompassed roughly the current states of New Mexico and Arizona. The colonization of the Kingdom of New Mexico in 1598 came rather late in Spain's imperial expansion in the Americas. By this date Spaniards had been in the New World for more than a century, and the Franciscan friars who were charged with the Christianization of the area had had seventy-five years of experience among the natives of central Mexico. In addition, the Europeans who conquered New Mexico in 1598 were not ignorant of what they would find there. Fifty-eight years earlier, in 1540, Francisco Vásquez de Coronado had led a grand expedition into New Mexico in search of the legendary cities of gold that, according to the 1539 report of Fray Marcos de Niza, were to be found at Cíbola. When the gold proved to be nothing more than the sun's reflection on sandstone walls, New Mexico's brilliance quickly faded from the popular imagination. What the conquistadores encountered, then, was a land inhabited by approximately 100,000 Pueblo Indians, so called by the Spanish because their multistoried dwellings resembled Aztec *pueblos* (towns). The Pueblo Indians were primarily sedentary horticulturists who resided in 150 or so distinct towns best thought of as independent city-states.[1]

The dream of discovering a *new* Mexico more magnificent than the one that already existed was still alive. Largely under the auspices of the Franciscan order, which was eager to expand into new missionary fields and anxious to convert the souls of New Mexico's inhabitants, several expeditions were sent to reconnoiter the upper Río Grande Basin in the 1580s.[2] These explorers took copious notes on the indigenous cultures they encountered, describing social organization, religious life, the native pantheon of gods, and social habits and mores. With this information the soldiers and friars orchestrated the 1598 conquest, staging a spectacular theatrical production for the Pueblo Indians.

From the moment the *españoles* reached the New Mexico banks of the Río Grande in 1598, everything the Pueblo Indians saw and heard was a carefully choreographed political drama intended to teach them the meaning of their own defeat, of Spanish sovereignty, and of the social hierarchies under Christian rule. The European actors in this conquest theater gave dazzling initial performances. The Puebloans watched in attentive shock. At first they were undoubtedly a bit confused, but in time they understood the dramatic messages, for the narrative of this drama was a triumphal history of the conquest of Mexico as the Europeans wanted it remembered.[3]

The Spaniards correctly assumed that New Mexico's native residents had learned of the 1523 Aztec defeat through word of mouth.[4] To make the Pueblo Indians believe that their own conquest and subjugation in 1598 was a continuation of, if not identical to, the Aztecs' submission in 1523, Don Juan de Oñate, the leader of the conquering expedition to New Mexico, and the friars staged for the Pueblo Indians the most vivid episodes of that earlier encounter.

In these initial conquest dramas the Spaniards played themselves as well as the defeated Aztecs while a native audience looked on. In time the actor-audience relationship of the 1598 conquest dramas was reversed; the natives played themselves as the Spaniards looked on. When the Pueblos performed the dances, dramas, and pantomimes of the conquest, they continually relived their own defeat, humiliation, and dishonor, and openly mocked themselves with the caricatures of "Indians" the conquistadores so fancied. Today, ironically, in many of New Mexico's villages a memory of the Spanish conquest lives on in military dramas still enacted in seventeenth-century attire. How pleased Oñate and the Franciscans would be now if they could only see the spectacle. For what they projected in 1598 as a highly ideological view of history became fixed as an integral and "authentic" part of native ritual.

The orchestrated conquest of New Mexico was staged with what already had become legendary props. Oñate carried the banner of "Our Lady of the Remedies," the same one Hernán Cortés had carried into Tenochtitlán in 1519.[5] By Oñate's side marched a group of Tlascalan Indian allies, members of the same Indian group that had befriended Cortés in his defeat of the Aztecs.[6] They were accompanied by a native maiden named Doña Inés, who Oñate hoped would be seen by the Indians as "a second Malinche." Doña Inés, a native of Pant-ham-ba Pueblo (near Galisteo, New Mexico), had been abducted by Gaspar Castaño de Sosa during his unauthorized 1590 expedition into New Mexico and taken back to central Mexico. When Oñate obtained his license to colonize the area, he demanded of the king that the "Indian woman who was brought from New Mexico" be given to him. Oñate expected that just as Malinche had acted as Hernán Cortés's mistress, interpreter, and advocate before the native lords, so would Doña Inés act for him.[7] Finally, twelve Franciscans played the twelve Franciscan "apostles" who in 1524 initiated Mexico's spiritual conquest.

The first act of the New Mexican conquest took place near modern-day El Paso, Texas, on April 20, 1598. There Oñate received four native emissaries from a nearby village and immediately dressed them as Spaniards, cloaking their nakedness and showering them with gifts. In doing so, Oñate conformed to the European diplomatic convention that an inferior host always donned the clothes of the superior guest. Eighty years earlier, Montezuma, the Aztec emperor, had greeted Hernán Cortés in a similar fashion, wearing the red cap and seated in the chair that Cortés had sent him. In 1598 Oñate impersonated Cortés reenacting episodes from the conquest of Mexico as a way of communicating to the Puebloans the significance of what was transpiring. Indeed, whether in Mexico or New Mexico, or anywhere in between, these episodes, mythologized and transformed through oral transmission, would become the basic repertoire of conquest theater.[8]

On April 30, 1598, Oñate constructed a chapel for the natives. A solemn high Mass was celebrated, and after the sermon the soldiers enacted a drama for their aboriginal audience. The play recounted the most important historical event in the spiritual conquest of Mexico—the arrival of the twelve Franciscan "apostles" in Mexico City in 1524 and the spectacular greeting they received from Hernán Cortés. Cortés had gathered the lords and common citizens of Tenochtitlán so that they could witness how he greeted the twelve Franciscans who had just arrived. He approached the friars on his horse, dismounted, fell on his knees, and kissed their hands and feet. Cortés then ordered the *caciques,* or Aztec lords, to do likewise.[9] Among the Pueblo Indians in 1598, Oñate behaved just as Cortés had in 1524, intentionally projecting an image of himself as the new Cortés. Oñate approached the twelve friars, knelt, kissed their hands and hems, and then ordered the natives to do likewise. In the play's closing scene, the Spanish soldiers who played "simple natives," writes Gaspar Pérez de Villagrá, the expedition's chronicler, "reverently approached on bended knee and asked to be received into the faith, being baptized in great numbers."[10]

The exaggerated didactic gestures of such greetings, particularly the kneeling and kissing of hands and feet, were "necessary," insisted New Mexico's first missionaries, "since it was the first time [such a] proud and bellicose people had seen it." Kneeling before the Spaniards was a radical and humiliating gesture for the Pueblo Indians. Never had they approached their leaders, or even their gods, on bended knee. Now, not only were they expected to kneel before the Franciscans, but every time they greeted a friar they were to kneel and kiss his hands and feet. By so doing, said Fray Estevan de Perea, the Indians would "understand the true veneration that they should show the friars whenever they met them."[11]

When *The Arrival of the Franciscan Apostles* ended, Oñate again fell to his knees, lifted his eyes toward heaven, and loudly prayed: "O, holy cross, open the gates of heaven to these infidels. Found churches and altars where the body and blood of the Son of God may be offered in sacrifice . . . and give to our king and to me . . . the peaceful possession of these kingdoms and provinces." Firing arquebuses to evoke the heat of battle and the power of Spain, Oñate ceremoniously erected a cross as a sign of Christ's victory over the enemy, and then moved on. In the narrative sequence of this first act of conquest theater we see quite poignantly an articulation of clerical fantasies: their hope that the Pueblo Indians would reverently greet them on bended knees and graciously bow to accept the waters of baptism. In this case behavior was being taught in theater before it was actually enacted and made into history—a history that would then be reenacted as first imagined and represented in drama.[12]

Oñate's expedition traveled north from the El Paso area along the banks of the Rio Grande to Santo Domingo pueblo. There, in early July 1598, Oñate gathered the chiefs of thirty-one of the surrounding villages to swear obedience and vassalage to the king. Through Tomás and Cristóbal, two Mexican Indians who had remained at Santo Domingo during the 1590 Castaño de Sosa expedition, Oñate explained that the king had sent him for "the salvation of their souls, because they should know that their bodies had also souls which did not die even though the bodies did. But if they were baptized and became good Christians, they would go to heaven to enjoy an eternal life of great bliss in the presence of God . . . [if not] they would go to hell to suffer cruel and everlasting torment." The chiefs promised to obey Oñate as their temporal lord and Fray Alonso Martínez, the Franciscan commissary, as their spiritual leader. The Puebloans demonstrated their obedience by kneeling and kissing Oñate's hand and then Martínez's. The ceremony of submission at Santo Domingo ended with a Mass. [13]

From Santo Domingo pueblo Oñate's expedition proceeded north to Ohke, which he renamed San Juan de los Caballeros. Once all the chiefs of the surrounding villages had gathered there, Oñate staged the medieval military drama *Los Moros y Cristianos* (*The Moors and the Christians*). The play, set in Reconquest Spain, depicts the theft of the holy cross by the Moors, its heroic recapture by the Christian soldiers, and the final submission and acceptance of the cross by the infidels. The mock battle depicted in the play was staged with opposing troops of "Christians" and "Moors" played by Spanish soldiers. More often than not, the Christians were led by a man playing Saint James and the Moors were led by Pontius Pilate. [14] Here, in this drama, was a struggle not unlike those of the medieval Crusades. The play created a world divided between good and evil. The cross of Christ represented goodness and life. The Spanish soldiers were Christ's messengers spreading the news of salvation to heathens engulfed in darkness and evil. The infidel Moors submitted to the spiritual superiority of the Christians. Divine aid allowed the Spanish to triumph over the sinister forces of darkness. [15]

In the narrative of his expedition Oñate reports that when the play ended, the chiefs swore obedience and vassalage to Spain's king and to him, humbled themselves before the friars, and then returned to their pueblos accompanied by a friar who would preach the gospel to them. Thrice Oñate warned them that "if they failed to obey any of the *padres* or caused them the slightest harm, they and their cities and pueblos would be put to the sword and destroyed by fire." [16]

The dreamy world of thespian pretense that imagined a kingdom safe for Hispanic dominion was shattered on December 4, 1598, when Indians from Acoma pueblo killed thirteen Spanish soldiers. The hostilities began when the soldiers stopped at Acoma seeking maize, blankets, and sexual favors from the women. When these demands were not speedily met, the soldiers ascended the mesa on which Acoma pueblo sat and tried to seize what they wanted. Acoma's warriors defended themselves, killing several Spanish soldiers and putting the rest to flight. Retaliation was swift. A punitive expedition of seventy soldiers—more than half of the Spanish force in the province—was sent to Acoma on January 12, 1599, to wage a certified "just war" without mercy. The early Spanish chroniclers of New Mexico inform us that during the heat of battle, God sanctioned the brutalities committed in his name, sending Santiago (Saint James) and the Blessed Virgin Mary to the soldiers' aid. Saint James assailed Acoma's Indians with even greater gusto and flourish than had been displayed by those who impersonated him on the stage. Riding atop "a white horse, dressed in white, a red emblem on his breast, and a spear in his hand," Saint James killed the infidels "like a whirlwind," with "a maiden of most wondrous beauty" at his side. [17]

When the fighting at Acoma ended, eight hundred native men, women, and children lay dead. Eighty men and five hundred women and children were taken as prisoners to Santo Domingo pueblo, where they were tried for murder and sentenced. All the men and all women over the age of twelve were condemned to twenty years of slavery among New Mexico's settlers. In addition, all men over the age of twenty-five had one of their feet severed. Children under the age of twelve were distributed as servants to monasteries and households where they would "attain the knowledge of God and the salvation of their souls." Oñate hoped that with these punishments Pueblo resistance to the Spanish presence would cease forever. Various Puebloans later testified that after Acoma's defeat they realized that they did not have the strength to resist the Christians. [18]

The initial series of dramas that would shape the historical narrative of New Mexico's conquest was repeated over and over again in the routine of colonial life so that the Pueblo Indians learned them and internalized their explicit messages. Thus, whenever a village celebrated its founding, the feast day of its patron saint, or the arrival of the provincial governor or the ecclesiastical prelate, a set of ritual formulas evocative of the 1598 conquest was ceremoniously enacted. As in 1598, when the Puebloans greeted the Span-

iards, later resisted them in warfare, and finally submitted, so too during
these yearly events the Pueblo Indians relived their defeat, performing in
highly abbreviated form an image of their past.

The shape this encapsulated history took was a greeting, a symbolic battle,
and a submission.[19] First the Pueblo Indians greeted their Spanish overlords
with varying degrees of pomp and pageantry, just as they had in 1598—if
the visitor was a priest, by kissing his feet; if a civilian, by kissing his hand.
Next came a mock battle. In 1599 the Spanish had unleashed their fury
against Acoma, but for the purpose of teaching the Puebloans the proper
relations of super- and subordination under Christian rule, a host of didactic
plays served the same function. *The Moors and the Christians* was a favorite.
The colonists tell us that whenever it was performed in New Mexico, it was
full of "loud acclamations from the soldiers, with salvos of arquebuses, and
skirmishes and horse races." *Farolitos* and *luminarias,* the decorative lanterns
still used to announce a major feast or celebration, then evoked the fires of
warfare and conquest. The didactic play of the day, whatever its theme, always ended on a common note: the Indians' defeat and their acceptance of
Christian rule.

Greeting, battle, and submission marked the founding of Our Lady of
Guadalupe mission near El Paso in 1668. After the friars had been welcomed
on the outskirts of the town, "twelve dozen firecrackers, a beautiful castle,
two mounted horsemen, rockets, bombs and bombards were fired." The
Manso Indians then bowed their heads in submission and received the waters
of baptism.[20]

The ways in which the Spaniards fashioned a historical consciousness
among the Pueblo Indians of their own conquest and humiliation were also
vividly expressed in the *autos sacramentales,* didactic religious plays based on
New and Old Testament narratives and on popular Christian traditions. Historians and literary critics for some time have regarded the *autos* either as
simple theatrical works or as quaint folkloric curiosities, ignoring their powerful political content and the values their rhetorical gestures were intended
to communicate. The text of every *auto* had a subtext embedded in the costumes, generational casting, and dramatic actions. Every text had its context.
Drama was not the entertainment we know today but a moving political and
pedagogical instrument.[21]

The explicit purpose of the *auto* was to indoctrinate the Indians with
a highly ideological view of the conquest, simultaneously forging in their

minds a historical consciousness of their own vanquishment and subordination from the Spanish point of view. Here, in this theatrical production, was
a world safe for Hispanicism. Here the Pueblo Indians ridiculed themselves
by donning the "Indian" costumes the friars and soldiers had concocted and
deemed appropriate for their subjects, and by accepting their own vanquishment. Today we can see how successful the colonizers were in perpetuating
their view of history by watching the Matachines dance performed on Christmas Day or by attending Santa Fe's yearly fiesta to see the costumes and hear
the words of the conquistadores.[22]

The *autos sacramentales* not only instilled into the Pueblo Indians a historical consciousness shaped by the conquerors, they also attempted to teach
them the rudiments of Christian history and myth. Before the conquest the
Pueblo Indians had a vibrant ritual life which included dance dramas, pantomimes, and a wide array of ceremonial events. For evangelization purposes
the missionaries supplanted the indigenous ritual calendar with a Christian
ritual cycle that, at least in external forms and paraphernalia, looked as similar as possible to the native one. The naïve theory that guided this conversion
strategy presupposed that the psychological appeal of Pueblo ritual was to be
found in the magnificent external trappings: in the songs, prayers, costumes,
and masks. Replace these, the friars thought, with similar actions and gestures, and a convergence of meanings would surely follow.[23]

The Pueblo ritual year consisted of two six-month halves—a winter cycle
and a summer cycle. Winter began with the solstice on December 21 and
ended on June 21, when the summer solstice initiated summer. Christianity's
early fusions with European cosmological religions resulted in some temporal
similarities with the Pueblo schedule, thus making the "transformation" of
Pueblo to Christian somewhat easier. The Christmas season coincides with
the winter solstice; Holy Week and Easter follow on the heels of the vernal
equinox; and the feast of Corpus Christi in mid-June, the culmination of the
Christian calendrical year, is too close to the summer solstice to be purely
accidental.

The Franciscans' reorientation of Pueblo ceremonialism away from nature's
rhythms and toward the events in Christ's life began with the celebration of
Christmas during December. The winter solstice had always been a time
when each town's clans and esoteric societies joined together to celebrate their
unity. Under Christian rule, during roughly the same period the friars staged
a sequence of *autos*. First there was a performance of *El Coloquio de San José* on

December 16, telling of Saint Joseph's selection as Mary's husband. *Las Posadas,* about Mary and Joseph's search for shelter, was also staged on that night and on the eight nights that followed.[24]

On Christmas Eve the *auto Los Pastores,* a shepherds' play, was performed, followed by the *Misa de Gallo* (Cockcrow Mass) and ending with kissing the infant Christ's feet at the Nativity crèche. *Los Pastores* was staged by dividing the males of the indigenous community into three age-stratified groups: angels (boys), devils (old men), and shepherds (adolescents). The play opens at a shepherds' camp. The Star of Bethlehem (a child carrying a large star) appears to announce Christ's birth. Meanwhile, in Hell, Lucifer (an old man dressed in black and sporting a horned mask) decries the Messiah's birth and with a group of devils and sins (also played by old men) plots to wage war on the infant and his mother. Back at the campfire, a Franciscan hermit arrives and, with Saint Michael and a chorus of angels (played by boys dressed in white), leads the shepherds to Bethlehem. But Lucifer, the other devils, and the sins block their way. The angels and devils fight, and Lucifer and his minions are vanquished and exiled to Hell. The hermit and shepherds then proceed to Bethlehem, worship Christ, and offer him cornmeal, gourds, cloth, and dances.[25]

Los Pastores, which announced Christ's birth, was but a pretext for the Pueblo Indians to mimic the ideal society the Franciscans envisioned. Whatever the words of the play—which the Indians were not initially prepared to understand anyway—the generational casting of devils and angels left no doubt that the struggle depicted was between seniors and juniors, between Pueblo religion and Christianity; and the latter always triumphed. From the Pueblo point of view, the Nativity play was not unlike their own war epics, which described the birth of new war gods. To the Pueblo Indians the war gods were known as the Twin War Boys, or the sons of Father Sun. They were rowdy and troublesome boys, equated with the forces of nature (lightning and thunder) and always depicted astronomically as comets or the Morning Star.

The parallels between the War Boys and Christ must have been striking. Christ too was the son of God the Father, whose power was often portrayed as similar to the sun's. The Star of Bethlehem announced his birth. In infancy he was the Prince of Peace and in adulthood Christ the King. His followers wielded swords and lightning (gunpowder), and even the monsters (horses) were at his command, ready to kill whoever failed to accept Christ as Lord.

These parallels undoubtedly explain why at Santo Domingo pueblo the Ahyana War Dance and at Jémez Pueblo the Bow War Dance are still performed on Christmas morn to honor the newly born war god, Jesus Christ.[26]

The Indians' defeat with the advent of the new warlord Christ was further underscored on Christmas Day with the performance of *Los Matachines,* a dance drama that recounts the defeat of the Aztec emperor Montezuma, his baptism and acceptance of Christianity, and his obeisance before the mendicant fathers—all fictional events, but nonetheless fundamental to the Christianization project. The dance begins with a procession into the church courtyard by El Monarca (Montezuma), followed by a retinue of guards called Matachines. Next to Monarca stands Malinche, a young girl dressed in white who represents Doña Marina, Hernán Cortés's mistress, symbolically the first Mexican Indian to accept Christianity. Monarca and Malinche are flanked by four war chiefs, El Toro (a bull), and two Abuelos (grandfathers).[27]

The Matachines dance progresses through various episodes. First, the Matachines, the Abuelos, the war chiefs, and El Toro pay homage to Monarca. Malinche, standing in front of the church, approaches Monarca, who offers her his gourd rattle and palm, symbols of his magical powers. Malinche rejects the gifts but engages Monarca in a dance, slowly leading him into church, where he accepts baptism. Then an enraged bull, symbol of the native pantheon of gods, enters, threatening Monarca, the Abuelos, and the war chiefs. The Abuelos wrestle the bull and kill him. When the slaughter is complete, the dancers form themselves into a moving cross and enter the church, thereby symbolically accepting Christianity and rejecting their idolatrous past.[28]

The Christmas cycle ended on January 6, the feast of the Epiphany, with a performance of the *Auto de los Reyes Magos,* recounting the adoration of Christ by the Three Kings. This play begins with the triumphal entry into the village of three richly cloaked Magi bearing gifts of gold, frankincense, and myrrh. Following the Star of Bethlehem, the Magi approach the crèche, offer homage, obeisance, and gifts to Christ, and then kiss the babe's feet.

For the friars who staged this drama, as for the Pueblo Indians who observed it, the explicit message conveyed by the star, the triumphal entry normally reserved for such luminaries as the governor and the Franciscan prelate, the rich gifts, and the kissing of Christ's feet was that foreign chiefs acknowledged Christ as a powerful lord. Also not to be lost was the poignant generational symbolism. Mighty kings had humbled themselves before an infant. What a didactic sight that must have been![29]

The timing of the Christmas liturgies and the native winter solstice celebrations was so close that the two became conflated in the Indian mind. Winter was a masculine period when Pueblo hunters and warriors sustained their villages through hunting magic and knowledge of the animal world. The portrayal of Christ as a war god (in Pueblo culture warfare and hunting were conceptually linked) and the prominence of farm animals in the Nativity plays, and particularly around the crèche, reinforced these links.

Christ's incarnation and birth were but a necessary prelude to the highest drama of the year, his crucifixion and death. All Christian history dates to that momentous day. The Gospels tell us very little about Christ's birth, adolescence, and adulthood, but with excruciating detail, almost hour by hour, they recount his Passion and death.[30]

For the Franciscans, who were particular devotees of the crucified Christ, Lent, particularly the period between Palm Sunday and Good Friday, was a period of intense prayers, fasts, and bodily mortifications. The ritual surrounding Christ's crucifixion and death was, like the Nativity, organized around a sequence of didactic plays staged between Palm and Easter Sundays. The stations of the cross, representing fourteen episodes in Christ's final days—his condemnation to death; his carrying of the cross (John 19:17); his assistance by Simon of Cyrene (Mark 15:21); his meetings with the holy women of Jerusalem (Luke 23:27–31), with his mother (John 19:25), and with Veronica; his three falls en route to Calvary; the stripping and nailing to the cross; his death, deposition, and burial—were the basic themes of these Holy Week *autos*.[31]

The celebration of Mass on Holy Thursday night, commemorating Christ's last supper, formally initiated the ritual of the Passion. Like Christ stripped by his accusers, when Mass ended that night the mission's main altar was stripped of its linens and ornaments. That night, the night Christ reflected on his own death in the Garden of Gethsemane, was a time of great solemnity. The mission bells were silent, and only the raucous noise of *matracas* (hand clackers) and the doleful laments of *pitos* (flutes) pierced the silence of the night.

At noon on Good Friday the congregation gathered at church and in procession carried statues of the crucified Christ and his mother atop platforms through a village circuit that led to a symbolic Mount Calvary. First in the procession was Doña Sebastiana, a figure representing *La Muerte,* the Angel of Death. Doña Sebastiana, holding a drawn bow and arrow, rode in a wooden cart calling Christians to martyrdom in the name of Jesus Christ. Behind Sebastiana in the Good Friday procession was a figure of the crucified Christ. Candle-bearers walked at his sides. Behind them a string of active penitents staggered under the weight of enormous crosses. The 1655 Good Friday procession at Curac and Tajique pueblos included more than six hundred Indians carrying "large and small crosses on their shoulders." The Hopi celebrated Christ's Passion in similar fashion that year, dressed "like penitent hermits walking about praying in penitence, carrying crosses, large beads, and wearing haircloth shirts."[32] Periodically the procession stopped to view tableaux of the stations of the cross. When the performance at each station ended, the penitential procession resumed its course. When the procession reached Golgotha, a deathly hush fell over the crowd. Now Saint John's Passion (18:1–40, 19:1–42) was read before a statue of the crucified Christ. The crowd retired for a few hours and then at day's end reassembled for the *Santo Entierro,* the deposition and burial of Christ. The image of Christ was taken off the cross, his crown of thorns and the nails were removed, his hinged arms were lowered to his sides, and the statue was laid in an open coffin. In a torchlight procession the coffin was carried back to the village church and placed in the niche where it rested throughout the year. With this return, the commemoration of Christ's death ended.[33]

To the Indians who saw the Good Friday ritual, Jesus' power and the might and sanctity of his earthly representatives, the Franciscans, were readily apparent. Here too, it seems, was a rite of political authority, an interpretation that flows from a confrontation that took place at Isleta pueblo in 1660 when Fray Salvador de Guerra emerged from his convent one day to find his neophytes performing the *katsina* dance,[34] which he had strictly prohibited. When his repeated exhortations to cease dancing were ignored, the friar stripped naked before the natives, began violently beating himself with a whip, placed a rope around his neck and a crown of thorns on his head, and then crisscrossed the pueblo carrying an enormous cross. At the sight of this mad display the Indians immediately stopped their dance, and some, moved to tears by the sight, asked the friar's forgiveness. The others retreated to the safety of their homes, fearing that the Christian soldiers might shortly arrive.[35]

The feast of Corpus Christi, devoted to the living presence of Christ in the Eucharist, culminates the Christian liturgical year. Corpus Christi comes on the first Thursday after Trinity Sunday, a movable feast that falls anywhere from May 21 to June 24. The Catholic church established this feast in 1264 primarily to supplant pagan observances of the summer solstice. The main symbol of the feast of Corpus Christi is the Eucharist displayed in a sunburst-shaped monstrance. The host that Christians venerate on this day is a symbol of their social union, representing not only the organic unity of the mystical body of Christ but an image of a united church as well.[36]

We know very little about how Corpus Christi was celebrated in seventeenth-century New Mexico, but that it was observed there is little doubt. The existence of Blessed Sacrament confraternities, church inventories that list ritual paraphernalia used specifically on this feast, and Governor Bernardo López de Mendizábal's 1660 complaint that he wanted to be greeted by New Mexico's Indians with the same pomp that greeted the Blessed Sacrament on the feast of Corpus Christi (a desire that won him prosecution before the Inquisition) all attest to the celebration of this feast. If Corpus Christi was observed in New Mexico as it was elsewhere in Spain and New Spain, a solemn high Mass and a procession through the town's streets with a consecrated host were the main events of the day.

The ritual function of the Mass was to create peace and unity among the community's various parts. When the Eucharist was carried through the streets, the town's various elements were integrated into one, but within the procession itself, an image of differentiation and social hierarchy reflected the divisions that existed in the body politic. Precedence in the retinue was based on rank and status. Along its processional circuit the Blessed Sacrament stopped at the houses of notables while ignoring those of lesser men. And even the Indians had a specialized role that day, staging such dramas as *Adán y Eva, Los Moros y Cristianos,* and Saint Francis's sermon to the birds before a monstrance that glistened like the sun.[37] When the celebration of Corpus Christi ended, the major feasts of the Christian liturgical year were complete.

This short and schematic analysis of the history of conquest theater and didactic religious plays in colonial New Mexico leads us to some obvious conclusions. First, it has always been the privilege—indeed, the ideological mission—of conquering and dominant classes to recast history. We have seen how a highly ideological version of the conquest of Tenochtitlán by Hernán Cortés, only partially rooted in fact, was taught to the Pueblo Indians. In this case, ideological fictions and fantastic projections took on a life of their own while historical facts were obscured or forgotten. The memories that remained in the Pueblo Indian mind as the texture of history were fantasies of the conquistadores and their clerical orchestrators.

This recognition leads to a second point. Folklorists and literary scholars of Hispanic texts in the Southwestern United States, or any part of Spanish America, have been oblivious to the politics encoded in the texts and to the political goals of what seem to be coincidental narrative structures and stagings. Intellectuals have been all too willing to read superior European reflective imaginations and intellectualizations into native silences.[38] I have suggested here that the written words of conquest narratives and dramas had disciplinary powers. What is passed over as form and creativeness in the representation of the state and status hierarchies under colonial rule is the ways in which the pen could fix and perpetuate humiliations. The politics and practices of discipline and marginalization are read mistakenly by scholars as reflection and intellectualization. If we do not understand this antecedent, then we too become the dupes of the Spanish conquistadores, retelling their lies, privileging their utterances, and yet again enforcing, some five hundred years later, the brutality of the conquest of America's native peoples. On the other hand, most of Spanish America's native peoples have seen through these charades and constantly subvert the original meanings of conquest dramas with comic gestures, inverted utterances, and burlesque behavior of every sort, depriving the Spanish conquerors of the ideological hegemony they thought they had fixed permanently through force.[39]

Finally, there has been too much uncritical acceptance of the choreographed "Indians" of the Spanish imagination as the true and authentic essence of native groups. The utter idiocy of this mistake surfaces most poignantly when modern scholars look at the artifacts of conquest drama—scripts, costumes, behavior, and so on—and find in them the "authentic" ethnographic raw material of the past. How truly ironic it is that the imaginary caricatures of "Indians" that the conquistadores fashioned as a way of obliterating linguistic and cultural distinctions are thus transformed into our own *real* Indians. "Indians" did not exist before America's conquest. The native peoples of America were known by the languages they spoke, by the places they inhabited, or by other symbolic aspects of their social existence. By creating "Indians" as a category, the Spanish conquerors homogenized these identities to obliterate the past. And thus when Spanish soldiers played Indians for their native

audiences, mimicking "Indian" manners, wearing "Indian" clothes, and behaving as they thought Indians should behave, they were simply acting as
their clerical stage managers demanded. The political objective here should
not elude us; the conquerors meant to create in Pueblo Indian minds stereo-
typed memories of their humiliation and submission before a superior Christian force, memories of native failures as the Spanish wanted them remembered, and scripts for how colonized people should act.

Had the world of conquest theater been fact instead of fantasy, the history
of the relationship between the conquerors and the conquered might have
constantly repeated itself according to prescribed formulas. In the case of New
Mexico, it did not. In 1680 the Pueblo Indians revolted and sent those colonists who survived the natives' fury scurrying for cover, robbing the colonists
of all the pretense and fantasy they had carefully projected in their dramas.

NOTES

This article was written while I was a Fellow at the Center for Advanced Study in the
Behavioral Sciences in Stanford, California. I gratefully acknowledge the support provided by the Andrew W. Mellon Foundation. I also thank Richard Trexler, whose
splendid work on conquest theater in central Mexico inspired this essay, and Kathleen
Much for her editorial hand.

1. Edward P. Dozier, *The Pueblo Indians of North America* (New York: Holt, Rine-
hart and Winston, 1970), 29–70.

2. George P. Hammond and Agapito Rey, eds. and trans., *The Rediscovery of New
Mexico, 1580–1594: The Explorations of Chamuscado, Espejo, Castaño de Sosa, Morlete,
and Leyva de Bonilla and Humaña* (Albuquerque: University of New Mexico Press,
1966).

3. Richard Trexler, "We Think, They Act: Clerical Readings of Missionary Theatre in 16th Century New Spain," in *Understanding Popular Culture*, ed. Steven L.
Kaplan (Berlin: Mouton, 1984), 189–228.

4. During his 1540 expedition to New Mexico, Francisco Vásquez de Coronado
discovered that the Pueblo Indians were aware of the Aztecs' defeat and fully expected
that their country too would be conquered. See George Hammond and Agapito Rey,
eds. and trans., *Narratives of the Coronado Expedition, 1540–1542* (Albuquerque: University of New Mexico Press, 1940), 175.

5. José Espinosa, ed. and trans., *First Expedition of Vargas into New Mexico, 1692*
(Albuquerque: University of New Mexico Press, 1940), 59; and "The Virgin of the
Reconquest of New Mexico," *Mid-America* 18 (1936): 79–82.

6. Marc Simmons, "Tlascalans in the Spanish Borderlands," *New Mexico Historical Review* 39 (1964): 101–10.

7. On Doña Inés, see George P. Hammond and Agapito Rey, eds. and trans., *Don Juan Oñate: Colonizer of New Mexico, 1595–1628* (Albuquerque: University of New Mexico Press, 1953), 48, 321. Oñate was quite irritated at Doña Inés because she spoke only Tano, and none of the other Pueblo languages, and because few Pueblo Indians seemed to remember the details of her 1590 abduction. So much for the calculated ploys of political theater!

8. Gaspar Pérez de Villagrá, *History of New Mexico, 1610* (Los Angeles: The Quivira Society, 1933), 129; Hammond and Rey, *Don Juan Oñate,* 315; Richard Trexler, *Public Life in Renaissance Florence* (New York, 1980), 432; and "We Think, They Act," 191; Hubert H. Bancroft, *History of Arizona and New Mexico 1530–1888* (Albuquerque: Calvin Horn, 1962), 199.

9. John Phelan, *The Millennial Kingdom of the Franciscans* (Berkeley: University of California Press, 1970), 33; Trexler, "We Think, They Act," 191.

10. Pérez de Villagrá, *History of New Mexico, 1610,* 129.

11. Fredrick W. Hodge, George P. Hammond, and Agapito Rey, eds. and trans., *Fray Alonso de Benavides' Revised Memorial of 1634* (Albuquerque: University of New Mexico Press, 1945), 88, 214.

12. Pérez de Villagrá, *History of New Mexico, 1610,* 136; Trexler, "We Think, They Act," 189–203.

13. Hammond and Rey, *Don Juan Oñate,* 339–40.

14. Robert Ricard, *The Spiritual Conquest of Mexico* (Berkeley: University of California Press, 1966), 186–87.

15. This summary of *The Moors and the Christians* is based on several extant versions of the play deposited at the Museum of New Mexico's library (Santa Fe, New Mexico) in the archive of the Works Progress Administration, #5-5-3:26, #5-5-6:6, #5-5-21. See also Thomas Pearce, "Los Moros y los Cristianos: Early American Play," *New Mexico Folklore Record,* 2:58–65; Charles Martin, "The Survival of Medieval Religious Drama in New Mexico" (Ph.D. diss., University of Missouri, 1959), 86, 152; Sister J. McCrossan, *The Role of the Church and the Folk in the Development of Early Drama in New Mexico* (Philadelphia: University of Pennsylvania Press, 1948), 2; Juan Raél, *Hispanic Folk Theatre in New Mexico* (Stanford: Stanford University Press, 1969); Ramón A. Gutiérrez, "Marriage, Sex and the Family: Social Change in Colonial New Mexico, 1690–1846" (Ph.D. diss., University of Wisconsin, 1980), 105.

16. Pérez de Villagrá, *History of New Mexico, 1610,* 149.

17. Hodge et al., *Benavides' Revised Memorial,* 214.

18. Hammond and Rey, *Don Juan Oñate,* 427; Pérez de Villagrá, *History of New Mexico, 1610,* 264.

19. Trexler, "We Think, They Act," 195.

20. Hodge et al., *Benavides' Revised Memorial*, 214; France V. Scholes, "Documents for the History of the New Mexican Missions in the Seventeenth Century," *New Mexico Historical Review* 4 (1929): 196–97.

21. Colonial Mexican theater can be studied in Marilyn Ekdahl Ravicz, *Early Colonial Religious Drama in Mexico: From Tzompantli to Golgotha* (Washington, D.C.: Catholic University of America Press, 1970); Fernando Horcasitas, *El Teatro Náhual: Epocas novohispana y moderna* (Mexico City: Universidad Nacional Autónoma de México, 1974); P. Constantino Bayle, *El Culto del Santísimo en Indias* (Madrid: Consejo Superior de Investigaciones Científicas, 1951), esp. 341–461; Manuel R. Pazos, "El teatro franciscano en México durante el siglo XVI," *Archivo Iberoamericano* 11 (1951): 129–89; Luis Weckmann, *La herencia medieval de México* (Mexico City: El Colegio de México, 1983), esp. 2:641–59; George M. Foster, *Culture and Conquest: America's Spanish Heritage* (Chicago: Quadrangle Books, 1960), esp. 158–226; José Revello, "Orígines del teatro religioso en la América colonial," *Razón y fe* 135 (1947): 220–34, 335–47.

22. On colonial New Mexican theater see Richard Stark, *Music of the Spanish Folk Plays in New Mexico* (Santa Fe: Museum of New Mexico Press, 1969); Aurelio Espinosa, *The Folklore of Spain in the American Southwest* (Norman: University of Oklahoma Press, 1985), 201–13; Ronald Grimes, *Symbol and Conquest: Public Ritual and Drama in Santa Fe, New Mexico* (Ithaca: Cornell University Press, 1976).

23. Inga Clendinnen, "Franciscan Missionaries in Sixteenth-Century Mexico," in *Disciplines of Faith: Studies in Religion, Politics and Patriarchy,* ed. Jim Obelkevich, Lyndal Roper, and Raphael Samuel (London: Routledge and Kegan Paul, 1987), 229–44.

24. Arthur L. Campa, *Spanish Religious Folktheatre in the Southwest* (Albuquerque: University of New Mexico Press, 1934), 8.

25. Edmund Munro, "The Nativity Plays of New Mexico" (M.A. thesis, University of New Mexico, 1940); Martin, "The Survival of Medieval Religious Drama in New Mexico," 120–40; Thomas Pearce, "The New Mexican Shepherd's Play," *Western Folklore* 15 (1956): 77–88; Works Progress Administration #5-5-3:16, #5-5-3:26; Aurora Lucero-White, "Los Pastores de Las Vegas" (M.A. thesis, New Mexico Normal University, Las Vegas, 1932); I. Rapp, "Pastores," *El Palacio* 11 (1921): 151–63.

26. Elsie Clews Parsons, *Pueblo Indian Religion* (Chicago: University of Chicago Press, 1939), 534, 896.

27. Montezuma's acceptance of Christianity and baptism are memorialized in numerous myths and dramas, which have no basis in fact. One suspects that the story was fabricated by the friars to facilitate Indian conversions, for when a monarch or

chief accepted Christianity, his subjects and retainers usually followed. Montezuma's failure to accept baptism has been studied by José Fernando Ramírez, "Bautismo de Moteuhzoma II, Noveno Rey de México," *Boletín de la Sociedad Mexicana de Geográfica y Estadística,* 1st ser., 10 (1863).

28. Flavia Waters Champe, *The Matachines Dance of the Upper Rio Grande* (Lincoln: University of Nebraska Press, 1983); Gertrude P. Kurath, "The Origin of the Pueblo Indian Matachines," *El Palacio* 64 (1957): 259–64; John D. Robb, "The Matachines Dance—a Ritual Folk Dance," *Western Folklore* 20 (1961): 87–101.

29. Peter P. Forrestral, trans., *Benavides' Memorial of 1630* (Washington, D.C.: Academy of American Franciscan History, 1954), 59; Martin, "The Survival of Medieval Religious Drama in New Mexico," 144–51; Elizabeth Foster, ed. and trans., *Motolinia's History of the Indians of New Spain* (Albuquerque: University of New Mexico Press, 1950), 93; Richard Trexler, "La Vie Ludique Dans la Nouvelle-Espagne— L'Empereur et Ses Trois Rois," in *Les Jeux à la Renaissance,* ed. P. Aries and J. Margolin (Paris: Librairie Philosophique J. Vrin, 1982), 81–93.

30. Jaroslav Pelikan, *Jesus Through the Centuries: His Place in the History of Culture* (New Haven: Yale University Press, 1985), 95.

31. The stations of the cross were introduced into Christian devotion by Saint Francis and were popularized by the Franciscans. A set of stations hung in the nave of every moderately equipped Franciscan mission. During Holy Week the village itself became the sacred space for the dramatization of their narrative.

32. Hearing against Nicolás de Aguilar, May 11, 1663, Archivo General de la Nación (Mexico City), *Inquisición,* 512:99.

33. Declaration of Fray Nicolás de Villar, September 27, 1661, Archivo General de la Nación (Mexico City), *Inquisición,* 596:14; McCrossan, *Development of Early Drama in New Mexico,* 144; Thomas Steele, trans., *Holy Week in Tome* (Santa Fe: Sunstone Press, 1976), 128–52. A statue of the *Santo Entierro* is still found in the Santa Cruz parish church. See *La Iglesia de Santa Cruz de la Cañada* (Santa Cruz, N.M., Parish, 1983), 54, 95; José E. Espinosa, *Saints in the Valley: Christian Sacred Images in History, Life and Folk Art of Spanish New Mexico* (Albuquerque: University of New Mexico Press, 1960), pl. 32; George Kubler, *Religious Architecture of New Mexico* (Albuquerque: University of New Mexico Press, 1972), pl. 112. Similar *Santo Entierro* coffins exist in many colonial Mexican churches. See Sonia Roziere, *México: Angustia de sus Cristos* (Mexico City: Instituto Nacional de Antropología y Historia, 1967), pls. 111, 116, 118, 119, 121.

34. The *katsina* are the collective spirits of the ancestral dead, who are represented as clouds and potent rain spirits.

35. Declaration of Fray Benito de la Natividad, May 17, 1661, Archivo General de la Nación (Mexico City), *Inquisición,* 573:100.

36. Bayle, *El culto del santísimo en Indias,* 251.

37. Ibid., 193–94; Eleanor B. Adams and Fray Angélico Chávez, eds. and trans., *The Missions of New Mexico, 1776: A Description by Fray Atanasio Domínguez* (Albuquerque: University of New Mexico Press, 1975), 19n26; France V. Scholes and Eleanor B. Adams, "Inventories," 27–38; Hodge et al., *Benavides' Revised Memorial,* 109–24; France V. Scholes, *Troublous Times in New Mexico, 1659–1670* (Albuquerque, 1942), 21–22, 32n11; Francis G. Very, *The Spanish Corpus Christi Procession: A Literary and Folkloric Study* (Valencia: Tipografía Moderna, 1962).

38. Trexler, "We Think, They Act," 189–90.

39. Anita Brenner, *Idols Behind Altars* (New York, 1929); James C. Scott, *Weapons of the Weak: Everyday Forms of Peasant Resistance* (New Haven: Yale University Press, 1985); Victoria Bricker, *The Indian Christ, the Indian King* (Austin: University of Texas Press, 1981).

The *Comedia de Adán y Eva* and Language Acquisition

A Lacanian Hermeneutics of a New Mexican Shepherds' Play

MARÍA HERRERA-SOBEK

Adam's apple: The projection in
front of the neck formed by the
largest cartilage of the larynx.
Larynx: In man and other mammals,
and in amphibians it is the organ of voice.
—*Webster's Dictionary*

The lasting power of a creative work of art is directly proportional to its power to elicit some type of intellectual response from an audience. If a work of art elicits this "intellectual engagement" for a prolonged period of time, we may rightly infer that inscribed in it are kernels of "intuitions" revealing ingots of "truth" to a wide spectrum of peoples at various points in time and space. I submit that such is indeed the case with the New Mexican *pastorela Comedia de Adán y Eva,* a shepherds' play based on the Old Testament (Campa 1934 : 19–47).

Recent explorations into the human psyche are ferreting out new truths from ancient myths. A Lacanian hermeneutics of the play *Adán y Eva,* for example, yields a radically different interpretation of the Genesis myth. In this essay I analyze *Adán y Eva,* especially the New Mexican version, from a Lacanian perspective and demonstrate how it dramatizes men's and women's incursion into language acquisition.

It is my position that the myth allegorizes man's fall from a nonspeaking creature existing in paradisiacal splendor to a humanized speaking mortal. The drama unveils a conscious choice on the part of the protagonists to be Godlike in acquiring the ability to self-consciously exist, even though this means an unretractable leap into the awareness of finiteness, and thus the awareness of death. The rejection of language acquisition would have meant a continuation of life in a paradisiacal space of nonawareness. The acquisition of language ruptured the unifying bond between nature and human beings and catapulted humankind into the space of the suffering self and into an alienation from self, from others, and from nature.

Previous exegeses of the biblical myth of Adam and Eve in the Garden of Eden have underscored the element of sexual relations, or, more elegantly and metaphorically articulated, carnal knowledge, as the "original sin" that precipitated the Fall and subsequent expulsion of the two protagonists, our mythic forebears, from Paradise. A second equally popular interpretation likens the Fall to the acquisition of knowledge. That is to say, eating of the fruit of the Tree of Good and Evil (i.e., acquiring knowledge) catapulted the first couple out of the realm of innocence and into the vertigo of "sin." In the view of the French theologist-philosopher Paul Ricoeur, "The Yahwist would seem to have suppressed all the traits of discernment or intelligence connected with the state of innocence, and to have assigned all of man's cultural aptitudes to his fallen state. The creation-man becomes, for him, a sort of child-man, innocent in every sense of the word, who had only to stretch out his hands to gather the fruits of the wonderful garden and who was awakened sexually only after the fall in shame. Intelligence, work, and sexuality, then would be the flowers of evil" (1967:246). Ricoeur's analysis coincides with my position that sex or carnal knowledge is not necessarily the reason or the outcome of the Fall. He believes "the man of the first story [i.e., Adam] must have been an adult, sexually awakened; for he cries out in exultation, in the presence of his new companion: 'This is now bone of my bones, and flesh of my flesh: she shall be called Woman (ischa), because she was taken out of man (isch)'" (246). Indeed, Ricoeur does not even perceive the Adam myth as symbolic of the Fall. He elaborates: "The symbol of the fall, then, is not the authentic symbol of the 'Adamic' myth; moreover, it is found in Plato, in gnosis, in Plotinus. . . . When we have traced the roots of the symbolism of the Adamic myth back to the more fundamental symbolism of sin, we shall see that the Adamic myth is a myth of 'deviation,' or 'going astray,' rather than a myth of the 'fall'" (233).

He challenges J. Coppens's conceptualization of the Adam and Eve myth as symbolic of the acquisition of knowledge and more specifically disagrees that "the guilty knowledge is related to sexuality" (Ricoeur, 248). Coppens

rightly perceives the serpent as symbolic of the gods of vegetation and therefore of fertility and reproduction. At the same time he sees it as representative
of the divinities that sacralize sex and are associated with pagan cults. However, to view sexuality as the primary motivation in the Adamic myth is
perceived by Ricoeur as a "recessive interpretation of the sin of Adam" (249).
Instead he proffers the following: "It seems to me that the intention of the
text is to reduce the *content* of the fall to the extent of making it a peccadillo,
in order to emphasize the fact that man has broken the filial dependence that
united him to his Father. That is why, finally, the question of the tree is not
important as Zimmerli has clearly seen. . . . The decisive argument, in my
opinion, is the place of this story at the head of the series formed by Genesis
1–11. The sin of Adam is the first, in the sense that it is at the root of all
others: Adam breaks with God" (Ricoeur, 249).

Indeed, in the play *Comedia de Adán y Eva* Adán is portrayed as a sexual,
sensual being. Adán is certainly aware of Eva as a woman, a beautiful, entic-
ing woman. Surprisingly, he intuits that this charming, angelic-looking
woman will be the cause of his perdition, of his death. In the first scene of
the second act Adán is awakened by a chorus that foretells his approaching
change of fortune.

> Despierta jóven feliz
> No duermas porque el pecado
> Quiere hacerte desdichado
> y de feliz a infeliz.

> Awake happy lad
> Do not slumber for sin
> Wants to make you joyless
> And change your happiness to unhappiness.

> (Campa, 23)

Adán questions this tragic prediction and reasserts his firm stance against all
temptation; in particular, in his monologue he refers to his steadfast resolve
to obey the interdict and not eat of the forbidden fruit:

> No pienses triunfar de Adán
> Que yo sé bien que eres Caín
> Oculto en una manzana

Yo me guardaré tirano
De tus palacios y anzuelos
Previniendo mis desvelos
De los fatales acentos.
De mi vigor—Mas ¿Qué miro?

Do not think you'll triumph
Against Adam, I know well you are Caín
Hiding within an apple
I shall guard myself, tyrant,
From your palaces and hooks
Keeping awake and alert
From fatal accents [words].
From my vigor—But what do I see?

(Campa, 24)

At this point Eva enters, serving as the physical answer to the rhetorical question Adán had been posing a few minutes before her appearance. Her physical presence immediately brings about a change in Adán, and his firm resolve enunciated moments before begins to melt. In the play Adán reacts to Eva's presence as a fully awakened sexual man, just as Ricoeur envisions him.

(Entra Eva)
Que en esta deidad admiro
Un retrato de los cielos.
¿Quién eres ninfa graciosa?
Portento de la hermosura.
¿Eres acaso criatura
O eres deidad prodigiosa?
Si deidad a mi fe amorosa
Consagro humilde a tus plantas,
Pero en confuciones tantas.
Dime muerte de mi vida
Si deidad por qué humesida [homicida]
Si criatura por qué encantas
O eres ninfa divina
A que con luces bellas

Pueblas los cielos de estrellas,
Y sus liensos ilumina.
Habla, bella peregrina;
No tengas de mí recelo
Porque si yo mal no argullo,
O el cielo es retrato tuyo,
O tú eres el mismo cielo;
O eres tú quien los linderos
Pisan la sacra deidad,
O quien puso en realidad
La belleza a sus esmeros,
Porque esos tus dos luceros
Que son carta ejecutoria
De tu hermosura notoria
Como ellas sus glorias cantan,
Y a mí me canta que gloria
(Cantan adentro)
Eres más o dura suerte
Porque con solo mirarte,
Ya me sentencian a muerte.
Y así para más no verte
Suplico a tu gran clemencia
Me conceda la licencia
Para ir mi suerte a llorar,
Pues ven mis ojos firmar
La sentencia de mi muerte.

(Eve enters)
In this deity I admire
A portrait of heaven.
Who are you graceful nymph
Portent of beauty?
Are you a human creature
Or a prodigious deity?
If a deity, my faithful love
I humbly consecrate at your feet,

But in all these confusions
Tell me death of my life
If a deity why a murderess?
If a human creature why do you enchant?
Or are you a divine nymph
Who with beautiful lights
Sprinkles the heavens with stars
And its mantles illuminates?
Speak, O beautiful pilgrim;
Do not be fearful of me
Because if I am not mistaken,
You are a portrait of heaven,
Or you are heaven itself;
Or is it you whose path
Follows the sacred deity,
Or it was you who in reality
Put beauty to do its charms,
Because those your two stars
Which are a missive of death
Notorious for your beauty
Like them they sing your glory
(Singing inside)
And, oh, what glory sings to me
You are more than misfortune
Because by only seeing you,
You sentence me to death.
And thus so as not to see you
I beg your great clemency
To grant me permission
To cry about my misfortune,
For my eyes already see
The signing of my death.

(Campa, 24)

Adán's monologue, which foreshadows his coming misfortune, evinces a baroque literary style of expression. It is a felicitous coincidence that the subject matter of the play (death) and a literary style merged to reinforce the message of the work. This sixteenth- and seventeenth-century literary style is noted for its incorporation of a wide variety of rhetorical devices, and the anonymous author of this *pastorela* employed a wide range of these devices to produce the effect he or she wanted. One of the major characteristics of the baroque style is the emphasis given to the senses in its imagery. Among the rhetorical devices employed is the extensive use of metaphor, oxymoron, antithesis, repetition, parallelisms, enumeration, ellipsis, hyperbole, anaphora, and, of course, the "conceit," which may be defined as a striking word picture. Harold B. Segel, in *The Baroque Poem,* lists the salient characteristics of the baroque style:

1. an interest in the concrete and specific; i.e., the particular over the general
2. military images—used extensively in religious, meditative, and amatory poetry and reflecting the strife-torn character of the age
3. multiple-sense imagery expressing the sensuousness of much baroque art
4. classical mythology, a legacy of the Renaissance but used by baroque poets with levity and in incongruous, nonclassical contexts
5. a rich palette of colors drawn from the world of nature (e.g., flowers) and from precious stones (rubies, emeralds, pearls, diamonds)
6. the play of light and dark, or *chiaroscuro*
7. the opposition of hot and cold (e.g., fire:snow)

Furthermore, in amatory poetry death is frequently associated metaphorically with the beloved. The separation of the lovers is experienced as a disunion of self, as a threatening feeling akin to the death of the subject. Only in merging with the other does the self experience wholeness and harmony. The *Comedia de Adán y Eva* focuses on death because the expulsion from Paradise is conceived as a death inflicted on the soul. Death appears in the play as a leitmotif associated with Eva and her beauty.

In Adán's monologue we encounter various rhetorical techniques typical of Renaissance and baroque literature. Eva is addressed as a nymph or goddess. The antithesis "Dime muerte de mi vida" ("Tell me, death, of my life") is used to link Eva with their (Adán's and Eva's) inevitable death. Anaphora is found in the parallel phrases "Si deidad por qué humesida / Si criatura por qué encantas" ("If a deity why a murderess / If a human creature why do you enchant"). Adán continues to view Eva as a deity and through hyperbolic imagery again associates her with a nymph or goddess:

O eres ninfa divina
A que con luces bellas
Pueblas los cielos de estrellas
Y sus liensos iluminas?

Or are you a divine nymph
Who with beautiful lights
Sprinkles the heavens with stars
And its mantles illuminates?

Adán reiterates Eva's role as the harbinger of death through metaphors linking the eyes and death: "Porque esos tus dos luceros / Que son carta ejecutoria / De tu hermosura notoria" ("Because those, your two stars / Which are a missive of death / Notorious for your beauty"; Campa, 24). And again two lines repeat the metaphor of looks that kill: "Porque con solo mirarte / Ya me sentencian a muerte" ("Because just by looking at you / They sentence me to death"; Campa, 25).

Adán ends his monologue by underscoring the linkage between the gaze and death: "Pues ven mis ojos firmar / La sentencia de mi muerte" ("For my eyes already see / The signing of my death"; Campa, 25). The play on words and the rhetorical question are evident in the dialogue between Adán and Eva:

Eva:
Gallardo joven espera;
No te vayas, dueño mío;
No me mate tu desvío.
Oye aguarda y considera.

Adán:
Señora, ¿Quieres que muera?

Eva:
No, mi dulce esposo, no
Porque si el Alto me dio
El ser de tu mismo ser,
Dime ¿cómo podrá ser
Que te de la muerte yo?

Eve:

Handsome youth wait;

Do not leave, my love;

Do not kill me with your scorn.

Listen, wait, and consider.

Adam:

My lady do you want me to die?

Eve:

No, my sweet spouse, no

Because if the Almighty gave me

My being from your own being,

Tell me, how can it be

That I bring death to you?

(Campa, 25)

Adán realizes Eva is not a deity, as he first supposed, but an entity like himself. The theme of *engaño/desengaño,* of how the senses deceive, and the illusory nature of life is underscored:

Adán:

¿Has visto una concha bruta

Que a los ojos con que enfada

Que en vez de mostrar halagos

Mil deshalagos tuviera?

Pues así tú, amada esposa

Aunque tu bella escultura

Es vano es un desengaño

De una perla prodigiosa.

Goza mil veces dichosa

Perla que tanto te agracia

Con esmaltes inmortales,

Mas mira que tus cristales

No le manchen su desgracia.

Adam:

Have you seen a brute shell

Which displeases the eye

That instead of glorifying it
A thousand unflattering remarks reaps?
So it is the same with you, beloved spouse
In spite of your beautiful body
It is vain, it is an illusion
Of a prodigious pearl.
Enjoy a thousand times
That pearl which flatters you
With its immortal glimmer
But beware that your crystals
Do not stain its disgrace.

(Campa, 25–26)

A Lacanian Interpretation of Desire

Jacques Lacan's fundamental concepts of Desire and the Symbolic Order are essential to my revisionist interpretation of the Adam and Eve myth.[1] The French psychoanalyst has been greatly influenced by Georg Hegel's views vis-à-vis the concept of desire as an outgrowth of biological "need." Hegel first postulated the interconnection between need, desire, and the development of self-consciousness in the Subject (Hegel 1967). Parting from the premise that biological needs eventually give rise to the feelings of desire, Hegel extrapolated that desire in turn produces the self-consciousness of the Subject (i.e., the desire to eat something is a basic "I want," a basic affirmation of "I" in relation to "not-I"; thus, in desire the "I" is formed and revealed as a subject related to an object).

Alexandre Kojeve elucidates the Hegelian concept as follows:

Man's humanity "comes to light" only in risking his life to satisfy his human Desire—that is, his Desire directed toward another Desire. Now, to desire a Desire is to want to substitute oneself for the value desired by this Desire. For without this substitution, one would desire the value, the desired object, and not the Desire itself. . . . In other words, all human, anthropogenetic Desire—the Desire that generates Self-Consciousness, the human reality—is, finally, a function of the desire for "recognition." And the risk of life by which the human reality "comes to light" is a risk for the sake of such a Desire. Therefore, to speak of the "origin" of Self-Consciousness is necessarily to speak of a fight to the death for "recognition." (1969:7)

Lacan explicitly states that "it is a fight to the death, then, in the effort to reject a thingish or animal mode of consciousness" (Muller and Richardson 1982:65). In the New Mexican play both Adam and Eve experience a desire to be Godlike; to be fully recognized by the Other—by God—as equals even though both realize that they will die (i.e., they will evolve from one state of consciousness into another) in the process.

Lacan's second major postulate particularly useful in my analysis of the *Comedia de Adán y Eva* is his conceptualization of the Symbolic Order. The Symbolic Order may be viewed as the complex of human structurization that governs "not only the order of language, but the logic of mathematical combination, and the whole pattern of social relatedness that emerges under the guise of marriage ties and kinship relationships, superimposing the kingdom of culture on that of a nature abandoned to the law of mating" (Muller and Richardson, 77). It is the *name of the Father* (Muller and Richardson, 78). And it is the innate structure of language that will be the structuring agent of the Symbolic Order in its totality. That is to say, when human evolution led to the acquisition of language, language became an all-encompassing structure that superimposed itself on all our perceptions of reality. Lacan's theories are based on the belief that the underlying structure of human reality is modeled on the structure of language. Thus, since language is based on a system of oppositions (i.e., the twelve pairs of voiced and unvoiced phonemes), as the infant develops he or she will utilize this language paradigm to construct an instrument with which to conquer his or her desire for the absent mother. Lacan bases his theory on Sigmund Freud's early work on the infant's *fort/da* (gone/here) experience. The case presents a child playing a type of hide-and-seek game typical of infants in their developmental stage of language acquisition between the ages of six months and eighteen months. As the child repeats the presence-absence game he realizes he can master the absence of the mother through speech. Through language he or she acquires the ability to make present that which is absent. In other words, the mother is made present through the power of speech. Lacan perceives this all-important phase as the "birth of the symbol" (Muller and Richardson, 93). But it is also the child's first experience with *limit* (i.e., finitude, death), as experienced through separation from (hence, negation of) the mother. The child is said to be "born into language," and this "first experience of separation/limit/death" is also the moment at which "desire becomes human" (Muller and Richardson,

93). This is the first time *desire* is differentiated from *need*, and, as John P. Muller and William J. Richardson explain, "the child now experiences the otherness of the mother and with that not only his own 'lack of being,' but a desire for the mother which, in the Hegelian schema, becomes a desire to be desired by her in turn, i.e., to be the 'object' of the mother's desire" (1982; Lacan 1977:104, 319). The prelapsarian connection of being one with the mother is ruptured forever, and the child will henceforth begin to have the Hegelian Desire to be desired by his or her mother.

Furthermore, according to the Lacanian theoretical framework the replacement of the mother by a symbol may be considered equivalent to the "death of the mother," so that "the symbol manifests itself first of all as the murder of the thing, and this death constitutes in the subject the eternalization of his desire" (Lacan 1977:104, 319). Muller and Richardson add: "Death may be seen as ingredient to the experience of language: as radical limit, it is 'death' that the child experiences when the rupture of the symbiotic bond with the mother reveals the child's own 'lack of being,' i.e., finitude (Lacan 1977:105, 320); as negation of the thing it is 'death' that the child imposes on things by substituting for them the symbols of speech" (Muller and Richardson, 94). It is obvious that there is a close connection between death and the humanizing process.

The Play

The *Adán y Eva* drama is structured in four acts and eleven scenes, and the characters consist of Adán, Eva, Gran Poder (i.e., Jehovah), Lucifer, an Angel, Mercy, and Appetite. Briefly, act 1 introduces Lucifer and his scheming cronies Appetite and Sin. In act 2 we see a sleeping Adán awake and find Eva by his side. Act 3 depicts Appetite tricking Eva into eating the forbidden fruit; while in act 4 we encounter Eva seducing Adán into tasting the apple, the expulsion from Paradise, and the promise of eventual salvation through the birth of Jesus.

The structural axis of the play revolves about the twin themes of death and desire. Eva is conceptualized as an *humecida* (*homicida*, murderer), the bearer of death or language (i.e., language which in the Lacanian construct is equal to death); the foreshadowing of an approaching death is enunciated by the anonymous Greek-like choir singing the introductory *letras* (words):

Guerra es la vida del hombre
En la extensión de su imperio
De morir en la campaña
Irrevocable el decreto.

(Act 1, scene 1)

Despierta joven feliz
No duermas porque el pecado
Quiere hacerte desdichado
y de feliz a infeliz.

(Act 2, scene 1)

Infeliz mujer advierte
Que oculta en una manzana
Se vé la culpa tirana
Se vé la culpa tirana.

(Act 3, scene 1)

Nuestra madre Eva engañada
Por el astuto dragón
Comió en aquella ocasión
De aquella fruta vedada.

(Act 4, scene 1)

War is the destiny of man
In the extension of his empire
To die in battle
Is the irrevocable decree.

(Act 1, scene 1)

Wake up, happy young man
Do not sleep because sin
Wants to make you unhappy
And change your happiness to unhappiness.

(Act 2, scene 1)

Wretched women be advised
That hidden in an apple

Is tyrannical guilt
Is tyrannical guilt.

(Act 3, scene 1)

Our Mother Eve deceived
By the astute dragon
Ate on that occasion
From the forbidden fruit.

(Act 4, scene 1)

The word *muerte* (death) is reiterated *twenty-seven* times in the fairly short play (twenty-eight pages), underscoring its significance.

Desire is metaphorically refracted in Eva, who not only is emblematic of the desire of man for woman but is also the principal force desiring the forbidden fruit. It should be pointed out that the *manzana* is not the actual object Eva desires in this play, and therefore is not biological "need," but is merely the means through which she can achieve her specific goal of becoming "like God" (in other words, the Lacanian desire for "recognition" from the Other). Although Ricoeur does not incorporate a Hegelian or Lacanian analysis and certainly does not posit the Adamic myth as a fall into language acquisition as I am doing here, he does correctly intuit the significance of Desire in the myth: "At the same time as the meaning of the ethical limit becomes hazy, the meaning of finiteness is obscured. A 'desire' has sprung up, the desire for infinity; but that infinity is not the infinity of reason and happiness, as we have interpreted it at the beginning of this work; it is the infinity of desire itself; it is the desire of desire, taking possession of knowing, of willing, of doing, and of being: 'Your eyes shall be opened, and ye shall be as gods, knowing good and evil'" (Ricoeur 1969:253). Equally Lacanian in symbolism is the figure of Appetite, whose obvious connection to instinctual needs is explicitly formulated in his name and what it represents and through his discourse—the voracious ingestion of food. Appetite in this drama is the son of biological "need," for he portrays his mother as a voracious eater:

Me parió una buena vieja
Y de mi parto quedó
De tantos antojos llena
Que una vez se le antojaron

Comerse docientas yeguas
En salpicón, y cien burros
Guisaditos en conserva,
Y viendo que no podía
Envistiendo con mi suegra
Tragósela toda entera.

Una vez se le antojaron
Cuatro mil mulas rellenas
Doscientas gatas paridas
En pipián y en escabeche
Dos mil caballos asados
Y en gigote ochenta yeguas.
Y por última otra vez
Que lo diga la partera,
Se le antojaron diez cargas
De pinineos en conserva.
Fui por ellos y cogiendo
Pinineos y pinineos
Como granos de mostaza
En el hueco de una muela;
Las diez cargas se envocó
Y con grande esencia
Mi madre les da sepulcro
en su despensa.

A good old lady gave birth to me
And from my birth she became
Full of cravings
One time she craved
Two hundred mares
In sauce and one hundred donkeys
Fried in jam,
And seeing that she could not
Fighting with my mother-in-law
Ate her up completely.

One time she was craving
Four thousand stuffed mules
Two hundred pregnant cats
In *pipían* sauce and pickled
Two thousand broiled horses
And eighty mares in sauce.
And to top it off,
Let the midwife be my witness,
She craved ten loads
Of dwarfs in jam.
I went to get them
And grabbing dwarfs and dwarfs
As if they were mustard seeds
In a molar indentation;
The ten loads she swallowed
And with great ceremony
My mother kept them
In her pantry [stomach].

(Campa, 30–31)

In the first seduction Appetite seduces or tricks Eva into going to the forbidden tree by recounting his mother's great appetite, making the analogy that the ingestion of knowledge (i.e., language) is through the organ of the mouth. The two females are thus connected through the figure of Appetite. Appetite serves as an intermediary between the two women and also between Lucifer and Eva. For once Appetite seduces Eva into approaching the forbidden tree, Lucifer will be lurking behind the tree in the guise of a serpent. Here the second seduction takes place. However, the Serpent's seduction does not utilize the sense of taste as Appetite did; Lucifer's seduction appeals to a desire to be like the Other (i.e., God) and a desire for recognition.

Biological need would not be enough to express the Lacanian paradigm for language; the element of desire must be integrated within the signifying chain of metaphoric entities. This is exactly where the Serpent weaves the link between Eva-Need (Appetite) and Desire (Serpent). The wily Serpent (Lucifer), recognizing this desire, acquaints Eva with the supposed power of the apple:

Ese omnipotente Dios
Como sabe que en esta manzana
Está otra suprema grandeza;
Por eso manda que no comaís de esa
Fruta bella. Cómela que te aseguro
Que como deidades eternas
Tú y tu esposo como Dios
Sin ninguna diferencia
Y te digo la verdad
Tu harás lo que te paresca.

That omnipotent God
Since he knows that in this apple
Enclosed is another Supreme being;
That is why he orders us not to eat from that
Beautiful fruit. Eat it for I assure you
You and your husband like
Eternal deities, like God
Will be without a difference
And I tell you the truth
You can do as you please.

                                  (Campa, 33)

The Serpent encodes a complex of symbols. J. E. Cirlot in his *Dictionary of Symbols* says the snake is "symbolic of energy itself—of force pure and simple" (285). It is linked with both life and death, with fertility and destruction, with the principle of evil, with the primordial strata of life and primal and cosmic forces. Snakes were frequently associated with ancient goddesses and women in general (Artemis, Hecate Persephone, Medusa, Gorgon, and so forth). The play further refers to Lucifer as the "Dragon": "Nuestra madre Eva fue engañada / por el astuto dragón" ("Our mother Eve was deceived / by the wily dragon") and thus further underscores the relationship between primordial forces and their evolution. Again according to Cirlot, the dragon is emblematic of "forces which have been mastered, controlled, sublimated and utilized for the superior purpose of the psyche and the development of mankind" (287). Carl Jung further elaborates this important symbolic entity by stating that "the dragon is a mother-image (that is, a mirror of the maternal principle of the unconscious)" (Cirlot 88).

Paul Ricoeur provides a Freudian analysis of the significance of the Serpent, relating it to the topic of Desire. He views it as a quasi-external entity incarnating temptation as a "sort of seduction from without" (Ricoeur 1982:256). He further elaborates: "The serpent, then, would be a part of ourselves which we do not recognize; he would be the seduction of ourselves by ourselves, projected into the seductive object" (256). And furthermore, it is our own "bad faith" that latches on to the quasi-eternality of desire in order to use it as an excuse for defecting to freedom. Temptation, which has the attribute of being simultaneously inside and outside our being, is perceived through this self-deluding excuse as being outside ourselves and our control. As the old cliché cleverly intones: "The Devil made me do it!" It is clear, then, that the Serpent "represents the psychological projection of desire. He is the image of the 'fruit'—plus the bad faith of the excuse. Our own desire projects itself into the desirable object, reveals itself through the object; and so, when he *binds himself*—and that is the evil thing—a man accuses the object in order to exculpate himself" (Ricoeur 257).

As the wily Serpent tempts Eva, her willpower collapses. She hesitates only a moment in her deliberations, and then the *desire* to be like God overwhelms her:

> Pero sobre todo es el sí, que el alma llega
> comeré de esta manzana aunque mi esposo
> me enseña y me guardó de ella.
> Es porque no sabe lo que dentro se encierra.
> Un chiste secundéis cuya promesa resuena
> Tan dulcemente en el alma,
> Que juntando en mi concepto
> Dos contras dos afectos.
> De vivir si no la como,
> De reinar si como de ella.
> Quiero por reinar comerla
> Que por una gloria vea
> Aunque la vida, se pierda.

But above all it is the positive response that fills my soul
I shall eat of this apple even though my husband
Taught me, admonished me against it.
It is because he does not know what it encloses.
A joke it may be whose promise resonates
So sweetly in the soul,
That joining conceptually
Two opposites with two effects.
To live if I do not eat it,
To rule if I do eat it.
I want to rule so I'll eat it
That I may see glory but once
Even though I lose my life.

(Campa 34)

This strophe portrays Eva as consciously making a decision to evolve from an undifferentiated "animal-like" life of innocence to a life of self-conscious knowledge, even though it will "kill" her. Lacan insists that it is through the acquisition of language, or "being born into language," that humans become conscious of the concept of finitude, of death, for inscribed in the concept of life and following the Saussurian conceptualization of language as a system based on oppositions, it is inevitable that humans will also realize its opposite—death.

Language is a social entity: in order for language to flourish it needs an interlocutor. Thus Eva seeks to share her newly acquired skill with Adán. In her role as possessor of language Eva will link language with the feminine, and we will speak of our first language as our mother tongue. However, since the Symbolic Order displaces the feminine with the masculine, with the Law of the Father, the Garden of Eden drama can also be perceived as a change from a matriarchal structure to a patriarchal structure.

Cognizant of the great force of desire, in this case the desire to be like the Father—like God—Eva uses this argument when she induces Adán to partake of the fruit:

Mi bien, mi señor, y mi esposo
¿No te estimula mi afecto;

No te mueve mi respeto
A que logremos los dos
Ser paralelos a Dios?
Sobre el monte de la luna
Así me lo prometió,
Aquel oráculo a voz
Diciéndome que como Dios
Habías de ser tú y yo.

My Beloved, my Master, and Husband
Aren't you moved by my love;
Aren't you moved by my respect
For the two of us to achieve
Equality with God?
Above the moon forest
That is how it was promised to me.
The voice of the oracle
Telling me that like God
You and I would be.

(Campa 35)

It is through language—the voice of the oracle—that Eva will acquire God-like qualities; that is, human characteristics.

Adán, intuiting that to ingest the forbidden fruit is to perish, articulates his premonition but cannot resist his desire (just as a normal baby cannot resist the desire to fall into language—to acquire language); he bites the proffered fruit. Unfortunately, by falling into language immediately, "death" overtakes the two. "Mas ¿Qué miro? ¡Yo estoy muerto! / Tan desnudo y descompuesto" ("But what do I see? I am dead! / So nude and so undone"). Eva reiterates her awareness of having fallen into another state of consciousness; into "death": "El alma ya desfallece / Y que se ausenta parece" ("Our souls expire / And leave us it seems"; Campa, 36).

Once Adam and Eve enter into the realm of the Symbolic Order they are doomed forever to toil and suffer, for under the rule of the Law of the Father they are no longer free as animals are free; they are imprisoned in the grid of the Symbolic Order; or, as Fredric Jameson puts, it in the "the prisonhouse of language." From this time on, they are guided by the obsessive and unquenchable desire to return to Paradise, to that moment of plenitude and unity found in the preterit in which humanity and nature were one.

The Fall from Paradise—the alienation of humans from nature, from themselves, and from each other—began with the acquisition of language; for being born into language implied the formation of a barrier, the Lacanian bar, between the Signifier and the Signified, which only death can erase.

NOTE

1. For some elucidating works on Lacan see Jane Gallop, *Reading Lacan* (Ithaca: Cornell University Press, 1985); Anika Lemaire, *Jacques Lacan* (London: Routledge and Kegan Paul, 1970); Juliet Flower MacCannell, *Figuring Lacan: Criticism and the Cultural Unconscious* (Lincoln: University of Nebraska Press, 1986); and Mikkel Borch-Jacobsen, *Lacan the Absolute Master* (Stanford: Stanford University Press, 1991).

REFERENCES

Acuña, René. 1979. *El Teatro Popular en hispanoamérica: Una bibliografía anotada*. Mexico City: Universidad Nacional Autónoma de México.

Borch-Jacobsen, Mikkel. 1991. *Lacan the Absolute Master*. Stanford: Stanford University Press.

Campa, Arthur L. 1934. *Spanish Religious Folktheatre in the Spanish Southwest. University of New Mexico Bulletin,* Language Series 5, nos. 1 and 2.

Carreter, Fernando Lázaro. 1965. *Teatro Medieval*. Madrid: Odres Nuevos, 9–94.

Cirlot, J. E. 1976. *A Dictionary of Symbols*. New York: Philosophical Library.

Cole, M. R. 1907. *Los Pastores*. New York: Memoirs of the American Folk-Lore Society, vol. 9.

Donovan, Richard B. 1958. *The Liturgical Drama in Medieval Spain*. Toronto: Pontifical Institute of Medieval Studies, Studies and Texts 4.

Ducrue, Benno Iranciscus. 1967. *Ducrue's Account of the Expulsion of the Jesuits from Lower California (1767–1769)*. St. Louis: St. Louis University Press.

Engelkirk, John E. 1940. "Notes on the Repertoire of the New Mexican Spanish Folktheatre. *Southern Folklore Quarterly* 4: 227–37.

———. 1957. "The Source and Dating of New Mexican Spanish Folk Plays." *Western Folklore* 16: 232–55.

Felman, Shoshana, ed. 1982. *Literature and Psychoanalysis: The Question of Reading: Otherwise*. Baltimore: Johns Hopkins University Press.

Fernández de Lizardi, José Joaquín. 1965. "Pastorela en dos actos." *Obras*. Vol. 2: *Teatro*. Mexico City: Centro de Estudios Literarios Universidad Nacional Autónoma de México.

Fülöp-Miller, René. 1930. *The Power and Secret of the Jesuits*. Garden City, N.Y.: Garden City Publishing Company.

Gallop, Jane. 1985. *Reading Lacan*. Ithaca: Cornell University Press.

García Montero, Luis. 1984. *El Teatro Medieval: Polémica de una Inexistencia*. Maracena, Granada: Editorial Don Quijote.

Gillmor, Frances. 1957. "*Los Pastores* Number: Folk Plays of Hispanic America— Forward." *Western Folklore* 16: 229–31.

Happé, Peter, ed. 1984. *English Mystery Play*. New York: Penguin Books.

Hegel, G. W. F. 1967. *The Phenomenology of Mind*. New York: Harper Torchbook, Harper and Row.

Igo, John. 1967. *Los Pastores: An Annotated Bibliography with an Introduction*. San Antonio: San Antonio College Library.

Kinghorn, A. M. 1968. *Medieval Drama*. London: Evans Brothers.

Kojeve, Alexandre. 1969. *Introduction to the Reading of Hegel*. Ithaca: Cornell University Press.

Kolve, V. A. 1966. *The Play Called Corpus Christi*. Stanford: Stanford University Press.

Lacan, Jacques. 1977. *Écrits: A Selection*. New York: W. W. Norton.

———. 1981. *The Four Fundamental Concepts of Psycho-Analysis*. New York: W. W. Norton.

Lea, Aurora Lucero-White. 1953. *Literary Folklore of the Hispanic Southwest*. San Antonio: Naylor Company.

Lemaire, Anika. 1970. *Jacques Lacan*. London: Routledge and Kegan Paul.

Los Pastores (The Shepherds): An Old California Christmas Play. 1953. Reproduced from the original manuscript at the Bancroft Library, with a foreword by Lindley Bynum. Trans. María López de Louther. Hollywood: Homer H. Boelter.

Lucero-White, Aurora, ed. 1940. "Coloquio de los pastores." *Folklore of the Hispanic Southwest*. Santa Fe: Santa Fe Press.

MacCannell, Juliet Flower. 1986. *Figuring Lacan: Criticism and the Cultural Unconscious*. Lincoln: University of Nebraska Press.

McCrossan, Sister Joseph Marie. 1948. *The Role of the Church and the Folk in the Development of the Early Drama in New Mexico*. Philadelphia: University of Pennsylvania Press.

MacGregor-Villarreal, Mary. 1984. "Celebrating *Las Posadas* in Los Angeles." *Western Folklore* 39(2): 71–105.

María y Campos, Armando de. 1985. *Pastorelas Mexicanas*. Mexico City: Editorial Diana.

Menéndez Pidal, Ramón, ed. 1900. "Auto de los reyes magos." *Revista de Archivos, Bibliotecas y Museos* 4: 453–62.

Morner, Magnus. 1965. *The Expulsion of the Jesuits from Latin America*. New York: Alfred A. Knopf.

Muller, John P., and William J. Richardson. 1982. *Lacan and Language: A Reader's Guide to "Écrits."* New York: International Universities Press.

Oinas, Felix J. 1978. *Folklore, Nationalism, and Politics*. Bloomington: Indiana University Folklore Institute.

Palomar, Margarita. 1989. *Pastorelas*. Guadalajara, Jalisco, Mexico City: Editorial Conexión Gráfica.

Pearce, T. M. 1956. "The New Mexican Shepherds' Play." *Western Folklore* 15: 77–88.

Pradeau, Alberto Francisco. 1959. *La expulsion de los Jesuitas de las provincias de Sonora, Ostimuri y Sinaloa en 1767*. Mexico City: Antigua Librería Robredo de José Porrúa e Hijos.

Raél, Juan B. 1965. *The Sources and Diffusion of the Mexican Shepherds' Plays*. Guadalajara, Jalisco, Mexico City: Libreria La Joyita.

Ricoeur, Paul. 1967. *The Symbolism of Evil*. Boston: Beacon Press.

Ríos, José Muro. 1985. *Pastorela de Amozochil*. Guadalajara, Jalisco, Mexico City: Gobierno del Estado de Jalisco.

Robb, J. D. 1957. "The Music of *Los Pastores*." *Western Folklore* 16: 263–80.

Robe, Stanley L. 1954. *Coloquio de Los Pastores from Jalisco, México*. Los Angeles: University of California Folklore Studies 4, University of California Press.

———. 1957. "The Relationship of *Los Pastores* to other Spanish-American Folk Drama." *Western Folklore* 16: 281–89.

Romero, R. A. 1985. *La Aurora del Nuevo Día en los Campos de Belén*. Mexico City: Antonio Venegas Arroyo. Obra nacional de la Buena Prensa, A.C.

Romero Salinas, Joel. 1984. *La Pastorela Mexicana: orígen y evolución*. Mexico City: SEP Cultura Fondo Nacional Para el Fomento de las Artesanías, Fonart.

Rose, Martial. 1969. *The Wakefield Mystery Plays*. New York: W. W. Norton.

San Martin, Beatriz [vda. de María y Campos.] 1987. *Pastorelas y Coloquios*. Mexico City: Editorial Diana.

Segel, Harold B. 1974. *The Baroque Poem*. New York: E. P. Dutton.

Sturdevant, Winifred. 1927. *The Misterio de los reyes masgos: Its Position in the Development of the Medieval Legend of the Three Kings*. Baltimore: Johns Hopkins Studies in Romance Literature and Languages 10.

Thomas, R. George, ed. 1966. *Ten Miracle Plays*. Evanston, Ill.: Northwestern University Press.

Torres Marín, M. 1971. *Auto del nacimiento del Niño Dios en el portal de Belén*. Bilbao, Spain: Colección Mensaje.

Valdez, Luis. 1989. *La Pastorela: The Shepherd's Play*. Program Notes, San Juan Bautista, California.

Woolf, R. 1972. *The English Mystery Plays*. London: Routledge.

PART II   SOURCES OF RECONSTRUCTION

Poetic Discourse in Pérez de Villagrá's
Historia de la Nueva México

LUIS LEAL

One of the salient characteristics of Latin America's colonial literature (of which the American Southwest's colonial heritage is an integral part) is the incipient *mestizaje,* or racial and cultural mixture, that appeared in its forms and, even more significantly, in its thematic content. This is patently evident in Gaspar Pérez de Villagrá's epic poem *Historia de la Nueva México,* which I will examine in this essay.

Pérez de Villagrá, a Spanish captain born in Puebla de los Angeles in 1555, actively participated with Juan de Oñate in the conquest of the northern regions of New Spain in 1598. His poem *Historia de la Nueva México* (1610) is a historical account of the conquest of New Mexico written in the characteristic form of epic poetry common in the Renaissance: hendecasyllabic verse separated into cantos; in this case thirty-four cantos.

Villagrá's work was not the first in Hispanic-American literature to utilize poetic discourse to narrate a history. The two discourses intertwined in the composition, historical and poetic, are the same we find in Alonso de Ercilla's *Araucana,* whose first part appeared in 1569; in the unfinished epic-historic poem *Nuevo Mundo y conquista,* written by the Mexican author Francisco de Terrazas; and in Antonio de Saavedra Guzmán's *El Peregrino Indiano,* which was published in Madrid in 1599 and describes Hernán Cortés's conquest of Mexico.

With the possible exception of *La Araucana,* all of these works have been categorized as true historical documents. None, however, has been classified as a "true" poetic composition by those critics who, no doubt inspired by classic literary criteria, demand that the literary work should not violate the concept of unity in all its forms—generic, thematic, or disciplinary— and that verse and prose should not be integrated in the same composition.

The American historian W. H. Prescott asserts that Saavedra Guzmán, author of *El Peregrino Indiano,* was more of a chronicler than a poet. And regarding the author of *Historia de la Nueva México* the editor of the 1900 edition, Luis González Obregón, observes: "Of Villagrá may be repeated what is said of the author of *El Peregrino Indiano,* D. Antonio de Saavedra y Guzmán, that he was a poet-chronicler, but more of a chronicler than a poet." He adds that Villagrá's poem "is a history in rhyme, interesting because of the dates and facts which he gives. It would have been more interesting if, instead of writing in verse, he had written in prose. Unfettered by rhyme, this principal actor and eyewitness of the events he relates might have rendered an invaluable service . . . as did Cortés and Bernal Díaz del Castillo, . . . authors who also wielded the sword and the pen" (Hodge 1933: 24–25).

An even more acerbic criticism is Alfonso Reyes's dictum published in *Letras de la Nueva España:*

> The Cortesian cycle is initiated by Terrazas. Although lacking in *brío* it does have a certain amount of dignity. Soon—even though intermittently there will be exceptions—it begins to lose its impetus with José de Arrázola and with Antonio de Saavedra Guzmán's *El Peregrino Indiano.* The latter was the famous journal of daily operations written in verse, and penned during "seventy days of navigation with the constant swaying of the ship." Later the genre barely survives the "thirty-four mortal cantos" with which Villagrá laboriously stitched the *Historia de la Nueva México.* (Reyes 1948:76)

Even though Villagrá, in order to "stitch" (as Reyes so indelicately puts it) his *Historia* resorts to metered and rhymed verse, he also interpolates a long passage of prose at the end of the fourteenth canto regarding "how the new land was conquered and taken possession of," which in my view is the least interesting part of the work. This fact contradicts what González Obregón observes; that is, that if Villagrá had written a chronicle in prose instead of writing it in verse, such a work would have been more interesting. I doubt it. The *Historia de la Nueva México* is a literary artifact whose content is as historic as it is poetic, just as Ercilla's *Araucana* is. I should point out that

Villagrá was way ahead of his time, for it was not until the nineteenth century that the historical novel appeared in Europe. This subgenre became popular in Europe and in the rest of the Western world as a continuation of the Renaissance taste for historical accounts in poetic form. And it was not until the romantic period that American indigenist literature appeared in Europe—an indigenist type of literature already present in the works of Ercilla, Villagrá, and numerous other authors. The epic poem was transformed into the historical novel, with the only difference being that the first was written in verse and the second in prose. The "historical novel" subgenre culminated with such works as *I Promessi Sposi,* by Alessandro Manzoni, and Leo Tolstoy's *War and Peace,* both of which are frequently referred to by historians. Tolstoy's novel contains a minute description of the Battle of Borodino analogous to the description of the Battle of Acoma found in Villagrá's work, which has frequently been cited by historians interested in the history of the Southwest.

When the above critics and others, such as the Mexican Francisco Pimentel, speak of the poverty of poetics in Villagrá's *Historia,* they are expressing a personal value judgment regarding the aesthetic merits of the work. They do not, however, deny that the poem encompasses a literary discourse; that is, that it is an epic poem containing thirty-four cantos written in hendecasyllabic verse—be they perfectly rhymed and metered or not. Pimentel states that Villagrá's *Historia* is commendable for the "fidelity in which the historical events are rendered," but that it is "very prosaic, without any poetic fictions to adorn it; and it is written in an 'unstructured' verse, generally quite weak which makes the reading of the work tedious." He sums up by stating that the work "can only be appreciated by erudite scholars who are searching for obscure or hidden data as they would in any other historical chronicle" (Pimentel 1885:143). One cannot deny that there are few poetic images in Villagrá's work. But who can categorically affirm that the more poetic images a work contains the better the aesthetic quality of such a work? If such were the case, one would need only to count the number of images in a literary work and in that manner establish its aesthetic value. But that is not the case.

No one can deny that Villagrá's poem contains lively passages encompassing mythic themes such as the one describing the Aztecs' migration from their remote place of origin: "aquella parte donde el norte esconde, / del presuroso Boreas esforzado, / la cóncava caverna desabrida" ("That region where the North lays hidden / From the vigorous northwind, Boreas, / The unpleasant concave cavern") until they arrive at the location indicated by their god:

Viéredes una tuna estar plantada,
y sobre cuyas gruesas y anchas hojas,
una águila caudal bella disforme,
con braveza cebando se estuviera,
en una gran culebra que a sus garras,
veréis que está revuelta y bien asida.

You will see a cactus planted
And upon whose thick and wide leaves
Perches an eagle, with beautiful uneven feathers,
Fearless she feeds
Upon a great serpent in whose talons
She is encoiled and firmly grasped.

There they shall build "la metrópoli alta y generosa, / al cual expresamente manda, / que México Tenuchtitlán se ponga" (II.6r) ("A tall and noble metropolis / Which [their god] expressly bids / That Mexico Tenochtitlán be called").

During their pilgrimage they encounter a frightful "demon" in the guise of a woman. The baroque description leads us to believe it was probably Coatlicue, the mother of Huitzilopochtli, the Aztec war god, since Villagrá describes her thus:

En figura de vieja rebozado
cuya espantosa y gran desenvoltura,
daba pavor y miedo imaginarla
. . . .
El rostro descarnado y macilento,
de fiera y espantosa catadura,
desmesurados pechos, largas tetas,
hambrientas, flacas y fruncidas,
. . . .
sumidos ojos de color de fuego,
deforme boca desde oreja a oreja,

por cuyos labios secos y desmedidos,
cuatro solos colmillos hacia afuera,
de un largo palmo corvos se mostraban
....
encima de la fuerte y gran cabeza,
un grave peso casi en forma
de concha de tortuga levantada,
que ochocientos quintales excedía,
de hierro bien macizo y amazado.

                    (II.4v, 5r)

In the guise of an old and withered hag
Whose horrible great visage
Brought fear and fright just to imagine it
....
The horrid fleshless putrid face
A fierce and terrifying visage
Overflowing flaccid breast, with monstrous teats
Lean, emaciated and wrinkled
....
Her eyes, like glowing coals,
Misshapen mouth extends from ear to ear,
From whose parched monstrous lips
Four fanglike teeth protrude on either side
Huge as a man's palm and curled they leered
....
Atop her monstrous head she bore
A great object shaped not unlike a tortoise shell;
Weighing more than eight hundred quintals
An enormous mass of solid ore.

Another poetic element of great significance in Villagrá's work is the theme
of arms and letters so common in Renaissance literature. When Villagrá wrote
the *Historia de la Nueva México* he was waiting at the Spanish Court in hopes
of a reward for his participation in Juan de Oñate's conquest of New Mexico
in 1598. The *Historia* was well received and produced the desired results, as

evidenced by the fact that he was named *alcalde mayor* in a Guatemalan town. Fate decreed that he was not to fill this appointment, for he died during the voyage to Guatemala. While he lived, however, he distinguished himself in the military as well as in literary pursuits, even though Baltasar Gracián's assessment of Cortés can be applied to our author—that he "never would have been a Spanish Alexander or a New World Caesar, the prodigious Marqués del Valle, D. Fernando Cortés, if he had not changed his employment. At the most through his literary endeavors, he might have acquired a mediocre reputation, but through the military he was able to reach the peak of eminence" (Gracián 1944:29).

In practicing both arms and letters Captain Gaspar Pérez de Villagrá was the scion of illustrious predecessors. Among the many others who achieved distinction in Hispanic circles were Garcilaso de la Vega, Hernán Cortés, Bernal Díaz del Castillo, Alonso de Ercilla, and, of course, Miguel de Cervantes.

The similarities between Cervantes and Villagrá are particularly interesting: both were engaged in the military and in literature, and their works reflect ideas prevalent during their epoch. As soldiers, they both participated in bloody military encounters, Cervantes in the Battle of Lepanto and Villagrá in the Battle of Acoma. As authors, both described the total destruction of a town: Cervantes wrote about the destruction of Numancia, and Villagrá about Acoma. And by coincidence, Villagrá's *Historia* was published in Alcalá de Henares, Cervantes's birthplace, five years after the publication of the first part of *Don Quijote* and five years before the publication of the second part. It is precisely in part 1 of *Don Quijote* that we find the well-known speech regarding an individual's engagement in both military and literary endeavors. Did Villagrá read *Don Quijote,* and was Cervantes acquainted with the *Historia de la Nueva México*? We do not have any proof that either was acquainted with the other's work, but we can conjecture that Cervantes read Villagrá, since we do know he was an avid reader. And regarding *Don Quijote,* who could have escaped reading it at that time?

The subject of arms and letters made famous by Don Quijote had illustrious antecedents by 1605. As José Antonio Maravall observes: "[T]o compare and contrast the practicing of arms and letters was a frequent theme in humanist thought" (Maravall 1948:125). I shall cite a few examples from writers who treat the subject; some defend the involvement of arms while others support the involvement in literary pursuits, and still others praise both disciplines. In Spain, Antonio de Guevara, in his book *Libro áureo de Marco*

Aurelio, written during the period between 1518 and 1524, privileges letters above the military. "Few," he states, "have been lost because they practiced the art of writing and even less so those who have been won over by arms" (Guevara 1929:34). For Guevara, it is literature that brings honor to a nation; all those remembered from antiquity, he asserts, left their imprint and honored their country by distinguishing themselves in letters as opposed to the military (Guevara, 35).

During the same period Guevara was writing, an author of Italian origin, Baltasar Castiglione, was expressing the same ideas in his famous book *El cortesano,* which he completed in 1524 and published in Venice four years later. In Castiglione's view, literature ennobles gentlemen and courtiers. He specifically criticizes the French, who thought literature detracted from an individual's engagement in arms (see Castiglione 1942:85). For this author, the practice of literary pursuits is far superior to the practice of arms, because without the former, gentlemen could not praise their own merits. True glory, says Castiglione, is that which "is written in the memory of a literary work." And he adds, "But if someone wants to contradict me, I should not want to be brought to task on this and have my opinion obviated since it seems to me some negative effects do accrue in those who practice arms and are engaged in literature" (Castiglione, 86). Needless to say, this does not mean that the courtier should not know the art of weaponry; according to Castiglione, he should be deft in their use and practice, excellent at riding and handling horses, and skilled in all areas employing force and speed in running a lance, tournaments, and jousting. Castiglione was speaking from personal experience, as Menéndez y Pelayo indicates in his prologue to Juan Boscán's translation of the *Cortesano*: Castiglione "was a man of arms and of the court; he was skilled in all the sports and gentlemanly exercises . . . he was a lyric and dramatic poet and was the organizer of courtly festivals" (Castiglione 1942:viii).

A few years later, in 1546, Fernán Pérez de Oliva wrote his *Diálogo de la dignidad del hombre,* in which he presents two contrasting opinions: Aurelio's and Antonio's. The former is pessimistic; he can see only the drawbacks of both disciplines, while the latter tries to demonstrate the merits of both. Man, according to Aurelio, can only achieve understanding when he is old and near death. "And even then, he suffers a thousand defects when his senses fail him" (Pérez de Oliva 1982:86). And with respect to those engaged in warfare, "see them dressed in armor, earning their daily bread through theft, with fears of inflicting death on others and the dread of being killed themselves; constantly on the run, wherever fortune bids them, with constant tasks before them both day and night." Antonio answers, defending both literary and military endeavors and enumerating the positive aspects of each, pointing out that knowledge is "the Queen and Lady of all virtues . . . it teaches justice and tempers one's vigor" (Pérez de Oliva, 109); through her (knowledge), "kings and princes govern; and she is the one who founded the laws which rule mankind" (Pérez de Oliva, 109). Weapons are beneficent and useful because they safeguard all the good found in a republic. "Gentlemen are the mainstay in the safety and security of a town. . . . They dress in armor and suffer hunger and exhaustion in order not to bear the yoke of the enemy" (Pérez de Oliva, 112).

Cervantes takes up the theme of arms and letters in *Don Quijote* (part 1, chapters 37 and 38), but he seems to favor the practice of arms. Don Quijote begins his second speech by stating: "Quítenseme de delante los que dijeren que las letras hacen ventaja a las armas" (Cervantes 1950, 3:319; "Begone from my sight those of you who believe literature is more advantageous than arms"). Those who defend literary endeavors assert that "los trabajos del espíritu exceden a los del cuerpo, y que las armas sólo con el cuerpo se ejercitan" (3:320; "the tasks of the spirit exceed those of the body, and the tasks of arms require only the body"). Don Quijote defends the practice of arms by stating that it is not a "career for louts" and that the practice of arms "requieren espíritu, como las letras" (3:320; "requires spirit as well as do literary endeavors"). For Don Quijote, the goal of literature is justice and the goal of arms is peace. But as "el mejor bien que los hombres pueden tener en esta vida" ("the best thing man can have in this life") is peace, and because without arms peace could not be possible, we can deduce that the practice of arms is superior because without arms literature could not exist.

Why did Cervantes defend the practice of arms through Don Quijote's arguments? It is well known that Cervantes, like Villagrá, was first of all a soldier and second a writer. Perhaps, as his biographer Jaime Fitzmaurice-Kelly states, it was because toward 1585, the year *La Galatea* was published, Cervantes "was learning that with respect to earning a living the pen was a weaker tool than the sword: it was a lesson he learned hesitantly and grudgingly" (Fitzmaurice-Kelly 1944:90–91). His speech in defense of arms was the result of that bitter lesson. Cervantes's defense of the practice of arms certainly influenced later attitudes. As late as the nineteenth century we see the narrator-captain in Ignacio Manuel Altamirano's novel *La navidad en las montañas* (1871) telling a priest who offers him shelter: "I am a soldier, your excellency, and I will find to my liking anything you have to offer me. I am accustomed to hardships and privations. You well know what this difficult profession entails. That is why I will refrain from quoting a speech Don Quijote made in a style that would be impossible for me to imitate" (Altamirano 1940:58).

Villagrá agreed with Cervantes regarding the superiority of the practice of arms. His *Historia de la Nueva México,* as a literary piece and not a historical document, is a paean to both the practice of arms and to the conquerors of the New World who with their deeds brought glory to Spain. The poem begins with these verses, a distant echo of Virgil's poem (stanza 1, canto 1):

> Las armas y el varón heroico canto,
> el ser, valor, prudencia y alto esfuerzo,
> ....
> de aquellos españoles valerosos,
> que en la Occidental India remontados,
> descubriendo del mundo lo que esconde,
> plus ultra con braveza van diciendo.
>
> (Fol. 1r)

> Of arms I sing, and that heroic son.
> Of his wondrous deeds and of his victories won.
> ....
> I sing of the glory of that mighty band,
> Who nobly strive in that far distant land,
> The world's most hidden regions they defy.
> "Plus Ultra" is ever their battle cry.

That Villagrá privileged arms over letters is quite clear in these verses from a later canto:

> O soldados que al bélico ejercicio,
> sois con gran razón aficionados,
> advertir que es grandísima grandeza,

no ser nada muy pródigos en lengua,
y serlo por la espada es cosa noble.

(Fol. 120r)

Oh ye soldiers who with bellic war
With good reason are greatly enamoured
Be advised that it is of great worth
To know not to be prodigious in tongue
But 'tis noble to be so with the sword.

Oñate named the first town he founded San Juan de los Caballeros, an action that demonstrates his close affiliation (and that of his captains) with the Renaissance world. In the *Historia* Villagrá presents Oñate as the son of kings, a descendant of Cortés and Moctezuma, representatives of the two cultures that, upon uniting, gave form and spirit to the resultant Mexican nationality. And the same occurs with Captains Juan and Vicente Zaldívar, the nephews of Cristóbal de Oñate, the father of the general (Juan de Oñate):

Aquel gran general grande famoso
que Cristóbal de Oñate habemos dicho
que fue su claro nombre, y también tío
de Juan y de Vicente de Zaldívar,
el uno general de Chichimecas
y el otro explorador de aquesta entrada,
y padre de don Juan que fue casado,
con biznieta del rey, hija que he dicho
del buen Marqués, de cuyo tronco nace
don Cristóbal de Oñate descendiente
de todos estos reyes y no reyes.

(Fols. 26v, 27r)

That great and praiseworthy general
Whose name Cristóbal de Oñate I spoke of earlier
Of noble lineage he was,
The uncle of Juan and Vicente Zaldívar
One was a general of the Chichimeca tribe,

The other an explorer of this region
and the father of Don Juan who was
The husband of the great-granddaughter
of the last Mexican king
And the granddaughter of the Marquis
From this ancestry Don Cristóbal de Oñate was descended
A son of kings and nonkings.

All of these gentlemen are skilled in both arms and letters, although they prefer the first to the second, as Don Quijote did. In times of respite and in honor of a celebration or fiesta both skills were practiced in tournaments and festivities:

Unas solemnes fiestas que duraron
una semana entera, donde hubo,
juego de cañas, toros y sortijas
y una alegre comedia bien compuesta.

(Fol. 88v)

A week of celebration and festivities
Where we enjoyed
Tilting matches, bullfights, and *sortijas*
And a comedy especially composed for the occasion.

Villagrá is not referring here to the play written by the Sevillian Marcos Farfán de los Godos; he will tell us about Farfán's work in another place. Indeed, Farfán's *comedia* was presented when the expedition crossed the Río Grande, and this dramatic piece can thus be considered the first play staged in the United States. Villagrá describes how the dramatic enactment of the *comedia* came about: "y luego que acabaron los oficios, / representaron una gran comedia, / que el noble capitán Farfán compuso" (fol. 77v; "And after all the functions were set aside / A great and wondrous comedy was enacted / Penned by the noble Captain Farfán").

Perhaps other soldiers who accompanied Oñate also wrote literary compositions. We do not know. However, one of them, Juan Velarde, was appointed secretary: "pues por la pluma, / no menos era noble y bien mirado, / que por la ilustre espada que ceñía" (fol. 134v; "because of his skill with the pen / He was no less noble and well liked / Than for the illustrious sword he sported").

According to Don Quijote, those who practice arms suffer great penalties; they expose their lives to battles and for their troubles receive less recompense than those who practice the art of writing: "Alcanzar alguno a ser eminente en letras le cuesta tiempo, vigilias, hambre, desnudez, vaguidos de cabeza, indigestiones de estómago, y otras cosas . . . mas llegar uno por sus términos a ser buen soldado le cuesta todo lo que al estudiante en tanto mayor grado, que no tiene comparación, porque a cada paso está a pique de perder la vida" (Cervantes, 3:329; "In order to achieve eminence in literary endeavors one has to spend a lot of time, suffer sleepless nights, hunger, poverty, headaches, stomachaches, indigestion, and much more . . . on the other hand, in order to be a soldier it takes all the sufferings a student must endure and in greater degree which is really without comparison, because at each step of the way he is on the verge of losing his life").

Villagrá, likewise, in the twentieth canto tells us "of the excessive travails soldiers must endure" and of the meager salary they receive for their pains. In that same verse he complains that his poetry does not do justice to the great deeds those valiant soldiers accomplished:

De sus muchos quebrantos padecidos,
y por mostrar mejor si son soldados
. . . .
fuera bien se encargara, y escribiera
sus claros y altos hechos hazañosos,
mas como inculto, bronco y mal limado,
dellos informaré lo que supiere.

                                        (Fol. 108v)

Of the great hardships they suffered
And to better demonstrate their mettle as soldiers
. . . .
It would be of great value
If their great deeds and valorous actions
Were written for their glory, and even though I'm
Rough, unpolished, and unlettered
I shall relate what I have known of them.

Later on, he promises to do so in the second part of the *Historia,* which, unfortunately, was never published.

Muchos así las vidas escaparon,
temerarias hazañas emprendiendo,
y hechos hazañosos acabando,
cual cantaré señor si Dios me deja,
ver la segunda parte a luz echada,
donde veréis gran Rey prodigios grandes
de tierras y naciones nunca vistas,
trabajos y aventuras no contadas,
empresas inauditas y desdichas
que a fuerza de fortuna y malos hados,
también nos persiguieron y acosaron.

(Fol. 110r, v)

Many escaped with their lives in such a manner
Blazing their way with great and dangerous deeds
And forging glorious actions
Of which I'll sing, if God permits it,
In the second part of this work.
Where thou shall see, O Great King, of wonders
Of these distant and unknown lands,
And the adventures and travails of valiant men
Their prowess, audaciousness and even ill fortune
That through misfortunes and ill luck,
Also was wont to follow and inflict us.

Villagrá himself is an excellent example of a man who preferred the practice of arms but also cultivated the art of literature. His *Historia* is a testimonial to his qualities both as a soldier (he spent thirty years in the service of his king) and as a fairly accomplished poet. In the "Canción pindárica en loor del capitán Gaspar de Villagrá, y don Juan de Oñate, descubridor y conquistador de la nueva México," which Luis Tribaldo de Toledo used as a preface to the *Historia,* we read the following:

Vos Villagrá castellano
con la pluma y con la mano

fundáis la gloria española

....

pues hoy de vos nuevo Ercilla
corre esta voz por Castilla,
que nunca el tiempo consuma,
que en México la moderna,
será vuestra fama eterna,
por la lanza, y por la pluma.

You, Villagrá, noble Castilian,
With your pen and with your sword
Spain's glory have founded.

....

For throughout Castile today
Of you, new Ercilla, we hear,
And let it be known forever
That in modern Mexico the fame
Of your pen and your sword,
Will remain eternal.

And from the "Canción" dedicated to Don Juan de Oñate and written by Juan de Valdés Caballero, which also prefaces the work, the following closing verses appear in which Villagrá is praised for having been equal to the task of using the pen and the sword. Valdés Caballero first describes the feats of Oñate and afterward directly addresses the poet's achievements:

Y tu canción humilde que has subido,
a tan heroico y singular sugeto,
basta no desvanescas el sentido,
remite tantas glorias y alabanzas,
y plectro más subido y más perfecto,
vos capitán discreto,
que igualastes la espada con la pluma,
haréis la copia y la sucinta suma,
que llegue altiva al conquistado ocaso,
animaréis vuestro veloz pegaso.

And thy humble paean that elevates to such heights,

And sings of such heroic and singular person,

Do not weaken thy voice

Do continue singing of such glories and such praises

A plectrum more exalted and most perfect,

You my most discreet Captain possess

Who has proved equal to the sword and pen

You shall recount both part and whole

Let it reach the summits of the conquered West

Give loose rein to your fleet-footed Pegasus.

The final canto's description of the destruction of Acoma is without a doubt the most memorable and most important passage in the *Historia*. It is representative of the Chicano literature to come because it is a literature born in the heat of cultural conflict. In 1938 Mabel Major, one of the first critics to defend the colonial literature of the Southwest in her book *Southwest Heritage,* was ahead of her time in defending the work of Pérez de Villagrá, and one can consider her the first North American critic (who was not a historian) who recognized its literary value. "It is annoying to find American history and letters continually described as a style tradition with its genesis in the *Mayflower* and the Massachusetts Bay Psalm Book. . . . Villagrá's account of the heroic capture of Acoma by Zaldívar and seventy men bears comparison with the scaling of the heights outside Quebec by Wolfe if one keeps all the circumstances in mind" (Major and Pearce 1938:33).

Equally valuable are Villagrá's literary descriptions of the Southwest, the first written in poetic discourse. Among those regarding the fauna, his description of the bison is particularly outstanding. In describing this American animal he utilizes the image of the European bull, to which he adds other characteristics specific to the bison. The explorers encountered great herds of these animals as they trekked inland, northward bound.

Tanta suma y grandeza de ganados,

que fue cosa espantosa imaginarlos.

Son del cuerpo que toros castellanos

lanudos por extremo, corcobados,

de regalada carne y negros cuernos.

(Canto 17, 92v)

Such a great and grand herd of cattle,

That it was a horrifying spectacle even to imagine.

They are not unlike Castilian bulls

Quite woolly and hump-backed,

Robust flesh and black of horn.

Just as interesting are the descriptions of the great prairies where the bison roamed. Villagrá here uses a metaphor that Domingo Faustino Sarmiento later made famous in his description of the Argentine pampa in *Facundo* (1845). "Y gozan de unos llanos tan tendidos, / que por seiscientas y ochocientas leguas / un sosegado mar parece todo" ("And they enjoy such a great expanse of land, / That for six or eight hundred leagues / These plains resemble a sea at calm"). Anyone who loses his way in such expanses will be without hope: "en medio de la mar sin esperanza" (Canto 17, 93r; "in the middle of the ocean without hope"). And it is Villagrá who provides us with the first description of the *vaquero,* a person later to become one of the most popular prototypes of Southwestern culture, now better known as the cowboy. He also describes for us in anecdotal form the activity that would come to be known as the "rodeo":

Queriendo pues en estos grandes llanos,

el sargento mayor coger algunas

de aquestas vacas sueltas y traerlas

al pueblo de San Juan, porque las viesen,

mandó que una manga se hiciese

de fuerte palizada prolongada,

la cual hicieron con presteza,

. . . .

y luego que la manga se compuso,

salieron para dar el aventado

. . . .

Todos en buenas yeguas voladoras.

(Fol. 93r, v)

The sergeant, desirous of capturing some

Of these great bulls inhabiting the Great Plains

Who roaming loose he wanted to bring
To the town of San Juan, so we could see,
Ordered a strong stockade to be built
With the greatest of haste,
And after the stockade was built
They went forward to entrap them

. . . .

All this done on their fleet-footed mares.

The image Villagrá utilizes to describe the bison stampede is most original:

Y así como la manga descubrieron,
cual poderoso viento arrebatado,
que remata en un grande remolino,
así fue reparando y revolviendo,
la fuerza del ganado levantando.

(Fol. 93v)

And as soon as the stockade was discovered
As a strong gust of powerful wind engulfs
Or a raging whirlpool sucks, such was
The force which startled and drove the bison to stampede.

It is interesting to note, since it reveals the *mestizo* (mixed) origins of frontier culture, that Villagrá calls the Indians who were helping in the rodeo "cowboys." The author records how Oñate and his men encountered these cowboys in the plains:

Gran suma de vaqueros, que a pie matan,
aquestas mismas vacas que decimos
y dellas se sustentan y mantienen

. . . .

y tienen lindas tiendas por extremo,
y lindos y lucidos pabellones,
del cuero de las vacas, cuyo adobo,
es tan tratable y dócil, que mojado,

aqueste mismo cuero que decimos,
vuelve después de seco más suave
que si fuera de lienzo, o fina holanda.

(Fols. 93v–94r)

A great number of cowboys who kill on foot,
These same cattle herds we talked about
And from these they take their sustenance
. . . .
And they have such beautiful tents
and such splendid canopies
Made from the hide of these same cattle
Whose skin is so tender and so malleable
That when wet this same hide
Will be as soft as linen
Or fine Flemish lace when dried.

It is characteristic of Villagrá's poetic discourse to use aphoristic expressions and sharp commentaries concerning the life and culture he is observing. This indicates that he possessed a well-defined philosophy of life. At the same time, he tries to display his erudition by citing classic authors and famous books, or interspersing Latin phrases: "y así dice muy bien el Mantuano / o sacra hambre, de riquezas vanas" (fol. 11v; "And thus with such fine phrases Virgil speaks, / Oh those who hunger for vain riches").

Simultaneously, in the introduction of each canto we find passages with both a poetic and a historical content. In the introduction to canto 21 Villagrá utilizes a poetic discourse to express the conflict between Oñate's men and the Acoman peoples—that is to say, the conflict between Europe and America. In the passage below, representative of that type of discourse, there is not a single reference to historical fact.

O mundo instable de miserias lleno,
verdugo atroz de aquel que te conoce,
disimulado engaño no entendido,
prodigiosa tragedia portentosa,
maldito cáncer, solapada peste,
mortal veneno, landre que te encubre,

dime, traidor, aleve, fementido,
cuántas traiciones tienes fabricadas,
cuántos varones tienes consumidos,
de cuánto mal enredo estás cargado,
o mundo vano, o vana y miserable
honra con tantos daños adquirida,
o vanas esperanzas de mortales,
o vanos pensamientos engañosos,
sujetos siempre a míseros temores,
y a mil sucesos tristes y accidentes

Oh, unstable world, with misery filled,
Cruel master to those who know you,
Unacknowledged deceit not understood,
Prodigious and portentous tragedy,
Vile cancer, sly plague
Deadly poison, evil curse which engulfs,
Speak up, you traitor, perfidious, *fementido*
How many deceits have you concocted
How many gentlemen have you consumed,
In what vile deceits are you engaged
Oh wicked world, Oh vain and miserable
Honor with so much pain acquired,
Oh vain hopes of mortal men
Oh vain and treacherous thoughts
Always subjected to such miserable fears
And to a thousand sad and tragic accidents.

A few metaphors are reiterated consistently throughout the poem. One of these tropes is the ship at sea, symbolic of the flow of history (history being similar to a voyage on the high seas).

Llegados habemos gran señor al punto
y engolfados en alta mar estamos,
la tierra se ha perdido, y sólo resta,
el buen gobierno y cuenta de la nave.

(Fol. 26r)

Arrived we have, O Great King, to that most distant land
And engulfed on the high seas we tarry,
The land's been lost, and all we have,
Is the control of our ship afloat.

A literary analysis of Villagrá's *Historia* requires more attention than can be afforded here in these few pages. The quotes I have mentioned are only examples of what the poem entails vis-à-vis its literary form and content; they do not include the historical aspects encompassed with regard to the conquest of New Mexico. Villagrá, like Cervantes, was a writer who preferred the practice of arms to that of letters. However, as he was composing the poem, he was conscious that it would have a niche in the history of Hispanic literature. His presence in the poem, not as a soldier but as a poet, is clearly manifested in a number of the cantos. Alfonso Reyes has observed that "the history and epics regarding the conquest had a practical purpose which was to ask for a recompense. It sought a false equilibrium between the representation of reality . . . and a manner in which to exaggerate the debt" (i.e., feats accomplished in the name of the Crown; Reyes 1948:76). I must point out that Villagrá does not ask for a reward for his services, although he believes recompense is due to the soldiers who risked their lives in order to expand the Spanish Empire in the New World. His primary purpose in writing the poem was to inform the king of the conquest of New Mexico. The poem is dedicated to His Majesty Felipe III, and the poet assumes the king is listening to him, is the receptor of the poem. We know that because in the last canto he addresses the king with these words: "Y vos Felipe sacro, que escuchando / mi tosca musa habéis estado atento, / suplico no os canséis, que ya he llegado" (fol. 175v; "And O most sacred Felipe, who listening / to my rough, unpolished muse you've been attentive / I beg of you not to tire, for I am done").

Doubtless Villagrá had a desire to be remembered as a poet. If this had not been the case he would not have selected the verse form to relate the history of the destruction of Acoma, just as Cervantes previously had done with the Battle of Numancia. Villagrá was conscious of the similarity of the two events, and he refers to it in the last canto:

Sin cuya ayuda dudo, y soy muy cierto,
que aquella gran Numancia trabajosa,
cuando más desdichada y más perdida,

quedara más desierta y despoblada,
que aquesta pobre fuerza ya rendida.

(Fol. 177r)

Without whose help I doubt I could have made it
For that great Numancia
When it was most unhappy was most lost
And was left deserted and uninhabited
Even more than this my efforts now exhausted.

The laudatory poems written by his friends certainly afforded Villagrá great satisfaction. He died quite young and thus was not able to enjoy the praise granted him by some of his contemporaries. At the same time, he was spared hearing the negative barbs of some critics. In spite of the adverse criticism, though, the poem has survived; it has been republished and translated into English. If as a soldier Villagrá helped in the conquest of New Mexico, as an author he left us the *Historia,* thus planting the seeds of Aztlán's literary heritage. As Gabriel Gómez states in the laudatory *Canción* written in the dedicatory pages:

No de otra suerte al nuevo mexicano
libras tú del olvido,
después que valeroso le has vencido.

. . . .

salga tu libro al mundo,
admiración de ingenios superiores.
freno de detractores.
y Marón tenga su lugar segundo.
que si él cantó, tú solo
cantas a Marte y das batalla a Apolo.

(Fol. 182)

And in such a manner you have saved
The New Mexican from oblivion
After you so daringly have vanquished him.

. . . .

May your book see the world

And be admired by superior minds
Who'll stop inferior tongues from wagging
And Marón will take a second place
For if he sang, you alone
Sing to Mars and battle with Apollo.

Bancroft called Pérez de Villagrá our New Mexican Homer. If the aesthetic
value of Villagrá's work is not sufficient to make him deserving of such a
distinction, the fact that he was the first to sing in honor and remembrance
of the tragedy at Acoma (just as Homer sung about the Trojan War) should
grant him that title. But it really is not necessary to use such comparisons to
evaluate Villagrá's work. It is of sufficient merit to have been the founder of a
literature, the literature of New Mexico, for, as Luis Tribalo de Toledo puts
it in the preface to the *Historia:*

Long years ago, fate had decreed
That all these annals we should read
From the worthy pen of one
Who knows what happened where
These wondrous deeds were done,
For he himself was there.

NOTE

This essay was translated from the Spanish by María Herrera-Sobek.

REFERENCES

Altamirano, Ignacio Manuel. 1940. *La navidad en las montañas*. In *Aires de México*
(prose). Ed. Antonio Acevedo Escobedo. Mexico City: UNAM. "Biblioteca del
Estudiante Universitario," 18.

Bancroft, Hubert H. 1889. *History of Arizona and New Mexico*. Vol. 17 of *The Works
of Hubert H. Bancroft*. 24 vols. San Francisco: The History Company, 1883–90.

Castiglione, Baltasar. 1942. *El cortesano*. Trans. Juan Boscán, ed. Menéndez y Pelayo.
Madrid: S. Aguirre.

Cervantes Saavedra, Miguel de. 1950. *Don Quijote de la Mancha*. 8 vols., 5th ed.
Ed. Francisco Rodríguez Marín. Madrid: Espasa Calpe. "Clásicos Castellanos."

Ercilla, Alonso de. 1967. *La Araucana*. Part 1. Madrid, 1956; New York: Kraus Reprint Corporation, 1967 (facsimile copy of first two parts).

———. 1945. *The Araucaniad*. Trans. Maxwell Lancaster and P. T. Manchester. Nashville: Vanderbilt University Press, 1945.

Fitzmaurice-Kelly, Jaime. 1944. *Miguel de Cervantes Saavedra*. Buenos Aires: Clydoc.

Gracián, Baltasar. 1944. *El héroe; el discreto*. 4th ed. Buenos Aires: Espasa Calpe. "Colección Austral," 49.

Guevara, Antonio de. 1929. "Libro áureo [de Marco Aurelio]." *Revue Hispanique* 76: 1–319.

Hodge, F. W. 1933. Foreword to *History of New Mexico*, by Gaspar Pérez de Villagrá. Alcalá, 1610. Trans. Gilberto Espinosa. Los Angeles: Quivira Society.

Major, Mabel, and T. M. Pearce. [1938] 1972. *Southwest Heritage: A Literary History and Bibliography*. Albuquerque: University of New Mexico Press.

Manzoni, Alessandro. 1905. *I Promessi Sposi. Storia Milanese del Secolo XVII*. Rev. ed., ed. Alfonso Cerquetti. Milan: Ulrico Hoepli.

Maravall, José Antonio. 1948. *El humanismo de las armas en "Don Quijote."* Preface by Ramón Menéndez Pidal. Madrid: Instituto de Estudios Políticos.

Pérez de Oliva, Fernán. 1982. *Diálogo de la dignidad del hombre*. Ed. María Luisa Cerrón Puga. Madrid: Editora Nacional.

Pérez de Villagrá, Gaspar. 1610. *Historia de la Nueva México*. Alcalá de Henares: Luis Martínez Grande.

———. 1900. *Historia de la Nueva México*. 2 vols. Ed. Luis González Obregón. Mexico City: Imprenta del Museo Nacional.

———. 1933. *History of New Mexico*. Trans. Gilberto Espinosa. Los Angeles: The Quivira Society.

Pimentel, Francisco. 1885. *Historia crítica de la literatura y de las ciencias en México desde la conquista hasta nuestros días . . . Poetas*. Mexico City: Librería de la Enseñanza.

Prescott, W. H. 1844–46. *Historia de la conquista de México*. 3 vols. Trans. Joaquín Navarro. Mexico City: Ignacio Cumplido.

Reyes, Alfonso. 1948. *Letras de la Nueva España*. Mexico City: Fondo de Cultura Económica.

Saavedra Guzmán, Antonio de. 1880. *El Peregrino Indiano*. Madrid: Pedro Madrigal, 1599; reprint, Joaquín García Icazbalceta. Mexico City: J. M. Sandoval.

Terrazas, Francisco de. 1941. "Mundo Nuevo y Conquista." In his *Poesías*. Ed. Antonio Castro Leal. Mexico City: Librería de Porrúa.

Tolstoy, Leo Nikolaevich. 1952. *War and Peace*. Trans. Louise and Aylmer Maude. Chicago: Encyclopaedia Britannica. "Great Books of the Western World," vol. 51.

Fray Gerónimo Boscana's *Chinigchinich*

An Early California Text in Search of a Context

FRANCISCO A. LOMELÍ

> In principle, the cultures of the world, past and present, form
> an interconnected continuum, and it is somewhat arbitrary to
> dichotomize this continuum on the one specific issue of
> whether particular cultures do or do not have writing, and to
> call them civilized or uncivilized accordingly.
> — Alfred Luis Kroeber, "Ethnographic Interpretations, 1–6"

Literary history as a distinct pursuit in Hispanic or Chicano letters
marks a relatively recent development in scholarship. Before 1970 literary
historians did not see this field as unique; uncertainty and vacillation pre-
dominated with respect to the proper identification of early colonial or territorial texts. Oftentimes, these texts are examined in light of their relevance
to contemporary social experience as understood in modern times, and thus
their significance has been minimized. Critics of contemporary Chicano literature have generally centered their attention on more contemporary authors
and their works in the quest to define the here and now. The political urgency
of the tumultuous 1960s and 1970s did not permit philosophical evocations
or reflections into the remote past. Social issues demanded far more immediate attention than incursions into the "purely" esoteric or inherently intrinsic.
But as a sizable corpus of literary production has emerged and Chicano literature has gained wider acceptance nationally and internationally, critics have
increasingly become interested in examining these early literary antecedents.
Part of the new fascination with literary history is grounded in the opportunity to gain a better insight into our forebears' thoughts and imaginative
fancies. This colonial literary heritage suggests a basic truth: there is a continuous strand linking the past with the present, despite the tribulations of
political and economic oppression experienced by the Mexican people. More-

over, associating cultural hydroponics with Mexican displacement in the United States is both inaccurate and malicious, for the underlying sentiment denies a long-standing Mexican presence during the colonial period and before the area became the U.S. Southwest. When this historical fact is viewed in its full implications, early Hispanic works of literature become key links to our cultural legacy. It is vital, therefore, to reassess these early works and to examine their contents as testimonies of their time.

Luis Leal, a highly respected literary historian whose specialty includes the colonial literature of the Southwest, introduced an approach to the study of this literature that interfaces the cultural and historical dynamics of Mexico and the United States. In his pivotal study, "Mexican American Literature: A Historical Perspective" (1973), Leal provides useful parameters for the conceptualization of a literary history. He cites a comprehensive bibliography from the colonial period which includes little-known, and barely imagined, texts. His nomenclature for periodization establishes key variants and distinctive features of each historical period. Most important, his eclectic recourse to data from many areas and disciplines (such as history, lore, fiction, art, and philosophy) is effective in linking a complex network of interrelated components. This linkage provides a watershed framework through which we can integrate all genres of literary works from the Hispanic and Mexican Southwest.

Another important venture entails a recent development in the application of new critical approaches to the study of literary history. Concentrating on a specific area, such as narrative (e.g., autobiography), regional case models (e.g., New Mexico or California), contrastive gender modalities (Chicana literature), the difference between written and oral traditions (Jacques Derrida and Walter Ong), a single genre (e.g., theater), or theoretical comparisons of movements and schools (e.g., postmodernism), allows for much broader experimentation and examination.[1]

The field of historical inquiry in literature has been greatly affected by a cross-pollination of the aforementioned approaches in dealing with early texts from the Hispanic colonial period (1540–1821), the Mexican period (1821–48), and the different territorial periods, which vary from region to region (1848 to 1912). It is no longer sufficient to use a traditional historically oriented methodology because the results tend to be either faulty, misinterpreted, or incomplete. The most reliable praxis in achieving maximum results requires an interdisciplinary focus which demands a set of criteria that supersedes a single specialization. The examination of an early work, for example, requires knowledge of a whole array of fields to properly comment on its pretext, the text itself, and its context. A unique work that certainly contains the necessary features for challenging a critic or literary historian is *Chinigchinich* (pronounced chiñich-ñich; chiñich-ñix; chi-ñi'ch-ñich; chi-ñi'ch-ñish; or chee-ngich'-ngich), which was written by a San Juan Capistrano mission priest named Fray Gerónimo Boscana between the second and third decades of the nineteenth century.[2] It is representative of the type of intergeneric accounts produced during the first 350 years of colonization in the provinces of the *vasto norte* of New Spain, as described by Luis Leal in the case of California: "In general it can be said that California colonial literature is didactic in nature. It consists of diaries, letters, memoirs, *memoriales,* chronicles, histories, travelogues, *relaciones,* essays and a few scattered poems and plays. Written first by the explorers themselves and then by the missionaries, government officials, military men, and other non-professional writers, its immediate end is seldom aesthetic" (Leal 1987 : 24).

The variant ways of pronouncing its title are symptomatic of *Chinigchinich*'s elusiveness; the work has been subject to a number of concerns and polemics ranging from questions of textual authenticity (there is an undetermined number of manuscripts, although more than likely only two) to the reliability of the translations. Other questions relate to Boscana's intent and ulterior motive in writing the work, the testimonial accuracy of the subject's versions, and the author's own biased—or culturally conditioned—interpretations. Quite evidently, the many veiled truths (or untruths) juxtaposed inside and outside compound the problem of deciphering this *one* text. Part of the problem no doubt resides in its multigeneric makeup and its fluctuation from one genre to another. As a consequence, the modern reader might subject the work to unrealistic or unattainable expectations; for example, empirical data might be judged by nonscientific methods, and fictional material might be evaluated accordingly by possible scientific content. The issue of rendering *Chinigchinich* literally or figuratively becomes central to unraveling its intrinsic nature. How are these dilemmas and multiple dimensions to be reconciled? One approach is simply to read the available text(s) from a specific perspective instead of pretending to cover all options. Essentially an ethnographic and anthropological treatise on the Juaneño Indians from the San Juan Capistrano area in southern California, *Chinigchinich* clearly defies preestablished notions of traditional literary paradigms as well as common

ethnological methodologies, although a case could be made for either camp.
However, the principal aim here is to understand the work's underpinnings
from a literary perspective.

In his *Handbook of the Indians of California* Alfred Luis Kroeber claims
Boscana's memoir is "easily the most intensive and best written account of
the customs and religion of any group of California Indians in the mission
days" (1925:636). The official chronicler of Boscana's native city in Mallorca
(Lluchmayor), Bartolomé Font Obrador, further comments: "Nada de cuanto
fue escrito por los franciscanos que misionaron en California, incluyendo crónicas de viaje, diarios de expediciones, tratados varios, etc., puede compararse
al estudio especializado y sistemático del misionero de Mallorca (Font Obrador 1966:5; "Of the writings by Franciscan fathers who evangelized in California, including travel chronicles, expedition diaries, various treatises, etc.,
none can compare to the specialized and systematic study of the missionary
from Mallorca"). On another occasion Kroeber says that "his picture is much
the fullest, is spiced with concrete detail, but also is definite in its broad
contours, and, for his time and profession, is liberal and enlightened"
(1957:282). Carl Schaefer Dentzel perceives Boscana as a missionary with
a keen appreciation for the California Indians' native ways: "The Franciscan Father Boscana belongs to this enlightened group" (Moriarty 1969:viii).
John P. Harrington, in an annotated reprinting of *Chinigchinich,* underscores
a similar view: "The Relación Histórica . . . is easily and by far the most
ethnological of any of the essays or accounts written in the Spanish language
during the Spanish period of the history of the Californias" (Robinson
1978:96). In the accompanying preface to Harrington's 1978 annotated edition, William Bright classifies the priest's manuscript(s) as "ethnoscience"
(Robinson 1978:iii). In his earlier (1934) translation Harrington claims the
rights to a second manuscript by the Franciscan priest, adding: "There was
comparatively rich Spanish archival material to be found, consisting of
chronicles of voyages and land expeditions, church records, etc., but no other
good description of a tribe and its customs, although certain writings on
Lower California Indians constituted the nearest second to the Boscana
[manuscript]" (Harrington 1934:1). Boscana himself is credited by his first
translator, Alfred Robinson, originally in 1846, with having admitted the
following in his introduction: "Perchance some one may enquire how I have
obtained so much information relative to the secrets or religion of these natives when, up to the present time, no other Father has written on the sub-

ject" (Robinson 1978:17). A reasonable qualification is that Boscana was operating as a pioneer in a new area of knowledge while exploring many aspects shrouded in secrecy. His methods of observing rituals and ceremonies might appear anthropologically questionable and at times primitive or scientifically fallible, but he seems to have made concerted efforts to be faithful to what he saw and heard, despite his firm conviction not to succumb to a suspension of disbelief. However, his goal was not so much a scientific treatise as it was a sociological tract with which to decipher myth, worldview, and a totally different religion. His observations were made for the purpose of understanding the Juaneños so that he could proceed with his ultimate aim: to use the information as a didactic tool for Christian evangelization. In the process he delved amply into myth, cosmogony, legends, fantasy, the supernatural, customs, habits, and an extensive belief system, all of which were part of a rich oral tradition. Of pivotal importance is the fact that in writing *Chinigchinich* he was functioning as a scribe ("Since these Indians did not use writings, letters, or any characters, nor do they use them, all their knowledge is by tradition, which they preserve in songs for the dances" [Harrington 1934:5]) for events and the participants' thinking and their scope of reality. He thus fluctuates from the cognitive to the unknown, entering the domain of imagination and literature while blurring boundaries between the creative and the scientific. Besides, if the intrinsic makeup of *Chinigchinich* produces elusive conclusions, it is because we may be seeing an early precedent to the contemporary but enigmatic Carlos Castañeda and his *Teachings of Don Juan.* Or perhaps we may discover a late Fray Bernardino de Sahagún, whose documentation of Náhuatl cultures represents classic ethnographic work on sixteenth-century Mexico. Either way, Boscana also transgresses the traditions of his era by fusing genre boundaries and meshing disciplines—writing in a remarkably sui generis mode.

Chinigchinich represents a work difficult to classify within a single narrative structure or framework. It conforms quite well with the tone and tenor of the writings found during the colonial period vis-à-vis its wide-angle coverage of diverse topics, its various perspectives integrated into a text, and the utilization of set formulas. The work's objective appears multifold: at times the central narrative fluidly meanders between informing and speculating; and at other times Boscana denounces what he learns while almost admitting that he is awestruck by it all. Although his training and vocation cannot permit him to even consider accepting the Juaneños' belief system, he cannot help but demonstrate some degree of amazement for the profound meanings in the traditions they avow. He also manages to transcend the standard chronicle format because the engaging nature of the narrative is more important than the information related. In addition, he discovers along the way that the disclosures are grander than his capacity to relate them. What apparently begins as a matter-of-fact account in chronicle form becomes an autobiographical search for the right language to properly capture what he vicariously witnesses. The problem is an internal or psychological one as well as an external or social one. The text is as much about a limited narrator's perspective as it is about an indigenous people: his editorializing and judgments, his conjectures and intuitions, his intimations and perceptions. In other words, the unfolding of the narrator's circumstance and insightful optic override all the authentic ethnological data he can unveil. As an incredulous narrator, he is predisposed to defy and debunk what he is told, considering it *extravagancias,* superstition, and irrational behavior. He is intrigued, nonetheless, by the cosmic similarities between the Juaneños' cosmogony and that of Western civilization and how these are governed by unexplainable coincidences that transcend cultural lines. However, he does not always present counterarguments because he realizes the futility of dismantling an established belief system he is unqualified to judge. Perplexed by the unfolding of this incredible Indian lore and the firmness of his own theological doctrines, he exercises discretion and restraint through both overt and subtle signs of praise for another people's complex order of beliefs and practices.

The text constitutes a meticulous effort to reconstruct a people's sense of history and mythology through a systematic but pseudo- or quasi-anthropological approach, one influenced by the teller's religious or didactic agenda and Eurocentric point of view. Boscana notes: "By gifts, endearments, and kindness, I elicited from them their secrets with their explanations, and by witnessing the ceremonies which they performed I learned by degrees their mysteries. Thus, by devoting a portion of the nights to profound meditation, and comparing their actions with their disclosures, I was enabled after a long time to acquire a knowledge of their religion" (Robinson 1978:18). The work must be considered syncretic because a certain amount of assimilation had already taken place, and the two worldviews—Western and Juaneño—had begun to interface.

Given the flaws in his nonscientific strategies to extract socially verifiable evidence, Boscana nevertheless penetrates the cultural barriers of his time, which tended toward a stalemate between Native Americans and recently arrived Hispanic Mexicans. We find a work that involves itself more in uncovering an ethos than discovering the most expedient way to convert the Indians into something else. Although *Chinigchinich* lacks a conventional plot, it does offer multifaceted narrative strata without confining itself to conventional models. Its plurality of traditions plus its diversely hued construct help explain its fascination for readers: it offers infinite interpretations at various levels (especially if it is true that more than one text exists).

While he was assigned to the San Juan Capistrano mission between May 17, 1812, and February 4, 1826, Fray Boscana became intensely inquisitive about the Juaneño Indians, a group sandwiched between the Gabrielinos to the immediate north and the Luiseños to the south.[3] His religious fervor motivated his desire to decipher their forms of religion, symbolism, and iconography with an eye to adapting them to Christian teachings. To this end he proceeded to cultivate a series of informants whom he considered infallible given the circumstances of language differences and their ability to communicate, as well as his ability to understand: "I confess that it is difficult to be able to penetrate their secrets, because the signification of their usages and customs is not known to all of them" (Harrington, 5). Deviating at times from his initially stated objective, he nevertheless provided significant parameters for documenting the ethnohistory of an observed primeval culture. His original goal may have been a handbook on evangelization procedures for future priests who needed to become better informed about the Indians' "absurdities and extravagances," but he accomplished much more. He uncovered and reconstructed a rich and amorphous body of oral knowledge and bestowed on it a comprehensible meaning by tapping into an extraordinary wealth of anthropological, religious, orally literary, mythological, sociological, and purely cultural records as they were being transmitted from one generation to the next. The text(s) of *Chinigchinich* probably achieved more than the author intended with his fragmentary note-taking: perhaps he never fully conceptualized or realized the scope of what he had started. As a text(s) in the process of becoming, it contains the simultaneity and plurivalence of voices that congregate between the lines. The abrupt ending hints at an unfinished endeavor or an open book. Alfred Robinson, the first to locate a copy, asserted in 1846 that "it is uncertain if the Holy Father ever intended it [the manuscript] for publication. After his death in 1831, it was found among his effects, with other writings, which came into the possession of the Syndic of the Missions, who kindly presented it to me" (Robinson 1978:vi). The work's merit lies not so much in its intrinsic quality as in the potential it presents for interpretations; it is an unfinished product, raw data and notes.

The author's stated intentions also deserve some comment, although the issue becomes somewhat clouded when the two known translations, by Robinson and Harrington, are compared. In both extant translations Boscana explicitly proposes to write a "history," or *relación histórica*—without specifically stating what kind of history—of the local indigenous population. He then proceeds to salvage and deconstruct their belief systems, resorting to evangelical alternatives to further indicate the advantages of such an enterprise. Part of his aim involves comparing their previous state of "heathenism" with their present condition as Christians. His principal desire is to determine and make public their inner secrets in order to supplant these with elements of "an understanding of the true faith" (Robinson 1978:17). In one version he alludes to his project as investigating "to a moral certainty everything that is related in the present book" (Harrington, 5). Besides, the priest's sense of humility overtakes him, although his fascination oscillates between cultural curiosity and religious zealousness. He also reveals a personal clue that might be the key to his interest in Juaneño religion and myths. His inquisitiveness admittedly emerged as a result of having to fulfill an obligation when the government of Spain circulated a set of thirty-six ethnological questions to all civic and ecclesiastical authorities on October 6, 1812. This questionnaire reached San Juan Capistrano in 1814, and Boscana, along with another priest named Borfa, drafted a response as a part of a larger document called "Contestación al Interrogatorio."[4] If this did not directly effect his fondness for the Juaneños, it more than likely motivated him to become more precise about his observations while providing a format to do so. In Harrington's translation Boscana goes to great lengths to minimize his personal role in divulging such confidential material from privileged informants or chiefs, while apologetically referring to himself as a "pygmy" and asking pardon for his possible "arrogance and presumption" (Harrington, 6). The rhetoric of his introduction closely resembles passages common in narrative works at the time the Inquisition was in power. The Inquisition forced authors to hide as narrators behind others' views and perceptions as if they had had no part in what they wrote. Some authors fabricated smokescreens to divert attention from their real feelings, or they created a distance from their narrations by allowing characters and events to speak for themselves. Boscana's special affinity with the related data suggests a triple purpose: to disclose a "fabulous in itself" indigenous background, to pave the way for Christianization, and to reconcile or at least bridge the gap between the two religious systems.

Much speculation and mystery surround the enigmatic *Chinigchinich* because it has become known through second- or thirdhand sources. According to Robert F. Heizer, Eugene Duflot de Mofras was the first to refer to such a manuscript, in *Exploration du Territoire de l'Oregon, des Californies, et de la Mer Vermeille, Exécutée pendant les Années 1840, 1841, et 1842* from 1844.[5] Duflot de Mofras claims to have obtained a copy in 1834, which he calls "Historia de las costumbres gentilicas de los Indios de California" (1844:100). The key figure responsible for introducing Father Boscana's text, however, is Alfred Robinson, an employee of a Boston trading company who first translated it and inserted it as part 2 of his famous account *Life in California: During a Residence of Several Years in That Territory* (1846).[6] Later, Alexander S. Taylor reprinted Robinson's translation in the series "Indianology of California."[7] Other authors refer to it only in passing. The primary mystery, however, revolves around the location of an original copy of the manuscript. The incessant search has resembled a treasure hunt of legendary proportions, not to exclude the phantasmagorical. Scholars sense a plot for a mystery novel— one that contains many leads but eludes solution. Records indicate apparent purchases of extant copies since the 1830s, but again, no concrete evidence has been openly displayed. In 1934, John P. Harrington made headlines in ethnography with his important translation of what he termed a variant version: *A New Original Version of Boscana's Historical Account of the San Juan Capistrano Indians of Southern California*. Harrington, inexplicably, does not specify where or how he made his discovery, although he may have encountered an obscure copy at the Bibliothèque Nationale in Paris. As the only consolation, he provides a reproduction of a photostatic copy of Boscana's first page of the introduction to dispel doubts (?), thus revealing a faithful and literal translation—something Robinson also claimed. Adding more fuel to the mystery, Harrington's forthrightness becomes suspect, for he does not comment or elucidate anything about his 1930s finding in what is considered the most comprehensively annotated edition of *Chinigchinich* to date (Malki Museum Press, 1978). It seems that only Alfred Luis Kroeber is willing to divulge such secrets about Boscana's manuscript(s): "It was secured at Santa Barbara Mission in the early 1850's by L. de Cessac, brought to Paris, and acquired in 1884 from de Cessac's associate, Alphonse Pinart, by the Bibliothèque Nationale, where it became No. 677 of the Spanish and Portuguese manuscripts. It has been seen there recently by our colleague John Rowe and by Edward H. Carpenter, Jr., of the Huntington Library; the latter, in fact, secured a microfilm copy of it" (Kroeber 1959:283).

Another inherent concern with respect to Boscana's writings is compounded by the variety of liberties taken to paraphrase his work, oftentimes not allowing the opportunity to resolve the issue of authenticity in the composition, veracity, and/or perspective. To a degree, this has become part of a small network of ethnologists' elite lore. And the panorama of scholarly intrigue is further muddied by the real possibility that past ethnographers were not necessarily referring to the same text. Umberto Eco would certainly have a picnic with such a scenario. For example, Robert F. Heizer contended in 1976 what Bartolomé Font Obrador had already asserted ten years earlier: that Robinson and Harrington had access to two distinct manuscripts by the Franciscan friar, representing a most interesting dilemma for anyone attempting to comment on *a* definitive text. If it were true, then, according to Heizer, three distinct manuscripts about the same subject might exist: one translated by Robinson, one by Duflot de Mofras, and one by Harrington. This scholarly imbroglio leads to puzzlement, confusion, and infinite possibilities. No one has explicitly posited the possibility of more than three manuscripts by Boscana. We can say with some certainty that his writings were interrupted by his transfer in 1826 to San Gabriel mission, where he eventually died in 1831.

Since no third manuscript is accessible, comparison can be made only on the two known translations. In general, they contain essentially the same information, except that discrepancies such as omissions or additions are evident. Their compositions, for instance, not only reflect the translator's peculiarities and style, they actually denote substantial variances in content, amplification, and opinion. Perhaps they might most accurately be described as versions in progress, although the dates of their completion are also indeterminate. In Harrington's photostatic copy dating from 1934, the years 1812–22 are etched on the left margin in what appears to be a reference to the time of research: "Through labor and cunning during a period of more than ten years [marginal annotation: from 1812 to 1822], I have been able to investigate to a moral certainty everything that is related in the present book" (5). More than likely, it represents the duration of his collecting the ethnohistorical data, because Harrington's translation contains fewer post-1822 references than Robinson's, suggesting that the latter version was written later or subsequently brought up-to-date.

Boscana's texts elicit a number of questions regarding their intrinsic conceptualization. Judging from the external structure, it is not always clear if these divisions are intended as "several penetrating but all too short chapters" (Harrington, 1), topical notes, or skeletal frameworks. However, both texts were written to be read by someone, as can be ascertained by the references to the "reader"—not Boscana himself—and to a "book." An argument can be made that the texts remain untitled in the modern sense, but the tradition of that time assumes the title to be the long description (a sort of abstract) that introduces the text: *Relación histórica de la creencia, usos, costumbres, y extravagancias de los Indios de esta Misión de S. Juan Capistrano, llamada la Nación Acágchemem.*[8] Why Robinson designated the version he read with the succinct title *Chinigchinich* is not altogether clear, except to indicate a preference for either brevity or sensationalism. His fascination for this local godlike figure perhaps parallels Boscana's fascination, but it would have been inconceivable for a priest to name his original manuscript for a heathen god. Free from compromising theological predicaments, Robinson yields to a romantic spirit by focusing on the exotic qualities surrounding Chinigchinich.

As if Boscana's *relación histórica* were not already cryptic enough, each translator (Robinson and Harrington) has contributed to its legendary status by providing portions that the other does not contain. Curiously, despite the differences I have already mentioned, both versions contain approximately the same number of pages. This might be explained by the procedure of submitting a formal response to the 1812 questionnaire from the Spanish government. But nonsystematic discrepancies abound between the two versions, and together they contribute toward a more global portrayal of the Juaneño culture. The order of the chapters and the correspondence between the two translations is as follows (chapter titles are abbreviated):[9]

Robinson's translation	*Harrington's translation*
Introduction*	Introduction
I. Of What Race?	1. From What Race?
II. On Creation of the World	2. About the Creation
III. Creation of the World†	3. Life of Chief Ouiot
IV. Vanquech Temple	4. Instruction of Children

V. Obedience and Subjection

VI. Instruction of Children

VII. Matrimony

VIII. Mode of Life

IX. Feasts and Dances

X. Extravagances

XI. Calendar

XII. Indian Wars †

XIII. Funeral Ceremonies

XIV. Immortality of the Soul

XV. Origin of the Population

XVI. Character of the Indians †

5. Matrimony ‡

6. Manner of Life *

7. Obedience and Subjection *

8. Temple Vanquex

9. Feasts and Dances

10. Calendar

11. Extravagances

12. Burials and Funerals

13. Immortality of the Soul

14. Origin of Inhabitants

15. About Rancherías †

* There is a resemblance but with significant modifications.

† The chapter does not match any other.

‡ A sizable section remains untranslated or is transcribed in the original Spanish.

The major differences consist in the number of chapters (16 versus 15), the number of independent chapters not corresponding to any in the other translation (3 in Robinson's and 1 in Harrington's), and the minor shuffling of chapters more evident in the middle chapters and less so in the beginning and end chapters. The three autonomous chapters in Robinson's text ("Creation of the World," "Indian Wars," and "Character of the Indians") contribute information markedly different from Harrington's text for the specificity in their ethnohistorical revelations, including extensive commentary on myth and sociology with some allusions to what was then contemporary Mexico. On the other hand, Harrington's text essentially offers one independent chapter ("About Rancherías") composed as an unfinished note outlining the various nearby villages. In comparison, the last chapter in Robinson's text advisedly informs the reader of a completed attempt: "To complete this history and to give a relation of all my observations during a period of more than twenty years' residence in the province, it will be important to delineate the character of the Indians" (Robinson 1978:87).[10] Otherwise, the correlation is indeed close in the general treatment of the respective topics.[11]

However, close scrutiny reveals more subtle clues to the manuscripts' order of composition and their degree of polishing and focus or tonality. For example, in Alfred Luis Kroeber's view, Robinson's translation is "somewhat flowery, and we do not know what liberties he took with the vanished origi-

nal" (Kroeber 1959:282), principally because we do not have the original
with which to compare it. But Harrington's translation of Boscana's introductory comments offers more tentative statements about his procedure: "Since
no information is found as to where these people of California may have come
from, . . . it is necessary (for us) to walk *blindly,* traveling to and fro with
closed eyes after the truth, and perchance not knocking at her door for a long
interval . . . inasmuch as *this chapter is all by way of conjecture,* if I err in this
undertaking, it is not through will and caprice, but because of not being able
to discover the light in a place so dark, *going along groping blindly"* (Harrington, 7; emphasis mine). Harrington's manuscript also appears to include data
that have not been fully filtered through Christian doctrine and practices.
The religious biases are ever present in both, but Robinson's text is replete
with specific biblical references that are absent in Harrington's: Robinson's
chapter 4 mentions Deuteronomy, and chapter 8 inserts Adam ("It cannot be
denied that these Indians, like all the human race, are the descendants of
Adam" [55]). And whereas Harrington in the chapter title "Temple Vanquex" refers to the devil, Robinson calls him "Satanic Majesty"; and chapter
3 designates Ouiot, a figure later transformed into Chinigchinich, as a "mon-
ster." In other words, Robinson's text is more culturally and religiously
charged, at times falling prey to hyperbole with which to rebuff Juaneño
beliefs. For example, while Harrington's translation describes the dances as
"very decent and for a time entertaining" (38), Robinson's version characterizes them as "very modest and diversified by a number of grotesque movements" (57–58). In Robinson a potentially compromising observation by
Boscana is omitted ("spiritual souls, created in the image and likeness of
God"). When cannibalism is discussed, in Robinson's version a "large piece
of meat" is extracted from the victim, but in Harrington's it is a "small
piece." In Robinson the Indians are "compared to a species of monkey" (87),
but no such mention is made in Harrington; and a detailed scene of a deflow-
ering ceremony is included in Harrington but not in Robinson. In addition,
in Harrington more doubts emerge as to the effectiveness of priests in evan-
gelizing Indians, but such delicate assessments in Robinson are conveniently
diluted so as not to admit a losing battle.

In sum, it can be argued that Robinson's manuscript (1825–26?) postdates
Harrington's text (1822?), and, further, that the latter possibly served as a
working draft or manuscript in progress for the later version. A number of
textual hints seem to verify this fact. Robinson's text contains more compre-

hensive material [12] about the ethnohistory of the Juaneños (i.e., the bridal song missing in the Harrington text) and seems to have benefited from trial runs, such as Harrington's version may have been. Also, the former is safer than the latter in balancing praise with censorship of "heathen" practices. One obvious clue in the Robinson version is the inclusion of recent events in Mexico regarding its independence from Spain; another is the mention of a comet appearing in December 1823; but the clincher is a direct citation of September 1825. Since the historically recent information does not appear in the Harrington text, it can be surmised that the Robinson text constitutes the most up-to-date reflections and annotations. A much more subtle difference between the versions reconfirms this theory. The linguistic equivalent of -*sh* appears in the earlier Harrington text designated by the sign *x* (e.g., vanquex), corresponding to Boscana's background in the Catalonian language, coupled with the Spanish -*ch* (e.g., vanquech), indicative of the more modernized version. The differences suggest both greater care in the "final version" and that Boscana's Spanish was becoming Mexicanized after his long residence in the region. Robinson's rendering of "Chinigchini*ch*" (instead of "Chinigchini*x*," as Moriarty later proposed) represents the most recent method of transcribing the name into the Spanish system of sounds. This transliteration of two distinct sounds might be coincidence, but it seems consistent with other differences between the two texts.

Part of the intriguing fascination with *Chinigchinich,* aside from the aforementioned variants and discrepancies, still continues to be the fantastic stories and legends about a Juaneño people who seemed completely unacknowledged until Boscana delved into the oral tradition of their myths. He recounts and gives form to much of what is relayed to him through the optic of an amazed listener and witness. The abysmal cultural differences he experiences constantly keep him on the brink of disbelief. Thus, his natural reaction is to downplay the elements of mythopoetics conveyed to him because their unexplained origins threaten his own; his sense of otherness is a centerpiece in the narrative. Since he is set in his beliefs and accompanied by a strong sense of a messianic Catholic doctrine, he is not about to relinquish any ground to the inventive tales, which he regards as fictitious or preposterous, terming them *extravagancias*. To admit anything less would mean he has succumbed to their enchantment. For that reason he feels compelled to denounce, qualify, or further explicate his views. This is the dynamics that operates through the text(s). That is, there is a narrative focus function at all

times, characterized by a tug-of-war between awe and disbelief, personal in-
trusions—including rhetorical argument originating from the Bible—and
some posturing of civilized righteousness. While trying to deconstruct another culture's view of itself through unique but questionable folklore and
ritual, Boscana also measures the limits of his own belief system. Above all,
most of what he relates is told through colored glasses, and at times through
a glass darkly. In that sense, *Chinigchinich* entails the poetics of an outsider
trying to capture, encapsulate, understand, appreciate, and represent a culture totally different from his own. The text, then, is as much about the
Juaneño Indians as it is about their highest religious figure—and all of what
that signifies—through whom we can unravel the mysteries of human memory as it relates to their distinctive past.

Because Boscana cannot fully comprehend that the Juaneños sprang from
a non-European social context, his logical conclusion is that they must be
descendants of or similar to the well-known wandering Chichimecas, as described by Torquemada in his *Monarquía Indiana*. It becomes obvious that his
understanding of local anthropological development was insufficient to provide a model with which he could easily reckon. Here he exemplifies a central
Mexican bias as he remains puzzled over the incredible linguistic diversity
found locally, intimating a Tower of Babel syndrome while not recognizing
that the local Indian groups did not experience a massive social organization
of the magnitude found in Mexico. The following excerpt illustrates how he
associates the primeval disclosures with biblical knowledge at the same time
that he overtly creates a schism between the two:

> Although this chapter has for its title, the creation of the world, the reader
> must not suppose it has any relation to the account given by Moses in the first
> chapter of Genesis. I do not intend any such thing; but merely to make known
> the belief of these Indians in their heathen state. We must not be surprised, if
> there be found many contradictions and extravagances; for these rude Indians
> were ignorant of the true God, without faith, without law, or king, and gov-
> erned by their own natural ideas, or by tradition. (Robinson 1978:27)

The priest resorts to analogies to exemplify or deconstruct, but a partnership
in the realm of ideas is intrinsically established; the arguments for a supposedly unrelated worldview seem to crumble little by little. The Juaneños'
narratives of cosmogony become their own version of Genesis, and vice versa.
In addition, they have a highly detailed narration about a deluge and how

their central god, Chinigchinich (a trend toward monotheism?), evolved.
Also, the topic of the immortality of the soul evokes a lengthy disquisition
by the priest, who wishes to show it as a human trend not foreign to the
Indians. Through sometimes remarkable parallels we can deduce a universal
human frame of mind that explains the unknown through allegorical stories
or extended metaphors of epic proportions. All rational faculties seem to defy
the versions of the creation of the universe, mainly because they are intended
to be accepted as an act of faith couched within a given tradition. Boscana's
thinking process, entrenched in a Christian mode, leaves him unable to exercise his sense of faith on a foreign interpretation. What he does not realize
is that Juaneños could logically counter with their own perspective. But as
the privileged narrator of the text, Boscana has the upper hand, or the last
say; he can discount as well as judge by the stroke of a pen. The Juaneño
culture, in a very real sense, is at his mercy for he determines the definitions
and ultimate criteria. Thus the text(s) are governed by a subtle conflict between narrative frames: his own or the Juaneño story.

Boscana's text(s) do not embody uncontaminated[13] sources. His knowledge
of indigenous cultures was possibly rooted—at least by hearsay or lore—in
the known classics about the Náhuatls, including the Mayan *Popol Vuh*. The
conquest of Mexico was probably very much in his mind, and his recent
immigration into the Americas might have been influenced by conquest stories of fancy and drama. It is possible that he sought out proven models to
help him understand indigenous peoples so that he could produce a useful
didactic guide on the Juaneños. Without following the lead of a kinship
or link with Quetzalcóatl, this group's recorded oral history exhibits strong
similarities to other Mesoamerican creation stories. In addition, strong parallels are evinced with respect to Genesis. It is almost certain that a syncretic
version was passed down to Boscana. For example, the creation narrative indicates that "before this world was, there existed one above and another below" (Robinson 1978:27), which resembles the dual Mesoamerican deities
such as the Aztec Ometéotl. The two figures (heaven and earth) are brother
and sister (a resonance of Adam and Eve or, again, native dualities?). Out of
their relationship is born the first mortal, Ouiot, who later becomes the main
divinity and whose story parallels the myth of the poisoning and exile of
Quetzalcóatl. At one point, Boscana compares the following: "We have the
six productions of the mother of Ouiot, corresponding to the six days of the
creation of the world" (Robinson 1978:35). Ouiot later metamorphoses into

Chinigchinich, who, as a type of savior known through the process of pro-
phetic revelation, admits returning to his people to fulfill a new destiny. This
regeneration and transformation into a higher being of godlike qualities also
resembles the story of Jesus Christ as a messianic figure. Boscana lays the
foundation of a quasi-Christian allegory, but he also takes the necessary pre-
cautions not to associate the two too closely for fear of censorship or heresy.
In the Robinson text, the next chapter (missing in Harrington's version) continues to expand on the creation theory of the Juaneños; however, the entire
discussion revolves around its localized relevance, thus thwarting any suspicion as to what he may be espousing beyond the confines of Christian doctrine. Again, we are not dealing with an objective and comfortable narrator;
his theological principles are being encroached upon. Yet, while balancing
between what he hears and what he believes, he is still unable to prevent
himself from retelling the incredible legends and myths. His disbelief becomes the medium or discourse of the suggested affinities between the two
religious belief systems.

Boscana's explanations of Chinigchinich are fairly detailed descriptions of
his dress, manners, aura, origins, and behavior. Numerous times he hints
at philosophical affinities between Western and indigenous peoples, *but* he
makes certain not to intertextually associate religious figures from distinct
traditions, for he does not consider them equal. Chinigchinich is viewed as
an all-powerful, almighty, and omnipresent deity: "He saw everything, although it might be in the darkest night, but no one could see him. He was
a friend to the good, but the wicked he chastised" (Robinson 1978:29–30).
In another instance Boscana skillfully refrains from any reference to the Holy
Trinity although the analogies are unavoidable: "Chinigchinich was known
under three distinct names, as follows: *Saor, Quaguar,* and *Tobet.* Each one
possessing its particular significance, denoting diversity of a difference of
times. *Saor,* signifies or means that period in which Chinigchinich could not
dance; *Quaguar,* when enabled to dance; and *Tobet,* when he danced enrobed
in a dress composed of feathers, with a crown of the same upon his head, and
his face painted black and red" (Robinson 1978:30). Chinigchinich possesses
the attributes of a compassionate and enlightened god who has lived among
his people; for example, he has relieved them of ignorance, taught them to
dance, related how to cure the sick, encouraged them to build a temple,
preached a set of "commandments" (a religiously loaded biblical term for

Boscana?) for the youth, and, most important, provided them with words. It is noteworthy that Boscana rarely questions Chinigchinich's godliness, because he too recognizes and admires the degree of social organization achieved by the Indians through his inspiration. Rarely does he enunciate the words *false god,* and when he does, it appears to be used as a rhetorical tool to maintain a certain distance. Although he never explicitly admits it, he probably viewed Chinigchinich as a good starting point in the evangelization process toward Christianity. The more he was able to elucidate the legend and myth surrounding Chinigchinich, the more he could argue that the Juaneños were ready for the next stage of religious evolution. Besides, this god shares some points in common with the Christian God and Catholic rituals, as James R. Moriarty's summary makes clear:

> The religion of Chinigchinix had serious and emotionally moving ceremonies and rituals. It was founded on a group of laws which required fasting, self-sacrifice and absolute obedience. Inviolable secrecy on the part of its adherents added an aura of mystery and the allure of the supernatural, thereby drawing converts to it by these powerful psychological attractions. Finally, it contained perhaps the most important ingredient requisite for a conquering religion. Its prophet and founder gave the sanction of fear. Punishment and damnation were the lot of the disobedient and the unfaithful. Terrible avengers in animal and plant form descended on these unfortunates, causing them great physical harm and even death. (Moriarty, 11–13)

One remaining question not resolved by Boscana is whether the Chinigchinich cult designates him as a human prophet or a god who upon death ascended into a type of heaven. Both options seem to echo Christian logic. However, he does explicitly state that Chinigchinich was born at a *ranchería* (village) called Pubu. This deity thus supplied the Juaneños with both functions (prophet and god) without one being exclusive of the other. According to Kroeber, most of Robinson's and Harrington's theological suppositions ring with misleading interpretations clouded with rudimentary ethnographical documentation, leading him to suggest a plausible compromise: "Changichnish [*sic*] might be a reaction formation, an invention due to the imported stimulus, made by natives desirous of preserving their old religion; an imitation of the Christian God of the missionaries, whom they took over and furnished with a native name and added their own beliefs" (Kroeber 1959:291).

If that were the case, then Father Boscana was a pawn or a victim of his own curiosity. Either way, his work should not be considered a lost effort, for it laid the groundwork for dialogue and interchange on such matters as value systems and ways of articulating worldview. The codes, signs, and even symbols for both cultures might have seemed incomprehensible, but the initial step was taken to expose an intrinsically unique cultural tradition. The variant texts of *Chinigchinich* reveal that the Juaneños were in fact neither simple-minded nor primitive, as most presumed at the time. If Kroeber is correct, perhaps Boscana was suffering from a serious case of naïveté. However, the texts serve multiple purposes, such as allowing the humble priest to organize his thoughts through the prism of his eyes and his sense of the divine, marking a search for a systematic approach to penetrating beyond another culture's observable prima facie. In that regard, the texts created their own context—one in the process of becoming a genuinely syncretic fusion of the New World and the Old. When the original manuscripts in Spanish are located, we will not have to depend on intermediaries to transpose or translate meaning and signifiers. Therefore, now that the context has been established, perhaps the premise of the central thesis should be inverted: it is also a context in search of its texts, for these represent the best sources available to decipher a set of circumstances that rest on a series of ambiguities. Fortunately or unfortunately, the real truth lies somewhere in between: indigenous and European social-historical experience and their perspective (mystery and the fantastic versus faith and doctrine, respectively) depend on one another to better delineate what they are about.

NOTES

1. An example of each approach, respectively, might be as follows: Genaro Padilla and Ramón Saldívar for autobiography, Luis Leal and Francisco A. Lomelí for regional case models, Tey Diana Rebolledo and María Herrera-Sobek for the contrastive gender modality, Nicolás Kanellos and Yvonne Yarbro-Bejarano for theater, and Barbara Brinson-Curiel and José David Saldívar for theoretical comparisons of movements and schools.

2. I thank Professor Luis Leal for introducing me to this fascinating *relación histórica* by Fray Gerónimo Boscana through his extensive work in Chicano literary history and his conversations.

Fray Gerónimo Boscana (Jeroni Boscana in his native Catalán) was born on

May 23, 1776, at Lluchmayor, on the island of Mallorca off the coast of Catalonia; he was ordained in 1792 and sailed to Mexico in 1803. He arrived in Alta California in 1806 and served at La Purísima mission from that year until 1812. He then moved to San Juan Capistrano mission, where he served until 1826, although some historians also place him at San Luis Rey mission between 1812 and 1814. It is generally accepted that Boscana composed *Chinigchinich* while at San Juan Capistrano. He died at San Gabriel mission on July 5 or 6, 1831.

3. Considerable discrepancy surrounds the exact dates when Boscana arrived at and left San Juan Capistrano. Most authorities state that he served the mission for the aforementioned fourteen-year period after moving from La Purísima. However, John P. Harrington, in the Malki Museum edition of *Chinigchinich* (1978), says in a footnote that Boscana spent almost two years at San Luis Rey mission prior to 1814, as substantiated by his first entry signed in the San Juan Capistrano mission during the alleged two-year gap. Maynard Geiger, O.F.M., in *Franciscan Missionaries in Hispanic California, 1769–1848; A Biographical Dictionary,* confirms Harrington's position of Boscana's brief stay at San Luis Rey mission, except that Geiger proposes 1811–14 instead of Harrington's 1812–14. The confusion and doubt are partly based on Father Boscana's mobility during that two- or three-year period, during which he also performed services at San Diego mission on November 12, 1813, and San Fernando mission on April 7, 1812.

The Gabrielinos, Juaneños, and Luiseños shared more commonalities than differences as they interrelated and influenced each other—the Gabrielinos were generally regarded as the most advanced.

4. For further information on its contents see the document titled "Contestación al interrogatorio del año 1812 por el presidente (Fr. Presidente José Señan) de las misiones de esta Alta California, y los padres de las misiones de San Miguel, San Antonio, Soledad . . ."; a copy exists at the Mission of Santa Barbara under *Papeles Miscelaneos, Copias y Estractos hechos por E. F. Murry para la Bancroft Library,* tomo 7, 1887. Also consult Fray Zephyrin Englehardt, in *San Juan Capistrano Mission* (Los Angeles: Standard Printing Company, 1922), 58–60.

5. Mofras discusses Boscana in general terms on pages 362–80.

6. It was published originally in New York by Wiley and Putnam. Other subsequent editions have appeared: one in 1933 and another in 1947 (by Biobooks, Oakland, Calif.).

7. See *California Farmer* (San Francisco) 13 (1860).

8. It is immediately obvious that Alfred Robinson exercised poetic license in translating the title from Spanish—or he had another introduction available. For example, the semantic distance between *creencia* in the original and his use of "origin," and *extravagancias* and his "tradition," are either irreconcilable translations or ques-

tionable choices. The latter is confirmed when we see the original Spanish version in Harrington's 1934 edition. In other words, the descriptive titles in both versions seem exactly alike.

9. A similar listing is presented by A. L. Kroeber in "Ethnographic Interpretations, 7–11" in an important section titled "Problems on Boscana" (282–93). However, his comparisons are merely cursory and concentrate basically on two chapters.

10. If we take Boscana's comments literally, and there is no reason why we should not, then the Robinson version might have been completed after he transferred to San Gabriel mission in 1826. No other critic has suggested a post-1826 date. Boscana notes his residence in the province for more than twenty years at the time of writing his concluding remarks (he arrived in Alta California in 1806). Thus, the final version must have been written during the last five years of his life (before 1831).

11. In fact, according to Kroeber, who counted the approximate number of words ("Ethnographic Interpretations, 7–11"), the translations contain about thirty thousand words each. If Boscana intended his originals to be works in progress, why would the texts would be comparable in size ("58 octavo pages written in a rather neat hand" [Harrington, 1])?

12. This can be readily proven by reviewing Robinson's chapters 3 and 16, which are characterized by their ambitious nature in informational utility and global focus while meticulously delineating myths and their relevance or fallacies in relation to Christian beliefs.

13. Kroeber openly proposes the idea of a "corrupt text" (1959:286).

REFERENCES

Duflot de Mofras, Eugene. 1844. *Exploration du Territoire de l'Oregon, des Californies, et de la Mer Vermeille, Exécutée pendant les Années 1840, 1841, et 1842*. Paris: Arthur-Bertrand.

Englehardt, Fray Zephyrin. 1922. *San Juan Capistrano Mission*. Los Angeles: Standard Printing Company.

Font Obrador, Bartolomé. 1966. *El Padre Boscana, historiador de California*. Palma de Mallorca, Spain: Ediciones Cort.

Geiger, Maynard, O.F.M. 1969. *Franciscan Missionaries in Hispanic California, 1769–1848; A Biographical Dictionary*. San Marino, Calif.: Huntington Library.

Harrington, John P., trans. 1934. *A New Version of Boscana's Historical Account of the San Juan Capistrano Indians of Southern California*. Washington, D.C.: Smithsonian Miscellaneous Collections 92, no. 4.

Heizer, Robert F. 1976. "A Note on Boscana's Posthumous Relación." *Masterkey* 50 (July–September): 99–102.

Kroeber, Alfred Luis. 1925. *Handbook of the Indians of California*. Washington, D.C.: Bureau of American Ethnology, Bulletin 78.

————. 1957. "Ethnographic Interpretations, 1–6." *University of California Publications in American Archeology and Ethnology* 47(2):191–204.

————. 1959. "Ethnographic Interpretations, 7–11." *University of California Publications in American Archeology and Ethnology* 47(3):235–310.

Leal, Luis. 1973. "Mexican American Literature: A Historical Perspective." *Revista Chicano-Riqueña* 1(1):32–44.

————. 1987. "California Colonial Literature." In *In Retrospect: Essays on Latin American Literature (In Memory of Willis Knapp Jones)*. Ed. Elizabeth S. Rogers and Timothy J. Rogers. York, S.C.: Spanish Literature Publications Company.

Moriarty, James Robert. 1969. *Chinigchinix: An Indigenous California Indian Religion*. Los Angeles: Southwest Museum.

Robinson, Alfred. 1946. *Life in California: During a Residence of Several Years in That Territory*. New York: Wiley and Putnam.

————, trans. 1978. *Chinigchinich: A Revised and Annotated Version of Alfred Robinson's Translation of Father Gerónimo Boscana's Historical Account of the Belief, Usages, Customs and Extravagances of the Indians of This Mission of San Juan Capistrano Called the Acágchemem Tribe*. Annotated by John P. Harrington. Banning, Calif.: Malki Museum Press.

"¿Y Dónde Estaban las Mujeres?"

In Pursuit of an *Hispana* Literary and Historical
Heritage in Colonial New Mexico, 1580–1840

TEY DIANA REBOLLEDO

This essay is an attempt, in the face of little documentation and scarce research, to give a brief overview of the cultural images of Hispanas in the early history and literature of colonial New Mexico. Contemporary social historians such as Frances Leon Swadesh, Salomé Hernández, Deena González, and Ramón Gutiérrez researching Hispanic women and social life in the seventeenth, eighteenth, and nineteenth centuries have uncovered much information in unexpected sources.[1] Using muster roles, baptism certificates, marriage declarations, wills, Inquisition records, judgments, and other creative ways of exploring history, they have been able to circumvent the traditional canon to research the ways women participated in the exploration, colonization, and settlement of New Mexico. These historians and their exploratory investigations are bringing life and vitality into an area little known and almost forgotten. Of necessity the recuperative efforts need to be finalized before a complete theoretical basis can be fashioned, particularly because images of women have been primarily defined and described by narratives written by men and through male perspectives.[2]

If traditional history is the history of power narratives, defined as primarily political, economic, and military, how do we come to an understanding of the consciousness of a people, and of ordinary life? When conventional documentary evidence is not available, we must turn to evidence of a different kind: folklore, ritual, religious ceremonies, and even food preparation. It is a truism that historians and literary historians often find what they are looking for; therefore we can read histories and official accounts in new ways, or we can look to the creative ways already mentioned in order to find this "consciousness." As yet, no official "literary" texts written by women during the colonial period have been found; nevertheless we see glimpses and hints of their lives in songs and plays, *dichos, cuentos,* and *memorate* (sayings, stories, and memorabilia)—popular chronicles of local and limited origin in which people tell their own history. These *cuentos* and *memorate,* particularly those connected to the lives of women, are the literary texts I intend to discuss later in this essay. First, however, in order to understand the evolution of the material and the importance of these texts, the women in colonial New Mexico must be situated within their historical context. Because for the early period we have only narratives written by men, we must understand that the images of the women were always presented within male discourses and from male perspectives. Only when the oral tradition began to be transcribed could we even begin to hear the voices of the women themselves, albeit within mediated discourses (the mediator would be the person writing down the oral tradition).

The accounts of expeditions, *crónicas* of exploration, letters to the viceroy, and other documents that ascertain the place of the Spanish and Mexicans on the frontier of the New World would lead to us believe that only men and their horses accomplished the discovery, conquest, and settlement of these areas. While certainly the discoveries and conquests were led by military men and priests, shortly after the first expeditions to the north the areas were settled by colonists—families, which included a good number of women. As Salomé Hernández points out in her dissertation "Female Participation in Official Spanish Settlement Expeditions" (1987): "In the historiography of the Spanish borderlands, authors such as Bancroft, Bolton and Scholes have recounted the heroic adventures of frontiersmen, soldiers, settlers, and missionaries . . . yet in their studies they tend to imply that these intrepid male leaders succeeded in their endeavors without the aid of such seldom-mentioned persons as Indians, the servants, or women who accompanied them."[3]

Indeed, at least one woman accompanied the soldiers on Antonio de Espejo's early expedition to New Mexico in 1582. Miguel Sánchez Valenciano was accompanied by his wife, Casilda de Amaya, and three sons: an older son, Lázaro; Pedro, who was three and a half; and Juan, who was twenty months old. Diego Pérez de Luxán's account of the expedition says little of this

woman; nothing is revealed about how she endured the arduous journey across
the desert nor how she fared in the end. We do know that she became pregnant during the journey. In the course of the narrative we learn that some of
the people wanted to return to Mexico. Discouraged by the little progress
that had been made, they were unwilling to continue the search for mines.
One of the soldiers, Gregorio Hernández, told everyone it was possible to
escape from the land alive. He declared that he meant to take the priest and
Miguel Sánchez's wife, who was pregnant, back to the land of peace (Mexico).[4] After some discussion Miguel Sánchez Valenciano, four other men, and
the priest (Father Beltrán) went with him. We assume Casilda de Amaya and
her children also returned to Mexico.

This narrative does take note of the Indian women encountered along the
way, and meticulous detail is given to the adventure of one Francisco Barreto
and his attempts to retain control over an Indian women who had been
"given" to him and who was trying to escape. In this particular episode the
valor of the Indian women is remarkable:

> On the afternoon of the following Sunday there were peace parleys between us
> and the Corechos. It was agreed that they should return to us one of the Core-
> chos women given us at Mojose (belonging to one of the companions, Francisco
> Barreto, although she had fled from us the morning of the skirmish); and that
> we should give them a girl we had taken from them. . . . The Corechos deter-
> mined to put over a wicked plan . . . as they had sent the Indian woman
> belonging to Francisco Barreto to her land, they took one of their relatives and
> sent her over, wearing her feather crest so that we should not recognize her,
> with the intention of recovering their own girl and giving us nothing but a
> discharge of arrows. This was planned with the help of the interpreter, who
> was another Indian woman (belonging to Alonso de Miranda) and who was
> trying to escape. The Corechos clamored to make the exchange and Francisco
> Barreto took the woman interpreter as well as the one who was to be ex-
> changed, tied with two maguey ropes. He had left his sword and harquebus
> and had the Indian woman tied to his body, as a man inexperienced in
> war. . . . The Indians were leading them little by little into the sierra, holding
> the disguised woman. When they were about to deliver her, she pretended
> they had let her go. When Diego Pérez de Luxán perceived the scheme and
> saw that Francisco Barreto had come without arms, he urged that they go
> down. . . . Francisco Barreto, eager to recover his Indian woman, persisted;
> the treacherous woman interpreter was also urging it insistently. . . . Then
> Luxán made a leap, seized the disguised Indian woman by the hair, and at the

same time let loose the woman held by Francisco Barreto. The people shouted at Diego Pérez de Luxán, who ran down the sierra with both Indian women. The woman interpreter wrestled with him, took from him a knife that he carried in his boot, and threw it to the Indians. Then, like a lioness, she grasped his sword, seizing it by the guard, which Diego Pérez de Luxán could not prevent without letting the two Indian women escape, because his hands were occupied in holding them. He threw them to the ground and dragged them down the hill, even through the Indians shot many arrows and threw many stones to force him to let the women go. Then Francisco Barreto came and seized the disguised woman, but there was such a discharge of arrows that two pierced his right cheek and right arm. When they had reached the plain, the captain and other companions came to help. With all this, Francisco Barreto had to let go of the Indian woman; if he had not done so, the soldiers might have fared much worse; nevertheless they regretted very much having lost the woman in the skirmish. (Hammond and Rey 1966:201–2)

This narrative, like many other colonial texts, contains highly descriptive and creative passages which highlight the sense of adventure and discovery these soldiers possessed. While they took for granted the women who accompanied them, the men displayed great interest in the Indian peoples they came across. We therefore often know more about the Indian women than we do about the Spanish Mexicanas. For example, in an earlier account by Hernán Gallegos of the Chamuscado-Rodríguez expedition (1581) we discover that the people are handsome and fair-skinned. "The women part their hair in Spanish style. Some have light hair, which is surprising. The girls do not leave their rooms except when permitted by their parents. They are very obedient. They marry early; judging by what we saw, the women are given husbands when seventeen years of age. A man has one wife and no more" (Hammond and Rey, 86). Whether Gallegos was right or not about young women's lives and marriage customs, it is hardly surprising that the Spaniards took such an interest in sexual customs. They felt no hesitation in taking the Indian women both as servants and as lovers.

From the Juan de Oñate expedition to New Mexico in 1598 we know more about the number of carts and wagons (and their contents) and the quantity and quality of the horses and armor than we do about the women and children who accompanied them; for example, we know that forty-one reams of paper made the journey, as well as stuff for women's clothing. Documents mention the presence of forty-seven wives and Doña Inez, an Indian.

While officers were more likely to bring their wives than ordinary soldiers were, the names of only a few of these women are known (Hernández, 21). What the women experienced, except for a few heartrending scenes, has also been lost.

Eventually, colonies were founded at San Juan (some 25 miles north of what would be Santa Fe) and San Gabriel. Because settlement efforts were important to bring population to the frontier, women had to be recruited and brought in as settlers. They often walked from one to ten miles a day, had little food and water, and, as their husbands were military men—soldiers on a hard frontier—many soon became widows.[5] The women faced the hardships and dangers with great bravery. According to Gaspar de Villagrá's *Historia de la Nueva México,* when mutiny rose "and threatened disaster" on the arduous Oñate expedition to New Mexico, Doña Eufemia, wife of Alférez Francisco Sosa de Peñalosa, called the soldiers to task for their defections. Eufemia is described as a woman of singular courage and beauty, and of clear, fine, and perfect understanding. Recognizing that everyone was exhausted from so much exertion, she said to the men,

> Gallant soldiers, tell me what you consider the noble part of those brave hearts you showed when you offered yourselves to fight such a hard war, giving us to understand that it was no match for such strong effort and excellence. From your strong and courageous arms if now, without embarrassment or shame, as if you were women, you turn your backs on such a horrible thing.
>
> What reason do you have being men, giving up this responsibility you took, so that seeing such looseness and such dishonor, disgraced I feel you to be, full of shame and knowing to see in Spaniards such intent.
>
> When all faith is lost and everything is lacking we still have extensive land and a peaceful flowing river where we may build a great city in imitation and example of many others who thus immortalized their fame and name.
>
> Where can we go to be more worthwhile? Hold your steps, you don't want to stain yourselves with stains so infamous as will descend upon your children.[6]

Later in Villagrá's poetic narrative, Eufemia, her daughter, and twenty-two other women go to the rooftops of San Juan to aid in the defense of the town. They are thus portrayed:

> The Indians continued their alarms. The men were all well stationed and ready to defend the capital when the general noticed that all the housetops were crowded with people. He quickly sent two captains to investigate who they

were and what they meant. They returned soon, informing him that Doña
Eufemia had gathered all the women together on the housetops to aid in the
defense. Doña Eufemia had stated that they would come down if the general so
ordered, but that they wished to aid their husbands in the defense of the capi-
tal. Don Juan was very pleased at this display of valor coming from such valiant
female hearts, precious jewels, and he delegated Doña Eufemia to defend the
housetops with the women. Together the brave Amazons joyfully held their
posts and walked up and down the rooftops with proud and martial step.[7]

Clearly these Amazonian partners in conquest conformed with the heroic discourse that Villagrá was portraying. The Indian women described in Villagrá's
narrative did not fare so well.

In addition to the historical presence of women on the colonial frontier,
they also exerted influence through myth and popular belief. Religion was
important in the sustenance of the colonists and in the conversion of the
Indians. One incident, the miraculous conversion of the Xumana nation, is
attributed to a female, the Lady in Blue. In his *Memorial* (1634) Fray Alonso
de Benavides, a Franciscan, tells of a tribe of pious Indians who continually
requested a priest to come and live among them. When asked why they were
seeking to be baptized they told of a woman dressed in blue who talked to
them in their language. Upon seeing a portrait of a nun, Mother Luisa, in
the convent, they said, "que la mujer que les predicaba estaba vestida, ni
más, ni menos, como la que allí estaba pintada, pero que el rostro no era
como aquel, sino que era moza y hermosa, y siempre que venían indios de
aquellas naciones, mirando el retrato y confiriéndolo entre sí decían que el
vestido era el mismo, pero que el rostro no, porque el de la mujer que les
predicaba era de moza y hermosa" ("that the woman who preached to them
was dressed more or less like the one who was painted in the picture, but that
her face was not the same, but she was young and beautiful, and whenever
Indians from those nations came, they looked at the painting and, conferring
among themselves, they said that the dress was the same, but the face wasn't,
because the face of the woman who preached to them was young and beautiful"). This miraculous apparition was further complicated when newly arrived
friars declared that it "was common news in Spain that a nun named María
de Jesús de la Concepción, of the Discalced Order of Saint Francis, residing
in the town of Agreda in the providence of Burgos, was miraculously transported to New Mexico to preach our holy Catholic faith to those savage Indians."[8] When Benavides traveled to Spain in 1630, he visited with this nun

and became convinced that indeed she had bilocated to New Mexico and had converted the Indians: "She convinced me absolutely by describing to me all the things in New Mexico as I have seen them myself, as well as by other details which I shall keep within my soul. Consequently, I have no doubts in this matter whatsoever" (Hodge et al. 1945:95).

María de Agreda was twenty-nine years old in 1630 (although she had started her bilocations to New Mexico in 1620, when she was nineteen), and for some years she had been experiencing ecstasies. In 1627 she wrote a book, *The Mystical City of God,* detailing the life of the Virgin Mary, particularly the nine months she spent in her mother's womb. The book was condemned by the church for indecent language, and by her confessor, who thought that women should not write about spiritual matters, and she was ordered to burn it, along with the daily dairies she had kept of her bilocations to New Mexico. The story of her miraculous apparitions profoundly affected the consciousness of Hispanos in New Mexico and constantly reappears in later folk literature.[9] Nevertheless, questions remain about how and why her discourse was appropriated by Benavides and how the natives themselves utilized the discourse for their own purposes.[10]

Thus women played both a spiritual and a real role during this period of colonization. The reality was that New Mexico was a place of great hardship for both the new settlers and the old. In the early years the colonists often took grain, food, and other goods from the Indians, leaving many "Indian women stark naked, holding their babies to their breasts" (Hernández, 41). In 1680, after ninety years of settlement, the indigenous peoples finally rebelled against the harsh treatment and injustices. The rebellion was well planned and affected the lives of all of the twenty-four hundred or so settlers living in the area. Four hundred Hispanos died and two thousand survived, mostly women and children (Hernández, 55). Half of the group at first stayed in Santa Fe while the other half went to Isleta. Ultimately everyone retreated to El Paso, the women and children walking since there were only twenty carts (Hernández, 57).

Many women were killed during the Pueblo Revolt. The death of Francisca Domínguez, who lived on an estancia near Pojoaque pueblo, was reported by Francisco Naranjo, a Spanish-speaking Indian of San Juan pueblo, who saw her dead when he went to look for some cattle. He said she lay naked, her head crushed with a lance thrust into it and emerging from her throat, a child at her feet as though aborted.[11] Some of the women were captured. Fray Angélico Chávez records that "some young females were spared by the rebels to be kept as captives and these were rescued 13 years later, along with some half-breed children they had acquired in the meantime."[12] Reunited with their families in 1692 were Petrona Pacheco and three children, María Naranjo, Juana Hurtado, Juana de Apodaca, and others. These captivities are important to the literature. Even though they did not produce a "captivity narrative," the tales of the *cautivas* (captives) resulted in the songs known as *inditas*. These *inditas* are passed down from mother to daughter and honor and record the experiences of these women during their captivity. They may be one of the few creative forms that record the experiences of both Hispanic and Indian women of this time.

Many of the pre-1680 records in the colonial archives were destroyed. What little we know about the lives of women and their cultural and intellectual interests until the end of the colonial period generally comes from records and sources written after 1692. Yet, vignettes of what life might have been like before the Pueblo Revolt jump out at us from marriage records and other archival sources found in Mexico. Bigamy, sexual problems, accusations of witchcraft, and scandals abound in these documents. For example, Margarita Márquez, who married Geronimo de Carvajal in 1656, was involved in a scandalous incident with then Governor Manso, which included the fake baptism of one infant and the fake burial of another, so that her child by Manso could be spirited to Mexico City to be reared by his "natural father" (Chávez 1982:15). Hernando Márquez, who had figured in Oñate's muster lists, was dead in October 1628 when his brother Pedro accused a Mexican-Indian woman, Beatriz, of causing Hernando's death through witchcraft. Hernando had been living with Juana de la Cruz, who was also accused of hexing him after he spurned her. Alonso Martín Barba had been married to María Martín, who was allegedly poisoned by a María Bernal, with whom Alonso was having relations (Chávez, 71). The wife of Juan Griego put a spell on the wife of Bartolomé Romero II in 1628; and Isabel, the wife of Juan Rodríguez Bellido, whose name is on El Moro, Inscription Rock, was involved in witchcraft in 1607. In 1631 Juana de los Reyes and her sister Juana Sánchez were accused of using "bizarre" remedies to hold their husbands' affections (Chávez, 182). In 1695 Bartolomé de Anzures, who had been married for two years to Inés Martín, was involved in annulment proceedings on

grounds of his impotence. His wife claimed to be a virgin. Bartolomé was
not truly impotent, he said, but "suffering from a stricture resulting from
various experiences." The petition was denied, and the Franciscan custodian
gave Bartolomé four months to find medical aid (Chávez, 118). Word of these
incidents spread from one person to another and became embedded in the oral
literature in the form of *cuentos*.

With the Diego de Vargas resettlement effort in 1692, many of the women
and children returned to their homes in New Mexico, and many new settlers were recruited. Among these women—Hispanas, Mexican Indians, New
Mexican Indians, blacks, mulattas, *lobas, coyotas,* and mestizas (Hernández,
87)—were many widows and single heads of households.[13] They were strong,
independent women who ran households, worked in the fields, and managed
ranches in addition to bearing, raising, and educating their children. They
came from all social classes. The difficulties of life in the eighteenth century
precluded activities that were not directly concerned with survival. There
were few doctors in the region, and knowledge of medicinal herbs and curing
techniques was highly prized. There was no birth control, and we come across
records of women having eleven, twelve, thirteen children, but little indication of how many of them survived.

Recent scholarship has begun to trace women's lives and concerns through
court documents. Ramón Gutiérrez studied a 1702 court case on seduction
which illuminates not only the relationship between the sexes but important
social issues of the time.[14] This mediated text documents the voice of a young
woman, Juana Luján, who had been seduced by Bentura de Esquibel. He
promised to marry her, but Juana was not of the same social class and Bentura's father wished to stop the marriage. Bentura soon became betrothed to
another. Juana Luján, who was pregnant, asked the court to stop the marriage
because she already had a claim. Bentura claimed that Juana was not a virgin
when he seduced her, but Juana spoke out in her own defense:

> How can Bentura say I was not a virgin when he himself saw the evident sign
> of my virginity which was the blood that was left stamped on his shirt from
> our act. That same blood which I tried to wash out of the shirt because of my
> great remorse. . . . That Bentura has had a change of heart and now wants to
> marry Bernardina Lucero saying that she is honorable and Spanish, I can only
> say that I cannot dispute that Bernardina is indeed from a very honorable
> family; but that she is better than me in racial status is disputable, for I am as
> good as she. (Gutiérrez, 454–55)

Juana eventually gave up her claim. She had been threatened, and perhaps she also recognized that forced marriages are not happy ones. However, her independent resolve in standing up for herself and her family name is remarkable.

Intellectual Life for Women on the Frontier

Historians seem united about the dearth of "intellectual" life and literature on the colonial frontier. The priests were among the few who could read or write. Carefully annotated lists note others, particularly women, who were literate; for example, Doña Isabel de Bohorquez, married to Don Pedro Durán y Chávez, is listed as being able to read and write. The personal property of Governor Bernardo López de Mendizábel (1659–81) included many books. One suspicious volume in Italian, Ariosto's *Orlando Furioso,* was used by the Inquisition as evidence of heresy against his wife, Doña Teresa de Aguilera. It was also said that she read devotions to her attendants and presented them with copies of extra volumes; perhaps they too could read. [15] Many books were privately owned, but along with their own books government officials and members of the upper class had access to volumes kept in the library or archives of the Casa Real in Santa Fe. Among the listed books owned by the governors or friars, besides numerous religious tracts and breviaries in Spanish, we find *Don Quijote*; works by Quevedo; Ovid's *Metamorfosis*; Gracián's *El criticón*; Villagrá's *Historia de la Nueva México*; *Errores celebrados de la antigüedad,* "a book of astrology, natural secrets, and other curious things"; histories; and books on surgery, herbs, and matrimony. [16] These lists comprise the books whose titles were freely given up to scrutiny by the Inquisition; one wonders what books may have been read in secret. The lists tell us that along with well-worn devotional books in Spanish, romances, poetry, and plays were read, and also that children were taught to read. Certainly among the richer class, many were literate and brought books along with them as part of their few precious possessions. While France Scholes perceives of colonial New Mexicans as simple, illiterate folk, nevertheless his statistics, when read in another way, tell us that native New Mexicans were indeed receiving some sort of formal education. In the muster roles of 1680 Scholes says that of 147 persons able to bear arms, 131 were natives of New Mexico and 16 were from Spain and Mexico. Of the New Mexicans, 82 could not sign their names; indeed, that means that 46 *were* able to sign, a better percentage than the 3 of 16 Spanish Mexicans who could sign.[17] In fact, we know that there were creative endeavors in writing: "Both Peñalosa and López (governors of New Mexico in the early 17th century) dabbled in literary composition. Most of it, according to the documentary sources, was in the form of poetic satire against the clergy" (Adams and Scholes 1942:249–50). However, traditional historians like Mark Simmons have commented, "We look in vain for signs of creative endeavors in the literary arts. This is scarcely surprising since, by any standard, the colonial New Mexicans led an impoverished intellectual life. They never had a printing press, nor more than a handful of books, schools were practically non-existent, and the majority of the common people were illiterate."[18] Simmons, noting the efforts of the Inquisition to search for and destroy inflammatory books, says that

> these efforts by the Spanish Church and State to combat the spread of unortho-
> dox literature in an out-of-the-way place like New Mexico appear more ludi-
> crous than sinister. The simple frontier folk, concerned mainly with winning a
> living from the difficult soil and with preserving their lives in the face of
> constant Indian warfare, were hardly susceptible to subversion. They listened
> to the reading by the village priest or told tales around the campfire, and, for
> the time and place, that was all they required. For the most part, they were
> neither readers nor writers. (Simmons 1976:30)

This may be true if one equates intellectual life with written literature; none-theless, these colonial pioneers led complex and multifaceted lives, which included, as we shall see, various forms of creative endeavors.

Clearly, given the time and the place, women would have been even more at a disadvantage in terms of formal intellectual life than men. If we accept the gloomy perspective of conventional historians, women during this time were more creatures of procreation than of creation. But we have not yet discovered the letters written to families left behind or who had moved away, the diaries, the journals. Did these women never seek to capture and narrate their experiences? We know the women shared their experiences, their gossip, their needs. We know that from mother to daughter entire generations trans-mitted their recipes, the rituals of food, and special occasions on which it was served. With the scarcity of medical personnel, it was essential that women pass on their knowledge of herbs and cures. Sometimes they told stories about personal events which were picked up in the oral literature as universal events. Often they were "supernatural" things that might happen to ordinary women and men. Through these stories they have transmitted to us their consciousness and their fears. Through these stories we see a glimmer of what might have been recorded if there had been leisure to learn and time to write.

In the 1930s and 1940s the Federal Writers' Project sparked a great deal of interest in the Southwest.[19] In New Mexico, Arizona, and Texas the project gathered oral histories, trying to preserve the memories and culture of the "old-timers." Because Hispanic informants (many of them older women) were included in the project, valuable information about their lives, education, and traditions, as well as important folktales about women and their roles, were preserved.[20] In New Mexico the Federal Writers' Project yielded a source important to the preservation of Hispana culture: a collection of *cuentos* and *memorates*. Many of these folk stories (as well as songs) were told by women. Some of the texts are variants on European tales and have been studied by scholars eager to show their European basis. Fortunately, however, many of the these texts are very local and chronicle the lives of people living in remote areas such as the small villages in northern New Mexico. These *cuentos* and *memorate* not only portray dramatic situations in which women play an impor-tant part, they also contribute to some understanding of women's symbolic literary role during these times. If they could not read or write, women could still tell stories—stories fired with imagination and symbols and subse-quently passed down from generation to generation. Many contemporary Chi-canas are "first-generation" writers who are telling the *cuentos* of their mothers and grandmothers, thus preserving this oral tradition.[21]

The collection of creative material from the New Mexico Federal Writers' Project is very rich indeed. In general, the stories were told in Spanish and then translated, either by the interviewer or by the project director. Several women, including Guadalupe Gallegos, her granddaughter, Mary Elba C. de Baca, and Rumaldita Gurulé, as well as others, provided much information on a variety of topics. The New Mexico collection is particularly rich in women's materials because in 1940–41 Annette Hersch Thorp gathered ma-terials for a project (never completed) that was to be called "Some New Mex-ico Grandmothers." In addition, much of the collection of folktales came about because of several questions asked generally of all respondents in the project:

Are there any stories concerned with animals or animal life, or the relation between human beings and animals, which are *native* to your community?

Are there localized ghost stories, witch stories, etc.?

Are there any of the so-called "Tall Tales," where the storyteller gets the effect either through exaggeration or understatement, stories that are not in print but that are passed around by "word of mouth?"

Are there any persons in your community who are believed to possess power to see into the future? Tell some of the current stories about such persons.[22]

These standard questions clearly influenced the selection of informants as well as the type of material collected. Often, the stories were told by women, as Thorp indicates:

> Story telling was looked forward to on winter nights. All the family, big and little gathered around the fire-place, and by the light of a kerosene lamp, or ocote wood "pitch," would shell corn, or the women sewed, while some grand-mother or neighbor viejita "old woman" told stories until time for bed. The beds were made down on the floor. The colchons [sic] "Mattress" were stuffed with wool, and folded on bancos against the wall in the day time. At night they were laid on the floor. The stories that were told by these grandmothers were religious ones. About Santos, and the miracles they used to perform. And about brujas "Witches," and those who had been embrujada "bewitched." Bru-jas were taken for granted by all. The men as well as the women believed in brujas, and were careful not to offend anyone they were not sure of.[23]

Fortunately for researchers, the New Mexico project was careful to ascertain informants' names and genealogy. We are thus able to trace, with fair accuracy, stories that surely originated in the colonial period. One case in point is the material collected in Placitas by Lou Sage Batchen in 1938. Her informants included Rumaldita Gurulé, age 67, who was a descendant of one of the twenty-one families who received the San Antonio de las Huertas grant from the king of Spain in 1765; and José Librado Aron Gurulé, age 88, also a direct descendant of those families. We know that Placitas was founded in the very early nineteenth century and that references to the Las Huertas (abandoned in 1823) and El Oso settlements date the stories even earlier. In addition, the informants often stated that the stories were told to them as children by their grandparents. One story, "Petra's Faith," concerns the fears of a young woman living in a pioneer society and the way she dealt with them. Interesting in this *cuento* is the shifting of perspective from the male to the female, making it easier for the listener to identify with Petra.

It was in El Oso a very long time ago. Juan José built a house for his bride, Petra. He built it one room on the top of the other to keep them safe from the Indians and the wild animals. He brought Petra's two small brothers to stay with her for he was away much with his Patron's sheep and goats. But Petra was afraid. Every night when Juan José was away, she was sick with fear. She wanted to bring food and water to the top room and stay there with her brothers while her husband was gone, but that could not be. They must take the goats out where they could find grass and water, and whenever they went Petra was frightened at every noise she heard. The Indians and the wild animals might be coming. Then Petra prayed to the Holy Mother for a benediction. If the Holy Mother would bless her, she would no longer be afraid. . . . Then one bright morning she saw a halo. She could not see the head under it for the light, but she could see arms stretched forward and hands moving up and down in a benediction. "The Holy Mother! The Holy Mother! She gives me her benediction," Petra cried and ran toward it. Her small brothers called after her, "Ho, it is a hare. The sun on the fur, it makes the light." But Petra did not hear them. "I am not afraid any more," she sang out as the halo disappeared, she knew not where.[24]

Many of the stories contain humor and careful descriptions as the storytellers strive to recollect images of people and places long gone. The oral nature of the stories is also captured in the form of dialogue or stream-of-consciousness techniques. Often the "ordinary" incidents deal with a person and some supernatural event, or with some dramatic event of heroism and bravery.

Stories and beliefs about witches abound in New Mexico. The earliest written history of New Mexico contains accusations of witchcraft and mentions the belief and participation in "heathen" Indian rites, hexing, *mal de ojos* (evil eye), and miraculous apparitions. It may be that witch stories prevail more than others in New Mexico because of the merging of multiple cultures. One of the Placitas witch stories was told by Rumaldita Gurulé about her grandmother, Quiteria, who would have been born around the early 1800s; the other woman in the story, Doña Tomasa, was probably born about 1750. The story deals with generational change, the young replacing the old; its moral, however, is that in order to function, the new system must learn the ways of the old. Doña Tomasa continually outwits her young rival.

"Quiteria is the best nurse and she is young," the people said, and it made Doña Tomasa, the witch nurse, very jealous. So Quiteria was afraid of her and she tried to keep out of her way. The witch nurse might play an evil trick on her. Then one day somebody whispered to Quiteria that if she stood on Tomasa's shadow, Tomasa could not move and she would have Tomasa in her power. At noon one day Doña Tomasa came to visit Quiteria. Ah, thought Quiteria to herself, I must keep her until her shadow grows a little. So she invited the witch nurse to eat dinner with her. The woman was hungry so she stayed and drank the good atole and she ate the tortillas. But she was in a hurry and soon she was leaving. Quiteria picked up her new reboso and followed Tomasa out the door. "See how fine my new reboso is. Touch it," and Quiteria came very close to the witch nurse and stood on her shadow. The witch nurse tried to move. She could not. So she acted very natural as if she did not wish to go. She talked of the people to Quiteria. She talked of the crops. She rolled many cigarettes and smoked them. Hour after hour passed. Then she knew Quiteria was keeping her there on purpose. She must get away. She cried out, "I am sick. Run quick. Get me some water!" Quiteria saw that she looked very pale, so she ran into the house for the water. When she returned Doña Tomasa was gone.

As can be seen by this brief discussion, the images of Spanish-Mexicana colonial women are many and varied both in history and in the literature. And although no formal literature survives, we are able to approach their consciousness and their lives through a reading of the underside of history and the underside of story telling. We have much work to do: we need to storm the archives and reread the documents; we need to rethink the statistics in a positive way; we need to search our family trunks and our neighbor's family trunks. We need to dedicate ourselves to this important research. And I am positive that one day, perhaps soon, we will unearth a formal literature that will substantiate what we already know, que las mujeres estaban, y que estaban allí con y en fuerza.

Notes

1. See Frances Leon Swadesh, *Los Primeros Pobladores* (Notre Dame: University of Notre Dame Press, 1974); Deena González, "The Spanish-Mexican Women of Santa Fe: Patterns of Their Resistance and Accommodation, 1820–1880" (Ph.D. diss., University of California, Berkeley, 1985); see also Janet Lecompte, "The Independent Women of Hispanic New Mexico, 1821–1846," in *New Mexico Women: Intercultural Perspectives,* ed. Joan M. Jensen and Darlis A. Miller (Albuquerque: University of New Mexico Press, 1986). For more information on the general

problems of documenting Chicana-Mexicana history see *Between Borders: Essays on Mexicana/Chicana History,* ed. Adelaida R. Del Castillo (Encino, Calif.: Floricanto Press, 1990).

2. This work reflects an early attempt to assess the cultural and literary contribution of Spanish-Mexican women in colonial New Mexico. Since it was written the project has evolved into a full-length study of the role of Spanish Mexicanas in the Southwest. In the last few years much new research has been done on the role of women in early California by Antonia Castañeda and Genaro Padilla, but much remains to be done. In addition, the theoretical basis of women in cultural survival, the seizing of voice and subjectivity, and how women become subjects of history rather than images in history is outside the framework of this essay due to space constraints. It remains for a longer, more complete work now in progress.

3. Salomé Hernández, "The Present-day U.S. Southwest: Female Participation in Official Spanish Settlement Expeditions: Specific Case Studies in the Sixteenth, Seventeenth, and Eighteenth Centuries" (Ph.D. diss., University of New Mexico, 1987), 1.

4. George P. Hammond and Agapito Rey, *The Rediscovery of New Mexico, 1580–1594* (Albuquerque: University of New Mexico Press, 1966), 198.

5. Because church marriage records were meticulously kept, those desiring to enter into matrimony had to declare if they had been married before, to whom, and what had happened to the previous spouse. Much information about life on the frontiers has been retrieved from these records.

6. Gaspar Pérez de Villagrá, *Historia de la Nueva México* (Mexico City: Imprenta del Museo Nacional, 1900), 42–43; translation mine.

7. "These were the wives of the royal ensign, Alonso Sánchez, Zubia, Don Luis Gasco, Diego Núñez, Pedro Sánchez Monrroi, Sosa, Perreira, Quesada, Juan Morán, Simón Pérez, Asencio de Arculeta, Bocanegra, Carabajal, Romero, Alonso Lucas, San Martín, Cordero, the caudillo Francisco Sánchez, Francisco Hernández, Monzón, Alonso Gómez Montesinos, Francisco García, Bustillo, and the wife of the redoubtable Griego, who, like the brave and gallant chieftain he was, gave proof of his mettle" (Gaspar Pérez de Villagrá, *History of New Mexico, 1610* [Los Angeles: The Quivira Society, 1933], 224–25).

8. *Fray Alonso de Benavides' Revised Memorial of 1634,* ed. Frederick Webb Hodge, George P. Hammond, and Agapito Rey (Albuquerque: University of New Mexico Press, 1945), 93.

9. See, for example, Elba C. de Baca's "The Lady in Blue," in *Las Mujeres Hablan,* ed. Tey Diana Rebolledo, Erlinda Gonzales-Berry, and Teresa Márquez (Albuquerque: El Norte Publications, 1988), 10–11.

10. On this issue there has been some insightful research. María de Agreda became the confidante of King Philip IV and was a very powerful figure within the

church. For more information see H. D. Kendrix, *Mary of Agreda: The Life and Legend of a Spanish Nun* (London: Routledge and Kegan Paul, 1967).

11. Fray Angélico Chávez, *New Mexico Roots Ltd. 1678–1869* (Santa Fe: Catholic church, Archdiocese of Santa Fe, New Mexico, 1982), 28.

12. Ibid., xvii–xviii.

13. It is interesting to note the number of male settlers described on the lists and rosters as having scars and pockmarks on their faces—an indication of their military exploits and of the diseases that plagued them.

14. Ramón A. Gutiérrez, "Marriage and Seduction in Colonial New Mexico," in *Between Borders: Essays on Mexicana/Chicana History,* ed. Adelaida R. Del Castillo (Encino, Calif.: Floricanto Press, 1990), 447–58.

15. Eleanor B. Adams and France V. Scholes, "Books in New Mexico, 1598–1680," *New Mexico Historical Review* 3 (July 1942): 241.

16. Ibid., 257–64; see also Eleanor B. Adams, "Two Colonial New Mexico Libraries, 1704, 1776," *New Mexico Historical Review* 2 (April 1944): 135–67.

17. France V. Scholes, "Civil Government and Society in New Mexico in the 17th Century," *New Mexico Historical Review* 2 (April 1935): 100.

18. Mark Simmons, "Authors and Books in Colonial New Mexico," in *Voices from the Southwest.* Ed. Donald C. Dickinson et al. (Flagstaff: Northland Press, 1976), 16–17.

19. The Federal Writers' Project, a part of Franklin D. Roosevelt's New Deal program in the 1930s, assembled guides to the forty-eight states.

20. There is, of course, written material that chronicles the lives of early pioneer women and includes biographies of early Spanish-speaking women of well-to-do families who became civic leaders. Evelyn M. Carrington, ed., *Women in Early Texas* (Austin: Jenkins Publishing, 1975), is one such source. The education and lives of these well-known women were very different from the lives chronicled in the oral histories. Nevertheless, we get an insight into what the life of an upper-class girl was like: "From an early age the children were carefully trained: in the meticulous practice of their Catholic faith, in love, respect and implicit obedience to their parents; in the knowledge of, and strict adherence to family background and traditions; and in the elegant courtesy and social graces of the times" (Edith Olbrich Parker, "María Gertrudis Pérez Cordero Cassiano [1790–1983]," in Carrington, ed., *Women in Early Texas,* 51). These girls were carefully sheltered, never leaving the home without a chaperone or older companion. The history of María Gertrudis Pérez Cordero Cassiano goes on to say that "the Pérez girls were well educated, for women could own, inherit, administer, buy and sell property" (51).

21. The *cuento* is not just a female tradition; it is a tradition also incorporated into the writings of male authors such as Sabine Ulibarrí, Rudolfo Anaya, and Miguel Méndez.

22. Marta Weigle, ed., *New Mexicans in Cameo and Camera* (Albuquerque: University of New Mexico Press, 1985), xix–xx. This book is extremely useful in documenting the lives of the collectors of the New Mexico Federal Writers' Project as well as the lives of the people interviewed.

23. New Mexico Federal Writers' Project. Annette Hesch Thorp, December 17, 1940.

24. Lou Sage Batchen, New Mexico Federal Workers' Project History Archives, History Library, Museum of New Mexico, Santa Fe, 5-5-49, 1–6, 3.

Entre Cíbolos Criado

Images of Native Americans in the Popular Culture of Colonial New Mexico

ENRIQUE R. LAMADRID

Nuevo Méjico insolente
entre cíbolos criado,
¿quién te ha hecho letrado
pa' cantar entre la gente?

Insolent New Mexico
raised among the buffaloes,
who has educated you
to sing among the people?
—From a nineteenth-century *trovo* ballad

The construction of the Native American in the consciousness of the elite culture of Spain was based on a projection of existing categories of cultural otherness already filled by the Moors, the ancestral opponents of Christendom (Said 1979). But the American natives also exhibited pristine, less-civilized traits that added a mythic and natural quality to their humanity. At the first encounter, Columbus marveled at their communalism, generosity, and seeming lack of private property (including clothing). Later, when this behavior was repeated with the possessions of Spanish sailors, he denounced the same people as inveterate thieves, punishing them by amputating ears and noses (Todorov 1984:40).

The false dichotomy of "noble" versus "ignoble" savage appears in colonial discourse from the beginning and pervades it throughout. The direct and daily contact that Spanish colonists in America had with the natives led to the evolution of an analogous dichotomy, modified by experience and assimilation and manifested in their popular culture. With time, the elite concept of "noble savage" gave way to a popular concept of "spiritual savage," which resulted in a new *mestizo* syncretism. The shadow side of "ignoble savage" in the popular tradition was softened and transformed into a burlesque and carnivalesque mode; the "dangerous" Indian became the "ridiculous" Indian. The dyadic structure of the European paradigm remained but was modified in new surroundings. The literature and folklore of colonial New Mexico provides one of the best illustrations of this process.

The *Mestizo* Heritage of New Mexico

Nostalgic attempts to distill and exalt New Mexico's links with the Iberian peninsula have overshadowed the region's unique contribution to Hispanic popular culture: its *mestizo* (i.e., Indo-Hispanic) folklore. To be sure, peninsular forms persist in the region: strains of old romances such as "La Delgadina" and "Gerineldo" can occasionally be heard, and age-old traditional *coplas* (couplets) and *refranes* (proverbs) are still exchanged. Secular and religious folk dramas are regularly staged, and the tale types and motifs of oral narratives are predominantly European. Yet, similar inventories could be made for any other region of Spanish America. New Mexico is obviously much more than Spain on the banks of the Río Grande, yet since before the turn of the century, the existence of *mestizaje* (cultural and racial mixing) has been deemphasized or denied by laymen and scholars, whether it be the Indo-Hispano combinations of the colonial era or the Anglo-Hispano amalgamations of contemporary neocolonial times (Limón 1987). The colonial caste term *coyote,* still in popular use, applies then and now to the person of mixed cultural or racial stock—Hispanic plus other. *Coyotes de indio* and *coyotes de americano* designate those intercultural mediators whose individual and collective experience was and still is more the norm than the exception in what has always been a pluralistic frontier society (Lamadrid 1990). Although the written record of *mestizo* or *coyote* popular culture before 1821 is sparse, much can be inferred from literary and historical sources, and more can be extrapolated backward from 1850, when the advent of literacy in the region brought the first documentation of oral traditions.

The upper Río Grande has always been a cultural crossroads. Both the enclave of Keresan and Tanoan pueblos clustered along the river and its tributaries, and the remote western settlements of Zuñi and Moqui were surrounded on all sides by roving, generally hostile bands of Athabascan and Shoshonean peoples. With the Pueblo Revolt of 1680 behind them, Spanish

and Pueblos faced together the protracted siege of the nomads, which lasted
through the eighteenth century. As the military alliance of Pueblos and Spanish strengthened, their cultural accommodation and mutual tolerance grew.
The cultural environment of New Mexico was further enriched by an emerging class of *genízaros,* the captives, slaves, and orphans from nomadic tribes
detribalized as they were taken from the enemy. As *criados* (servants) living
in the intimacy of Spanish households, they became more thoroughly Hispanicized than the Pueblos. As they moved into society to populate assigned
military buffer zones, these New World janissaries evolved their own unique
style of Hispanicity and made a major contribution to the culture and folk
Catholicism of the region (Atencio 1985).

The volatile historical circumstances and cultural dynamics of a remote
frontier region like New Mexico are exactly what molded its unique popular
culture. Elsewhere in New Spain the assimilation of Indian groups was often
a ruthless project of cultural subjugation. The cultural *mestizaje* from such
zones appears repressed and subliminal when compared with the more pluralistic forms that emerged on the upper Río Grande. Since cultural pluralism
derives from cultural resistance, it is necessary to explore the elite and popular
concepts of Indians and Indian culture that developed in New Mexico.

Noble and Ignoble Savages: Elite and Popular Views Before 1680

The ideological baggage that the first colonists and governors brought with
them probably contained the same dichotomized preconceptions and stereotypes about Indians common in the rest of the colonies. Notions of the noble
versus the ignoble savage are classic projections of the European imagination
as it confronts cultural otherness. The articulation by social elites of these
ideas is well documented from the first chronicles of Columbus through the
famous debates of Fray Bartolomé de Las Casas and Juan Ginés de Sepúlveda.
The writings of explorers, churchmen, and intellectuals show a marked tendency either to idealize the Indians as noble savages or to denigrate them as
ignoble barbarians. To the humanist royal counselor Sepúlveda, the Indians
were only marginally rational beings. Only slightly better than beasts, they
were slaves to nature, giving the Europeans the right to impose even despotic
means such as servitude to oblige them to be authentically human—that is
to say, virtuous, industrious, and Christian. On the other hand, Las Casas,
the bishop of Chiapas, believed the Indians to possess great natural virtue,

ingenuity, and intellectual capacity, with a love for freedom and an orderly political life. Like the ancient Greeks, they were simply human beings at a different stage of development. Once given the opportunity of embracing the true religion, they would soon become exemplary Christians (Hanke 1965).

In the colonization and Christianization of the northlands, the philosophy and practice of the Jesuit missions to the Yaquis in Sonora were consonant with Las Casas's ideals. Unarmed and without military escort or Hispanic colonists to deal with, the Jesuits reorganized Yaqui society according to utopian models and their respect for the Yaqui culture (Spicer 1969). In New Mexico the fundamentalist strategy of the Franciscans was further removed from the precepts of Las Casas. Often at odds with the civil and military authorities who supported them, their persecution of native religious practices was paid for in 1680 in martyrs' blood.

Franciscan reports and memorials prior to the Pueblo Revolt reflect their intolerant zeal. In his report of 1630, Fray Alonso de Benavides, chief custodian of the faith in New Mexico, consistently refers to the Indians of the province as *bárbaros infieles* (barbarous infidels) raised up in the very claws of the Devil and subject to the evil whims of their sorcerer priests:

> Los traía el demonio engañados con mil supersticiones . . . desde que Dios los crió, sujetos al demonio y esclavos suyos hasta este tiempo, y todo poblado de estufas de idolatría, adonde jamás no sólo no se adoraba el santísimo nombre de Jesús, sino que no le conocían, ni su santísima cruz.
> The devil had deceived them with a thousand superstitions . . . since God raised them, subject to the devil and his slaves until these times, and covered everywhere with stoves [kivas] of idolatry, where not only has the most holy name of Jesus not been adored, but neither had his holiest Cross ever been heard of. (Benavides 1630:30–33)

It is difficult to determine how much of this zealous Franciscan spirit penetrated the popular consciousness of the colonists, but it must have had its influence. Soldier-poet Capitán Gaspar Pérez de Villagrá documents the enthusiasm of the colonists in the conquest dramas that were performed for the edification of the Indians (Pérez de Villagrá 1610; 1900:87–91). If the *Juegos de Moros y Cristianos* (Games of Moors and Christians) staged at the pueblo of San Juan de los Caballeros in the summer of 1598 at all resembled the contemporary spectacle of the same name in Chimayó, it certainly featured a good degree of religious and cultural chauvinism.[1]

The epic struggle between Islam and Christianity was still fresh in the imaginations of the colonists. Before Spaniards encountered American Indians, the Moors had occupied the role of cultural Other and enemy of the faith. Reveling in the defeat of Islam and triumphs of the past helped in facing up to the challenge of the present: the subjugation of the Indian. Thus the Spanish colonists reenacted the battles between Moors and Christians, galloping their horses back and forth and firing muskets as the Indians watched in fear and amazement. In the play *Moros y Cristianos,* the Moros deceive the Cristianos, stealing their cross by tempting a watchman with wine. In one scene a knight laments the theft of the cross while a sultan gloats over his prize:

Federico:

¡Alarma, noble español!

Que ya el turco se ha robado la Santa Cruz

Y ya tiene el castillo amurallado

Con ochenta mil soldados

Sin la guarnición de adentro

Que es de quinientos paganos.

Eduardo, borracho está,

Perdido y hasta descalabrado,

Riesgo corre de morirse.

Sultán:

Ya la prenda está ganada

Cautiva la prenda rica

Que entre los cristianos

Es la prenda de más estima . . .

Retírense a descansar y esta prenda

Como mía a cuidar.

Federico:

Sound the alarm, noble Spaniard!

The Turk has stolen the Holy Cross

And has the castle walled in

With eighty thousand soldiers

Not counting the garrison inside

Which is of five hundred pagans.

Eduardo is drunk,
Lost and undone,
And runs the risk of dying.

Sultan:
The prize has been taken
Captive the rich prize
That among the Christians
Is their most esteemed sign . . .
Retreat and rest and this prize
I will care for as my own.

                              (Lucero 1953:108, 109)

A furious battle follows and the cross is recaptured. The Moorish prisoners
are freed by the merciful King Alfonso, and the sultan begs to become a
Christian:

Don Alfonso:
¡Oh! soberano Estandarte.
¡Oh! triunfo de los cristianos.
Cautiva te veo ahora entre los moros
Pero ya ahora te veo entre mis manos.

Sultán:
Cristiano, ya tu valor
Me tiene a tus pies postrado.
Te pido por vuestra Cruz
Y por tu Dios venerado
Que me des la libertad
Que estoy desengañado—
Que sólo tu Dios es grande
Y Mahomá todo engaño.

Don Alfonso:
No me la dieron mis brazos
Sino la gran providencia de Dios
Y así por El por este Leño sacro
Te concedo libertad
A ti y a todos tus vasallos.

Don Alfonso:

Oh, sovereign Standard.

Oh, triumph of the Christians.

Captive I see you among the Moors

But now I see you in my hands.

Sultan:

Christian, your valor has me

Prostrate at your feet.

I beg you by your Cross

And by your venerated God

That you give me liberty—

Because I see the light

Only your God is great

And Mohammed is all lies.

Don Alfonso:

My arms did not give it to me

But rather God's great providence

And so through Him and this Holy tree

I grant liberty

To you and all your vassals.

(Lucero 1953:111–12)

The mercy bestowed by the Spaniards on their repentant foes did not go unnoticed by Indian observers. Those who did not submit to the true cross could expect the flash of cannons and the fury of the horses. Unlike the Indians in Mexico, the Puebloan peoples of the Río Grande were never interested in participating in *Moros y Cristianos,* which allowed the play to retain its intensely Spanish character. What is evident from these reported performances is the acceptance in the popular consciousness of the concepts behind the pontifical bulls *Veritas ipsa, Sublimis Deus,* and the brief proclamation *Pastorale Officium* of 1537, which affirm the capacity of the Indians as rational human beings to receive the blessings of the faith (Ortega y Medina 1987:34). If the colonists really believed that the Indians by nature could not participate in their faith, they would not have made such an enthusiastic effort to impress them.

In attendance at the performance of *Moros y Cristianos* on that midsummer day in San Juan pueblo (in the poetic imagination of Pérez de Villagrá) was Qualco, a spy from Acoma pueblo who reported to his people that the dreaded Spanish cannons and firearms produced impressive but harmless explosions. Unfortunately, this news *did* reach the Acomans; several months later, in the siege of the natural citadel of Acoma pueblo, defending warriors dashed un-afraid into the deadly gunfire, resulting in the bloodiest massacre in the his-tory of New Mexico. In his epic poem *Historia de la Nueva México* Pérez de Villagrá documents, embellishes, and attempts to legally justify the punitive expedition against Acoma. However, his portrayal of the Indians is more a reflection of his classical education than the consciousness of his comrades in arms. The articulation of the classic noble-ignoble dichotomy in the poem is both complete and ingenious. Native nobility is personified in the character of Zutancalpo, while the ignominious aspect is embodied in Zutancalpo's father, Zutacapán. Here New Mexico's Homer speculates on the father's dark character.

> Dime sobervia infame como ygualas,
> El poderoso cetro y Real corona,
> Con un tan bajo barvaro perdido,
> De barvara, y vil barvaro, engendrado . . .
> Digalo aqueste barvaro furioso,
> De tan humilde sangre produzido,
> Si como Luzbel quiere lebantarse,
> Y el govierno de todo atribuirse, . . .
>
> (Pérez de Villagrá 1610; 1900:113)

> Behold here this untutored barbarian born of ignoble savages! . . . O, blind ambition for worldly power sought for alike by the high and the low, the worthy and unworthy! A good example is this bloody savage, sprung from such ignoble forebears, and who like Lucifer seeks to reach such heights of power.
> (R. Espinosa 1933:185)

Like Julius Caesar and Thucydides before him, Pérez de Villagrá invents rather than reports the speeches of his adversaries. The vile Zutacapán is driven by "envy, jealousy, and vain ambition," individualistic motives that were surely as alien to his culture as the ideals of liberty he flaunts in his harangue:

Escuchadme varones y mugeres . . .
Será bien que perdamos todos juntos,
La dulze libertad que nos dexaron,
Nuestros difuntos padres ya passados,
No sentis los clarines y las cajas,
De la sobervia gente Castellana,
Que a toda priesa viene ya marchando,
Qual es aquel que piensa de vosotros,
Quedar con libertad si aquellos llegan.
Estando como estamos descuidados,
Tomad, tomad, las armas y esperemos,
La intencion mala, o buena, con que vienen.

(Pérez de Villagrá 1610; 1900:98)

Listen, O men and women. . . . Shall we allow ourselves to be so deprived of that sweet liberty we have inherited from our forefathers? Hear the trumpets of these haughty Castilians who march toward us! Who among you for a moment dreams of liberty if once they come among us, unprepared as we are? To arms! Let us await them and meet them, come they for good or evil! (R. Espinosa 1933:164)

Zutacapán's handsome son, Zutancalpo, is always the first to oppose his father with statesmanlike words of measured moderation. He praises the "Castillas" (Spaniards) as great, just, and possibly immortal warriors, lending credibility to Governor Juan de Oñate's contention that the atrocities against Acoma were actions in a "just war" that was precipitated by the reckless deeds of the Acomans:

Nobleza de Acomeses valerosos . . .
Bien os consta que entraron los Castillas
Segun grandes guerreros en la tierra,
Bien prevenidos todos con cuidado . . .
Y en pueblos que han entrado conozemos,
Que en paz gustosa a todos los dexaron,
Pues si ellos alcanzasen que nosotros, . . .
Y si aquesta no bien nos sucediese,
Y estos son como dizen inmortales,

Qual disculpa sera la que disculpe,
El ser todos nosotros los primeros,
En encender la tierra que de suio,
Esta toda gustosa y sosegada . . .

                    (Pérez de Villagrá 1610:99)

> Noble Acomans . . . we all know that these Castilians have come into our
> lands and proved themselves great warriors; and that they are always on guard
> and alert. . . . We know they have been received into many of our pueblos and
> have left our people in peace and well satisfied. . . . If, as is said, these men
> are immortal, who can ever forgive us the sin of starting a conflagration which
> we can never stop? (R. Espinosa 1933:165)

The inexorable course of events proves the truth of Zutancalpo's warnings.
Idealistic and brave to the end, he is given a hero's funeral while his
despised father's body is hacked to pieces by the distraught wives of his own
countrymen.

True to the Renaissance ideal of *armas y letras* (arms and letters), Pérez de
Villagrá not only immortalizes the battle in verse, he is one of its heroes.
However, he leaves completely intact and unresolved the dichotomy of the
noble versus the ignoble savage. Neither extreme in this conceptual dilemma
has much to do with actual Indians because the dichotomy itself is a creation
of the European mind. Even the Franciscan historian Lino Gómez Canedo can
argue that the majority of the Spaniards who actually lived in New Spain had
a "much less radical and much more realistic" view of the Indians that could
come only from living among them (Gómez Canedo 1960:30). If the colonists held any popularized notions of the noble-ignoble savage debate, the
social and political reality of New Mexico was bound to alter them.

Pueblos and Comanches: The Popular Culture of Warfare

For a century after Don Diego de Vargas returned to New Mexico in 1693,
the pragmatics of survival created a new cultural dynamic based on the en-
mities and alliances of the 1700s. Questions about the nobility or ignobility
of the Pueblos vanished as they became trusted military allies. The political,
social, and economic rapprochement was such that by 1812, the wealthy
rancher Pedro Pino could write in his report to the Cortes de Cádiz that the

Pueblos "casi no se distinguen de nosotros" ("are almost undistinguishable from us"), unusual words for a conservative monarchist (Pino 1812; 1849:2). Pino had harsher words for the Comanches, for his home community of Galisteo, south of Santa Fe, had been a favorite target for the bloody depredations of the previous century. After the reconquest there was no more appropriate model for the ignoble savage in New Mexico than the Comanche. However, Pino's descriptions of the Comanches and their culture neither idealize nor denigrate them. In the same report, Pino writes with an awe tinged with respect:

> El Comanche prefiere la muerte en vez de ser sujetado a la humillación. En la guerra nunca ataca a traición o con ventaja, sino siempre cara a cara y después de haber señalado con su silbato. Aunque su arma principal es el arco (o *pacta*), usa la lanza o arma de fuego como nuestros soldados, y con una cambiante táctica que impone a sus movimientos. Las guerras que han tenido con nosotros siempre han sido tenaces y sangrientas. (Pino 1812; 1849:85)

> The Comanche prefers death rather than be subjected to any humiliation. Never does he attack in war at an advantage or with treachery, but always face-to-face and after having given the signal with his whistle. Although his principle arm is the bow (*pacta*), he uses the lance or firearm like our soldiers, and with a changing tactic he imposes on his movements. The wars they had with us have always been bloody and tenacious.

Beginning with their appearance in Taos in 1705 and the first major attack on the pueblo in 1716, the Comanches, fierce new "lords of the plains," alternately traded with and raided Spanish and Pueblo settlements at will, carrying off captives, animals, and whatever else they wanted. Pushed out of their northern homeland, the Comanches had also migrated to the southern plains to seek a more constant supply of horses (Thomas 1932:15–25). Major military expeditions were led against them in 1719, 1747, and 1761 by Governors Don Antonio de Valverde Cosina, Francisco Marín del Valle, and Tomás Vélez Cachupín. The severe punishments inflicted on the Comanches only intensified the frequency and ferocity of their raids.

In 1774 Governor Pedro Mendinueta called the aging Indian fighter Don Carlos Fernández out of retirement in Santa Fe to lead a campaign of retaliation. The most feared Comanche of the era was named Tabivo Naritgante (Handsome and Brave), although he was known to the Pueblos and Spanish as Cuerno Verde, for the green horn that was part of his colorful costume.

Pedro Pino himself fought in this campaign and is suspected by scholars to
be the author of the heroic folk drama *Los Comanches*. Although Don Carlos
Fernández and Cuerno Verde never actually met on the field of battle, dramatic license united them in the play as characters representing the experience and dignity of old age versus the reckless energy of youth.

In contrast to the erudite hendecasyllabic cantos of Pérez de Villagrá's
poem, which was not yet known to the common people, the popular-style
octosyllabic verses of *Los Comanches* entered the oral tradition by the same
route as *Moros y Cristianos*. The spectacle, still performed in Alcalde, New
Mexico, begins with a stirring speech that many older Hispanos in the north
can still recite.[2] Here, a young Cuerno Verde exults in brash boasts and
bristling threats to inspire his warriors and intimidate his enemies:

Cuerno Verde:

Desde el oriente al poniente,
Desde el sur al norte frío
Suena el brillante clarín
Y reina el acero mío.
Campeo osado, atrevido,
Y es tanta la valentía
Que reina en el pecho mío . . .

. . . .

Ea, nobles capitanes,
Genízaros valerosos,
Que se pregone mi edicto,
Que yo como general
He de estar aprevenido . . .

. . . .

Que suene el tambor y pito.
¡Al baile, y punto de guerra!

Green Horn:

From sunrise to sunset,
From the south to frigid north
My shining trumpet sounds
And my steel reigns.
I campaign fearless and bold,

And the valor which reigns
In my heart knows no limit . . .

. . . .

Hey, noble captains,
Valorous janissaries,
Proclaim my edict,
That I as general
Will be ready.

. . . .

Sound the drum and flute.
To the dance, and ready for war!

(Campa 1942:25)

Here there is no preoccupation with nobility and ignobility, no Zutancalpo or Zutacapán, no talk of liberty, barbarism, fortune, vain ambition, or the work of Lucifer. If the poet is putting words into Cuerno Verde's mouth, it is because he actually heard the screaming battlefield harangues (although he did not understand the Comanche language). The dauntless bravura of the character in the play matches the historical descriptions of the chief himself and the fearless tactics of Comanche warfare.

In a purely fictitious confrontation, a dignified Don Carlos Fernández taunts Cuerno Verde face-to-face, boasting of Spain's wide dominions. The historical record shows that Don Carlos surprised and massacred a large group of Comanche families on September 20, 1774, on the *llano estacado* (staked plains) fifty leagues east of Santa Fe.

Don Carlos Fernández:
¿Qué no sabes que en la España
El señor soberano
De los cielos y la tierra
Y todos los cuatro polos
Que este gran círculo encierra?
Brilla su soberanía,
Y al oír su nombre tiemblan
Alemanes, portugueses,
Turquía y la Inglaterra,

Porque en diciendo españoles
Todas las naciones tiemblan . . .

. . . .

Siempre he pisado tus tierras
Aunque ya avanzado en años,
Y me veas de esta manera
Siempre soy Carlos Fernández
Por el mar y por la tierra,
Y para probar tu brío
Voy a hacer junta de guerra.

Don Carlos Fernández:
Know you not that in Spain
Is the Sovereign Lord
Of the skies and the earth
And all four poles
That this great circle encloses?
His sovereignty shines,
And on hearing his name do tremble
Germans, Portuguese,
Turkey, and England,
Because in saying *Spaniards*
All the nations tremble . . .

. . . .

I've always stepped on your lands
Though I am advanced in years
And you see me in this way
I am forever Carlos Fernández
By land and by sea,
And to test your vigor
I will make a council of war.

(Campa 1942:27−28)

In a confrontation in another part of the battlefield, a Comanche warrior
matches his valor against a Spanish soldier who mocks the (actual) Comanche

practice of gorging on buffalo lard before going into battle. Around them the
final battle rages.

Zapato Cuenta:
El oso más arrogante
Se encoge de mi fiereza
El tíguere en las montañas
Huye en la oculta sierra.
¿Quién se opone a mi valor?
¿Quién cautiva mi soberbia?

Don José de la Peña:
Yo quebrantaré la furia,
Que son la más alta peña
Soy peñasco en valentía,
En bríos y en fortaleza.
Esas locas valentías
Son criadas de la soberbia
Que tanto infunde el valor
En vosotros la manteca
Que coméis con tanta gula
Y con ella criáis la fuerza
De vuestras disposiciones.

Beaded Shoe:
The most arrogant bear
Shrinks from my fury
The lion in his mountains
Hides in the hidden ranges.
Who would oppose my valor?
Who would capture my pride?

Don José de la Peña:
I will break that fury,
That is the highest peak
I am a towering cliff of bravery,
In spirit and strength.
These crazy shows of bravura

Are the product of pride.
You get so much valor
From the buffalo lard
That you eat with such gluttony
And with it the strength of your
Dispositions grows.

(Campa 1942:35)

To provide some carnivalesque comic relief, an Indian camp follower named Barriga Duce begins to loot the battlefield, boasting of the booty he will take home to his wife and the green chile she will then cook for him.

Barriga Duce:
Que mueran, que para mí
Todos los despojos quedan.
Tiendas, antas, y conchelles
Para que mis hijos duerman.
Y la carne, a mi mujer
He de hacer que me la cuesa
Y me la guise con chile
Que es una comida buena.
¡Apriéntenles compañeros!
Que de eso mi alma se alegra.

Sweet Belly:
May all of them die
So the booty will be all mine.
Tents, hides and blankets
That my children can sleep in.
And the meat, I'll get my wife
To cook it for me
And prepare it with chile
Which is a good food.
Close on in, comrades!
That's what makes my soul happy.

(Campa 1942:40)

In the final scene, Cuerno Verde is vanquished, bringing the Comanche wars to their conclusion. The chieftain's death actually occurred below Pike's Peak five years later in 1779, when Tabivo Naritgante and fifty warriors charged headlong into the artillery fire of a Spanish force of over six hundred led by the newly appointed governor, Juan Bautista de Anza.

The touching scenes of repentance and forgiveness that characterize *Moros y Cristianos* are totally lacking in *Los Comanches*. Also lacking are the moral allegory and classical allusions that embellish Villagrá's siege of Acoma. Here the defiant Comanches are soundly defeated and the play is a victory celebration. Neither demon nor prince, Cuerno Verde appears as the haughty and formidable enemy that he truly was.

Because of its historical allusions, *Los Comanches* can be dated to approximately 1780. Also in this period can be found the origins of the *indita* (little Indian) ballads, so named by the people because the majority of the songs have to do with relations as diverse as warfare and love between españoles and indios. Some of the earliest and latest *inditas* are called *cautivas* (captives) because they sing of the travails of captive women on the frontier. In the continual depredations throughout the eighteenth century, captives were often taken and slavery was widespread.

In 1724 the Comanches decimated even the Jicarilla Apaches, carrying off half of their women and children and killing everyone else except for sixty-nine men, two women, and three boys (Bancroft 1889:239). In 1777 the town of Tomé south of Albuquerque suffered a particularly merciless attack in which every man, woman, and child was killed. Since men were usually killed in battle, any captives were likely to be women and children. Their sad lament could be heard in ballads and songs such as "La cautiva Marcelina" (in the version of Virginia Bernal of Ratón, New Mexico), the pathetic woman whose fate it was to witness the murder of her children and wander the plains with her captors with nothing to eat but mare's meat.

"LA CAUTIVA MARCELINA"

La cautiva Marcelina
Ya se va, ya se la llevan,
Ya se va, ya se la llevan
Para esas tierras mentadas
A comer carne de yegua,
A comer carne de yegua.

Refrán:

Por eso ya no quiero
En el mundo más amar,
De mi querida patria
Me van a retirar.

La cautiva Marcelina
Cuando llegó al aguapá,
Cuando llegó al aguapá
Volteó la cara llorando,
"Mataron a mi papá,
Mataron a mi papá."

[Refrán]

La cautiva Marcelina
Cuando ya llegó a los llanos,
Cuando ya llegó a los llanos
Volteó la cara llorando,
"Mataron a mis hermanos
Mataron a mis hermanos."

[Refrán]

La cautiva Marcelina
Cuando llegó al ojito,
Cuando llegó al ojito
Volteó la cara llorando,
"Mataron al Delgadito,
Mataron al Delgadito."

[Refrán]

La cautiva Marcelina
Cuando llegó a los cerritos,
Cuando llegó a los cerritos
Volteó la cara llorando,
"Mataron a mis hijitos,
Mataron a mis hijitos."

[Refrán]

"MARCELINA THE CAPTIVE WOMAN"

Marcelina, the captive,
Now she's leaving, they're taking her
Now she's leaving, they're taking her
To those faraway lands
To eat mare's meat,
To eat mare's meat.

Chorus:

That's why I no longer
Want to love in this world,
From my beloved homeland
They are taking me away.

Marcelina, the captive,
When she arrived at the cattail marsh,
When she arrived at the cattails,
She looked back crying,
"They killed my father,
They killed my father."

[Chorus]

The captive Marcelina
When she arrived at the plains,
When she arrived at the plains,
She looked back crying,
"They killed my brothers and sisters,
They killed my brothers and sisters."

[Chorus]

Marcelina, the captive,
When she arrived at the spring,
When she arrived at the spring,
She looked back crying,
"They killed Delgadito,
They killed Delgadito."

[Chorus]

Marcelina, the captive,
When she arrived at the hills,
When she arrived at the hills,
She looked back crying,
"They killed my children,
They killed my children."

[Chorus]

(Lamadrid and Loeffler 1989)

Known all over New Mexico, this ballad was collected as far south as Mexico City as late as 1914, in a version in which the female character is named "la infanta Margarita " (the princess Margarita) and whose refrain includes the memorable mention of mare's meat:

Margarita ya se va,
Ya se va, ya se la llevan,
A la sierra de los indios
A comer carne de yegua . . .

Margarita is already going,
She is going, they are taking her
To the mountains of the Indians
To eat mare's meat . . .

(Mendoza 1986:482)

There is no sure indicator of the direction of diffusion, north or south, but the ballad has all the indications of being of some antiquity. Many more recent captivity ballads still have enough points of temporal and geographical reference that they can be correlated with known historical events. "La cautiva Marcelina," however, is more regional than local in focus. In some areas it is sung with tragic overtones, while in others it has the same sarcastic or playful tone as a nursery rhyme (many of which are, in fact, fragments of old ballads). Since the focus of the ballad is on the individual suffering of *la cautiva,* there is no direct appraisal or particular condemnation of Indian cultures. What is significant about this particular ballad is its movement toward the first-person narrative style of the later *inditas.*

Eighteenth-century colonial records are filled with reports of captivity incidents, most involving women and children. The official documents are sparse, containing barely more than names of people and places. It is easy to imagine the multitude of personal captivity narratives that must have circulated. More difficult to determine are the attitudes that such anecdotes would express, since almost none were documented in any detail. Some later and better-documented oral captivity narratives from the nineteenth century suggest a marked tendency to interpret the experience of captivity from within a spiritual frame as an individual test of faith. The earliest North American captivity narratives from Puritans in New England and from French Jesuits in Canada are also spiritual. Subsequently, however, the stories of captives were consistently used for political propaganda to stir popular support and raise money for Indian campaigns (Levernier and Cohen 1977). In contrast, Hispanic New Mexican captivity narratives have consistently utilized a spiritual framework, right through the last Apache wars of the 1880s. Like "La cautiva Marcelina," New Mexican women seem to have been able to survive their ordeals and mourn their dead with faith and forbearance, somehow avoiding the condemnation or vilification of the Indians.

From Ignoble Savage to Funny Indian: The Comedy of Cultural Conflict

The elitist notion of the ignoble savage as an unfortunate, bestial, depraved being, worthy only of enslavement or extermination, disappeared quickly into the landscape. Villagrá's Zutacapán is the only character of New Mexican literature or folklore that even approaches ignobility. Despite all their real and legendary cruelty, not even the Comanches could fit this role. What emerged in popular culture was a comic portrayal of Indians that used denigrating sarcasm to express cultural conflict. The character of Barriga Duce in *Los Comanches* exemplifies this tradition. In performances, he plays both fool and coward, taunting the warriors, then hiding when the battles begin. In true Rabelaisian spirit, all he thinks about is his stomach and the goods he can pilfer from the dead. As the battlefield resounds with heroic speeches and combat, he makes lists of his booty and his wife's favorite recipes.

There are many popular verses that satirize Comanches in this vein. The following *verso* is sometimes used as a lullaby or to entertain children. The thought of the Comanche couple selling their child to satisfy their sweet tooth is both horrifying and humorous.

El Cumanchi y la Cumancha
Se fueron pa' Santa Fe,
Se fueron pa' Santa Fe,
A vender a sus hijitos,
A vender a sus hijitos,
Por azúcar y café,
Por azúcar y café.

The Comanche and his woman
Went to Santa Fe,
Went to Santa Fe,
To sell their little children,
To sell their little children,
For sugar and coffee,
For sugar and coffee.

    (A. M. Espinosa 1907:20–21)

Trading fairs at Taos, Santa Fe, and Pecos were well attended because, besides trade goods, hides, jerky, and horses, captives were brought in to be sold or ransomed. Other lullabies were a bit less unsettling, although here the child's restlessness is associated with roving Indians.

El indito anda en la Sierra,
El Comanche en la montaña,
Este niño no se duerme
Porque ha'garrado una maña.

The little Indian goes in the sierra,
The Comanche in the mountains,
This child does not sleep
Because something has got into him.

                (Mendoza 1986:468)

The military dominance of the Apaches by the Comanches is made light of in the following verse. Apache groups often complained to the colonial authorities about their suffering at the hands of the Comanches. Here the Apache is crying:

El Apache y el Comanche
Se citaron pa' la guerra,
Se citaron pa' la guerra,
El Apache gime y llora,
Y el Comanche se le aferra,
Y el Comanche se le aferra.

The Apache and the Comanche
Made a date for battle,
Made a date for battle,
The Apache groans and cries,
And the Comanche closes in,
And the Comanche closes in.

   (A. M. Espinosa 1907:20–21)

After the Comanches were pacified, the task of Hispanicizing and Christianizing them began, a process that never reached completion. As this humorous
stereotype shows, no matter how hard they try, the Comanches never succeed
in practicing Christian religion in a convincing way. Confession is a waste of
time for them, because they don't know how to pray.

El Comanche y la Comancha
Se fueron a confesar,
Se fueron a confesar,
Del camino se volvieron,
Porque no sabían rezar,
Porque no sabían rezar.

The Comanche and his woman
Went to confess,
Went to confess,
They returned by the same road,
Because they didn't know how to pray,
Because they didn't know how to pray.

   (A. M. Espinosa 1907:20–21)

The family relations of Indians were also frequent targets of satire. Missionaries had great difficulty introducing new marriage customs. When El Co-

manche and La Comancha finally agree to accept the sacrament of marriage, they are denied because they are first cousins. Any attempt they make to Hispanicize themselves is thwarted.

El Comanche y la Comancha
Se fueron a presentar,
Se fueron a presentar;
Salieron primos hermanos,
No se pudieron casar,
No se pudieron casar.

The Comanche and his woman
Went to present themselves,
Went to present themselves;
It turns out they were first cousins,
They couldn't get married,
They couldn't get married.

> (A. M. Espinosa 1907:20–21)

As traditional enemies of the Pueblos and Spanish, the Comanches and other nomads like Navajos and Apaches easily filled the category of cultural otherness that is so convenient to lampoon. However, even though the Pueblos were neighbors and allies of the Spanish, they did maintain a strong sense of cultural distinctness, mainly through religion. True syncretists, they added Christian saints and the Holy Trinity to their pantheon of deities but kept their sacred dances and ceremonies. Despite the strong alliance with the Spanish, they embodied enough otherness to also become targets of humor and satire, although never to the degree that the nomads did. Interestingly, much of the humor is erotic—expressive, perhaps, of the wish for a more intimate cultural relationship.

The "Indita de Cochití" is representative of a kind of raucous love song that is quite distinct from the *indita* ballads that speak of tragedies or the experiences of captives. The common point is that both types of *inditas* express experiences between Hispanics and Indians, although the aggressive role is reversed. In the *cautivas* Hispanas are carried off by Indian men. In the "Indita de Cochití" there is implied abuse of Indian women, with overtones of sarcasm rather than tragedy. In most of its many versions, the Indian girl is pregnant and is being abandoned not because she is Indian but because she "just isn't [right] for" the singer. The performance of this *indita* by José Domingo Romero of Las Vegas, New Mexico, is accompanied by peals of laughter and merriment.

"INDITA DE COCHITÍ"

Indita, indita, indita,
Indita de Cochití,
No le hace que seiga indita
Si al cabo no soy pa' ti.

Indita, indita, indita,
Indita del otro lado,
¿En dónde andabas anoche
Que traes el ojo pegado?

Indita, indita, indita,
Indita del otro día,
¿En dónde andabas anoche
Que traigas barriga fría?

"LITTLE INDIAN GIRL OF COCHITÍ"

Little Indian, little Indian,
Little Indian girl of Cochití,
It doesn't matter if you're Indian
If in the end you aren't for me.

Little Indian, little Indian,
Little Indian girl from the other side,
Where were you last night
That your eye is battered shut?

Little Indian, little Indian,
Little Indian girl from the other day
Where were you last night
That your belly is so cold?

(Loeffler 1992)

There may be love and erotic interest, but the Pueblo girl is an "indita del otro lado" whose otherness prevents the crossing of cultural boundaries; not because she does not want to cross them but because the singer does not. There is a sense of caste superiority expressed here, because if the Spanish man does agree to marry his *indita,* his status on the caste scale declines, while the status of his wife and child improves. In at least one version of "Indita de Cochití," however, love prevails, the boundary is crossed, and the *indita* becomes a lullaby to the *coyote* (mixed-breed) child of the union (Chávez n.d.).

In the popular culture of colonial New Mexico, the elitist concept of ignoble savage was transformed by historical experience into the ridiculous savage. The castigation of otherness through humor and sarcasm is one of many indications of the degree to which cultural boundaries were at least observed if not respected. New Mexican *mestizaje* occurs in a setting of cultural pluralism rather than cultural homogenization. "Los cañuteros" ("The Reed Game Gamblers") as sung by Abade Martínez of Alamosa, Colorado, is an erotic *indita* from the early nineteenth century or before that exemplifies this distinctive regional style of *mestizaje.* When Comanches came to the Río Grande valley community to trade, they often stayed for weeks. Ample time was spent striking bargains and deciding prices, and gambling and horse racing were favorite pastimes. The Comanches and many other Indian groups played a semisacred gambling game called the "bone game" whose sessions could last for days. In their enthusiasm for the game, bettors often wagered everything they owned. *El cañute* is a Hispanic adaptation of the bone game that was played through the beginning of the twentieth century. The game was played in winter, indoors, by two teams of four players. Each team would bury four hollow sticks, the *cañutes,* in a pile of sand; one of the hollow sticks had a smaller stick inserted into it. Each team alternated draws to find the *cañute* with the stick in it (R. Espinosa 1933). The chorus of "hállalo, hállalo, el palito andando" ("find it, find it, the little stick goes around"), repeats the object of the game, which has obvious erotic overtones.

"LOS CAÑUTEROS"

Allí vienen los cañuteros
Los que vienen por el mío,
Pero de allá que llevarán
Rasguidos en el fundillo.

Estribillo:

Hállalo, hállalo,
Cañutero sí, cañutero no,
El palito andando.

Parece que viene gente
Hay rastros en la cañada,
Parece que se lo llevan
Pero no se llevan nada.

[Estribillo]

Padre mío, San Antonio,
Devoto de los morenos,
Es verdad que alzamos trigo,
Pero todo lo debemos.

[Estribillo]

En el año de la nevada
Me enamoré de una tetona
En una teta me acostaba,
Con la otra me cobijaba.
De lo a gusto que dormía
Y hasta en la cama me meaba.

[Estribillo]

"THE REED GAME GAMBLERS"

There come the reed game players
Those that come for mine
But from there they'll only get
Scratches on their behind.

Chorus:

Find it, find it,
Cañutero yes, cañutero no,
The little stick goes around.

Looks like people are coming in,
There are signs in the canyon,
Seems like luck is with them,
But they don't have anything.

[Chorus]

San Antonio, my father,
The dark skinned are beloved to you
It is true we raise wheat,
But we are in debt for everything.

[Chorus]

In the year of the big snow,
I fell in love with a big-breasted woman,
On one I lay down, and covered up with the other.
I slept so well
I even wet the bed.

[Chorus]

(Lamadrid and Loeffler 1989)

Large groups of people would gather to bet, sing, and drink while watching the *cañuteros*. Personal items as well as sacks of beans or wheat would be bet. As it expresses with erotic humor the enthusiasm for this popular diversion, this *indita* also reveals the pride of the *mestizo* wheat farmer. He may be a poor mixed-blood, but at least he raises wheat, the staple that is as closely linked to Hispanic culture as corn is to Indian culture. The New Mexican *mestizo* is intimately nourished by both cultures, as evidenced in the following popular poem.

Pluralism is the product of resistance, which expresses itself culturally as confrontation, argument, and debate. A favorite popular form to express the competition of ideas, from philosophical to economic, was the *trovo*, or poetic duel. "El Trovo del Café y el Atole" expresses the competition between the native and the foreign. Mr. Coffee is sophisticated, stimulating, and worldly, but he is expensive. Ms. Atole finally wins the duel because she is both a popular beverage and she nourishes the people who use the sweat of their brow and not money to enjoy her.

"TROVO DEL CAFÉ Y EL ATOLE"

Por mi gracia y por mi nombre
Yo me llamo Don Café.
En las tiendas más hermosas
Allí me hallará usted.
A la América he venido
Y es claro y evidente,
Desde mi país he venido
A conquistar a tu gente. . .

Atole:

Yo también soy el Atole
Y te pondré mis paradas.
¡Qué bien mantengo a mi gente
Con tortillas enchiladas,
Con esquite bien tostado
Ahora te daré noticias.
Café, por comprarte a ti
Ya no se alcanzan pa' camisas.

Café:

Yo soy el Café
Y de todos conocido
En la América del Norte
De todos soy preferido.
En el mundo soy distinguido
Con satisfacción completa
En tacitas todos me usan
Bebiendo mi agüita prieta.

Atole:

Yo también soy el Atole
Y aquí te hago la guerra.
¡Qué bien mantengo a mi gente
Con sólo labrar la tierra!
Y tú, Café orgulloso,

Que sepa el mundo entero,
Sacrificas a mi gente
De comprarte con dinero.

"DUEL OF MR. COFFEE AND MS. CORN GRUEL"

By my grace and my name
I call myself Mr. Coffee.
In the most beautiful stores
There you will find me.
I have come to America
And it is clear and evident,
I have come from my country
To conquer your people . . .

Atole:

I am also Corn Gruel
And I will give you my points.
How well I maintain my people
With tortillas and chile,
With corn well toasted
Now I will give you news.
Coffee, in order to buy you
Nothing is left for shirts.

Café:

I am Coffee
Known to all
In North America
Of everyone I am preferred.
In the world I'm distinguished
With complete satisfaction
People use me in little cups
Drinking my dark water.

Atole:

I am also Corn Gruel
And here I give you battle.

> How well I maintain my people
> Only for working the land.
> And you, proud Coffee,
> May the whole world know,
> You sacrifice my people
> From buying you with money.

(Arellano and Atencio 1972 : 13–15)

In the *trovo,* the popular consciousness can be seen at work. Atole, the native product, wins the argument. She nourishes rather than impoverishes her people. All she requires in return is hard work and devotion. Atole, which is made with blue corn meal, is not only a contribution of indigenous culture, it represents a spiritual value within it. The *mestizo* may be proud to grow wheat, but he knows that his corn has the power to heal.

The Spiritual Savage: The Emergence of Hispanic Syncretism

The only classic European-style noble savage to appear in the literary and popular culture of New Mexico sprang from the imagination of Gaspar Pérez de Villagrá, who created Zutancalpo to add a Homeric touch of tragedy to the otherwise unthinkable massacre of Acoma. The young warrior's mouth was wishfully stuffed with generous and naïve expressions of tolerance, charity, and acceptance of the Spaniards. Pérez de Villagrá needed to create a balance and foil to the implacable Zutacapán, Zutancalpo's father. For every ignoble savage a noble one is needed to balance the scales of justice.

In New Mexico, some colonists may have shared Las Casas's belief in the natural virtue, ingenuity, and intellect of the Indians, but to invest too much trust in them in the dangerous new colony was to risk one's life. Besides, if the Indians really possessed an innate love for freedom and an orderly political life, then the shaky colonial institutions like the *encomienda* were bound to make them unhappy enough to protest the diminishing quality of their life.

The genuine affective links with Indian culture were made when the Spanish, by reason or necessity, came to identify with the Indians who surrounded them on all sides. This identification was hardest earned with Pueblo neighbors because it had to grow out of the respect the Pueblos had earned for themselves with an act of resistance and religious affirmation: the 1680 expulsion of the intolerant Spanish from the land. Times of privation or hardship lent themselves to the establishment of new bonds. Until very recently, in years of drought Hispanics living near San Juan pueblo would approach the Indian elders with petitions to *ir y traer la lluvia* (go and bring the rain); that is, to initiate a sacred rain pilgrimage to local mountain shrines to bring down the needed moisture (Ortiz 1981:8–17). Such practices are undoubtedly rooted in remote times. In many communities the saints, especially San Isidro, served as spiritual intermediaries between Pueblos and Spanish. The regional Matachines dance drama also has played a central symbolic role in expressing spiritual bonds between the cultures.

The omnipresence of diverse Indian groups in New Mexico was also a compelling reason to cling to Hispanicity as a matter of self and group definition. Cultural tenacity is strengthened in an isolated and threatening environment. The survival of peninsular forms in the folklore is proof of this factor. Unconsciously, the people knew who they were; they grew wheat, they were Christians, the body of Christ is made of wheat. They prayed to *santos* (saints) who favored them and brought them blessings. They had a strong code of honor, *hidalguía,* and the images and archetypes of these values were deeply embedded in the old Castilian songs they sang. *Sabían quiénes eran* (they knew who they were). Part of their identity was bound up in the land. As colonists, one of their dreams was to possess the land and pass it along as inheritance, to become *hidalgos, hijos de algo* (sons of something of great value). In New Mexico a transformation occurred in which the material commodity of land took on a deeper, more spiritual value. Colonists soon discovered their *querencia,* or newfound attachment to the land, which could not be defined in any less than spiritual terms. From their Indian neighbors they had learned that the land is sacred, *la madre tierra* (mother earth), the mother of us all.

On a spiritual plane, this subtle new fusion of New Mexican cultures can be seen at the shrine of the Santuario de Chimayó, where the sanctity of earth and the appreciation of its healing power are one. The faithful come as grateful pilgrims from all directions in search of the sacred earth of Chimayó, a Tewa (Pueblo) shrine with a sanctuary built on top, the most venerated spot in New Mexico. The local Penitentes, or penitent brothers of the Hermandad de Nuestro Padre Jesús Nazareno (Brotherhood of Our Father Jesus the Nazarene) include this prayerful promise as part of an entrance ritual: "Vesare esa Santa Cruz y vesare esta Santa Tierra de Rodias [*sic*]" ("I will kiss this Holy Cross and this Holy Earth on my Knees"; Steele and Rivera 1985:17). The shrine at Chimayó is intimately linked to the beginnings of the Penitentes in New Mexico. The special veneration of San Francisco is also widespread in the region, and the Franciscan concept of seeing God revealed in Nature is also in harmony with the basic landscape. The light of day is sacred, as praised in the *alba,* or song sung at daybreak, especially after *velorios* (all-night prayer vigils). This hymn is also associated with the *ángel de guardia* (guardian angel). Similar *albas* are sung in related ritual contexts in Spain, an indication that at least on some fronts, colonists were prepared for the more intense veneration of nature that they would find in Native American religions.

"CANTO AL ALBA"

Viva Jesús,
Viva María,
Cantemos todos
En este día.

Coro:

Cantemos al alba,
Ya viene el día.
Daremos gracias,
Ave María.

Bendita sea
La luz del día.
Bendito sea
Quien nos la envía.

[Coro]

Bendito sea
Su claridad,
Bendita sea
Quien nos la da.

[Coro]

Bendito sea
Sol refulgente,
Bendito sea
Sol del oriente.

"SONG TO THE DAWN"

Long live Jesus,
Long live Mary,
Let us all sing
On this day.

Chorus:

Let us sing to the dawn,
The day is already coming.
Let us give thanks,
Hail Mary.

Blessed be
The light of day.
Blessed be
He who sends it to us.

[Chorus]

Blessed be
The clarity,
Blessed be
He who gives it to us.

[Chorus]

Blessed be
The sun resplendent,
Blessed be
The sun of the east.

   (Lamadrid et al. 1991)

The Hispanic identification with non-Pueblo Indian cultures developed more easily, in part because of the more intimate social relations they experienced with Indian captives who joined Spanish households and families as *criados* (servants). Pueblo Indians were allies and trusted neighbors, but a *genízaro* with Comanche, Navajo, or Apache roots could be living under the same roof, taking care of the children and singing them native lullabies. Besides social intimacy, Hispanics also impersonated Comanches in secular and religious drama as well as in the Comanche dance, which is a true regional tradition enacted in the winter cycle of "enemy dances" in every Pueblo from Taos to Hopi (Clews Parsons 1939:1077).

After hostilities with the Comanches were resolved by the end of the eighteenth century, the Comanches continued trading and visiting the pueblos and plazas of the Río Grande valley. There is a flair and vitality in Comanche culture that both Pueblos and Hispanics recognized and admired in them as enemies and later as devoted trading partners. When the Comanches were reduced by the U.S. Army in 1875 and put on reservations, the yearly visits ceased. Ever since then, both Pueblo and Hispanic New Mexicans have emulated and honored them in their Comanche dancing.

Pueblo dancers who impersonate Comanches are allowed much more individual expression, both in the dances, which are similar to Pow Wow dances, and in the costumes, which use buckskin, beads, feathers, and horn and vary according to the personal tastes of the dancer. One dancer might have an eagle feather headdress while another wears horns. This individualism stands in sharp contrast to sacred Pueblo dancing, in which movements are collective and synchronized and costumes are uniform.

In the Hispanic Comanche dance found in western and northern New Mexico, Indian impersonators encounter Christianity in true Comanche style, by kidnapping the Christ Child on Christmas Eve from the house of the *mayordomo* (steward).[3] In a procession somewhat reminiscent of the Mexican *Las Posadas* (The Inns) ritual, the Indians dance in procession from house to house, finally entering the house where the Santo Niño is kept. In most performances a symbolic entrance ritual is performed at the door of the *mayordomo's* house, or at the threshold of the church in others. The Comanche chieftain sings:

Soy de la Sierra Nevada
Donde fui pintado león.
Vengo en busca del niñito
Y no hay quien me dé razón.

I am from the Sierra Nevada
Where I was painted as a lion.
I come in search of the little child
And there is no one who can tell me.

(Hurt 1966)

The entire group of Indian impersonators in buckskin and feathers then sing verses which include the following. The music, in true *indita* style, combines chromatic with pentatonic melodies, punctuated with shouts and syllable chanting, a Hispanic attempt to reproduce or at least emulate Indian music:

A las doce de la noche
Le hemos venido a buscar
Nosotros los Comanchitos
Le hemos venido a bailar.

Ya consiguimos la entrada;
Con gusto y con buen cariño
Pasaremos los Comanches
A ver a ese hermoso Niño.

Buenas noches les dé Dios
A toditos por igual,
Si nos reciben con gusto
Hemos venido a bailar.

No se asusten, caballeros
Porque venimos bailando;
Es promesa que debemos
Y ahora andamos pagando.

At twelve midnight
We have come to look for him
We the little Comanches
Have come to dance for him.

We have gained entry
With joy and loving

The Comanches will pass through
To see that beautiful Child.

May God give you good night
To every one the same,
If you receive us with gusto
We have come to dance.

Do not be afraid, gentlemen
Because we come dancing;
It is a promise that we owe
And are now paying.

(Hurt 1966)

The suspicious inhabitants of the house reluctantly offer the Comanches their hospitality. Once the dancers enter the house, they proceed to the altar and steal the Santo Niño. They flee, pursued by members of the audience. In the mock battle that follows, *la Cautiva* (the Captive Girl), the daughter of the chieftain, and other Comanches are captured and later ransomed. Additional music and verses accompany the various *desempeños* (bargaining sessions) in which the Santo Niño is recovered and *mayordomos* are chosen for the next year. The plot in this religious drama is loose, and it varies from community to community. The *indita* previously mentioned, "La cautiva Marcelina," is often sung during Comanche dancing. In other communities such as Ranchos de Taos, the dancing occurs on New Year's Day and uses music that is entirely pentatonic with syllable chant singing (Lamadrid 1992).

The practice of dancing to fulfill a promise and ask for miracles and blessings is done in the name of several saints. Matachines dancers make promises to dance for San Lorenzo if they are from Bernalillo or to San Antonio if they are from a community that celebrates his feast day. When their wives were in labor, nervous husbands used to dance and sing to San Ramón Nonato for a safe delivery and a healthy child.

Even though it dates from the end of the nineteenth century, nearly eighty years after the end of the colonial period, the "Indita de San Luis" is an excellent example of *mestizo* folklore. It was written to commemorate the final termination of colonial Spanish power in the Americas, the Spanish-American War. In 1898, many New Mexicans enlisted in the fight against Spain. The irony that the sons of conquistadores were now fighting Spaniards was not lost on the people of the day. Popular poet Don Norberto M. Abeyta from Sabinal, New Mexico, wrote the poem as a petition to San Gonzaga de Abaranda and the Virgin to intercede for a merciful end to the war (A. M. Espinosa 1985: 131–32). The poet's source of inspiration was the report of a miracle on the high seas in which a ship of New Mexican soldiers on the way to fight Spain was saved by San Gonzaga, who quelled a terrible storm. When this poem entered the oral tradition, San Gonzaga de Abaranda transposed to the more familiar San Luis Gonzaga, and the poem became the "Indita de San Luis," complete with *indita* chorus and a growing reputation for bringing *milagros*. People make devout *promesas* (promises) to dance for this patron saint of youth in return for blessings and miracles, which include everything from bringing rain to curing sickness and protecting soldiers. Manuel Mirabal of Albuquerque, New Mexico, the singer of this particular version of the "Indita de San Luis," is especially devoted because years ago the *indita* and the sacred healing dance that accompanies it cured his son, who was suffering from rheumatic fever.

"INDITA DE SAN LUIS"

De mis casa he venido
A pasear este lugar,
Dénme razón de San Luis
Que le prometí bailar.

Coro:

Yana heya ho,
Yana heya ho,
Yana heya ho.
Yana heya ho,
Yana heya ho.

En el marco de esta puerta
El pie derecho pondré,
Denme razón de San Luis
Y luego le bailaré.

[Coro]

San Luis Gonzaga de Amarante
Aparecido en un puente,

Esta indita te compuse
Cuando mi hijo andaba ausente.

[Coro]

San Luis Gonzaga de Amarante
Aparecido en la mar,
Concédeme este milagro
Que te prometí bailar.

[Coro]

Dicen que la golondrina
De un volido pasó el mar,
De las Islas Filipinas
Que acabaron de pelear.

[Coro]

Santo Niñito de Atocha
Tú solito no más sabes,
El corazón de cada uno
También todas sus necesidades.

[Coro]

"BALLAD OF SAINT ALOYSIUS"

From my house I have come
To visit this place,
Tell me about Saint Aloysius
I promised to dance for him.

Chorus:

Yana heya ho,
Yana heya ho,
Yana heya ho.
Yana heya ho,
Yana heya ho.

In this doorway
I will put my right foot,
Tell me about Saint Aloysius
And then I will dance for him.

[Chorus]

Saint Aloysius Gonzaga of Amarante
Appeared on a bridge,
I composed this indita for you
When my son was absent.

[Chorus]

Saint Aloysius Gonzaga of Amarante
Appeared on the ocean,
Grant me this miracle
I promised to dance for you.

[Chorus]

They say the swallow
In one flight crossed the sea,
In the Philippine Islands
They have stopped fighting.

[Chorus]

Holy Child of Atocha
Only you know
The heart of each of us
And all our needs.

[Chorus]
    (Lamadrid and Loeffler 1989)

The musical style of this *indita* juxtaposes chromatic European melodies with pentatonic Indian choruses. There is no better musical demonstration of the unique New Mexican style of pluralistic *mestizaje*. This kind of code switching and cultural borrowing is nothing new to Iberians, who for centuries tolerated each other's religions and cultures. The ancient *jarcha* and Mozambic *haragat* lyrics were sung bilingually with Arabic or Hebrew verses interspersed with refrains in the Ibero-Romance dialect (Hall 1974:117). That the power of a miracle that saved New Mexican soldiers fighting Spain on behalf of the United States would come home to combine with *mestizo* spiritual healing traditions to heal the sick and bring rain to the desert is a tribute to the syncretic power of popular culture in New Mexico.

After the elite culture of Spanish intellectuals, clergy, and bureaucrats was done idealizing and denigrating the natives of the New World, the popular *mestizo* culture of Hispanics in Aztlán learned not only to laugh at the otherness of the Indians but to share in and benefit from their spirituality. With a history of this kind of cultural adaptation, there should be little concern for the *coyotes de americanos* of contemporary times and their search to evolve and validate yet another layer of *mestizaje* under the new lords of Aztlán.

NOTES

A short version of this article was presented at a symposium held at the Universidad de los Andes, Bogotá, Colombia, October 15, 1991.

1. *Moros y Cristianos* is performed on horseback by a company of players from Chimayó, New Mexico, forty miles northeast of Santa Fe, for the Fiesta de la Santa Cruz, May 3; the Fiesta de Santiago, July 26; and on other special occasions.

2. Once performed in several communities involved in the Comanche hostilities, notably Ranchos de Taos and Galisteo, today *Los Comanches* is performed for the Fiesta de San Juan Evangelista, December 27, in Alcalde, New Mexico, thirty-five miles north of Santa Fe. Ranchos de Taos still has traditional Comanche singing and dancing, especially on New Year's Day.

3. The Comanche nativity play is said to have originated in San Mateo, New Mexico, sixty miles west of Albuquerque, and was performed extensively in that area, in Albuquerque, and in Taos until recent times. Contemporary performances are still found in the Estancia valley, forty miles east of Albuquerque.

REFERENCES

Arellano, Estevan, and Tomás Atencio, eds. 1972. *Entre verde y seco*. Dixon, N.M.: Academia de la Nueva Raza.

Atencio, Tomás. 1985. "Social Change and Community Conflict in Old Albuquerque." Ph.D. diss., University of New Mexico.

Bancroft, Hubert Howe. 1889. *History of Arizona and New Mexico*. Vol. 13 of *History of the Pacific States*. San Francisco: History Company.

Benavides, Fray Alonso de. 1630. *Memorial*.

Campa, Arthur L. 1933. "The Spanish Folksong in the Southwest." *University of New Mexico Bulletin,* whole no. 232, 4, 1 (November 15).

————. 1942. "Los Comanches: A New Mexican Folk Drama." *University of New Mexico Bulletin,* whole no. 376, Language Series 7, 1 (April).

Chávez, Alex. n.d. *El Testamento: Spanish Folk Music of Northern New Mexico and Southern Colorado*. LP FV 22376. Albuquerque: Kirt M. Olson Associates.

Clews Parsons, Elsie. 1939. *Pueblo Indian Religion*. Chicago: University of Chicago Press.

Espinosa, Aurelio M. 1907. "Los Comanches: A New Mexican Spanish Heroic Play." *University of New Mexico Bulletin,* whole no. 45, Language Series 1.

————. 1985. *The Folklore of Spain in the American Southwest*. Ed. Manuel Espinosa. Norman: University of Oklahoma Press.

Espinosa, Reginaldo. 1933. "Cañute." *New Mexico Magazine* 11(5): 16–17, 46–48.

Gómez Canedo, Lino. 1960. "¿Hombres o bestias?" *Estudio de Historia Novohispana,* vol. 1. Mexico City: Instituto de Investigaciones Históricas.

Hall, R. A. 1974. *External History of the Romance Languages*. New York: American Elsevier.

Hanke, Lewis. 1965. *The Spanish Struggle for Justice in the Conquest of America*. Boston: Little, Brown and Co.

Hurt, Wesley R. 1966. "The Spanish-American Comanche Dance." *Journal of the Folklore Institute* 3(2): 116–32.

Lamadrid, Enrique R. 1990. "Tierra de pícaros: La picaresca en el folclor y la reciente literatura de Nuevo México." In *Culturas hispanas en los Estados Unidos de América.* Ed. María Jesús Buxó Rey and Tomás Calvo Buezas. Madrid: Ediciones de Cultura Hispánica, 581–89.

————. 1992. "Los Comanches: The Celebration of Cultural Otherness in New Mexican Winter Feasts." New Mexico Festival of American Folklife 1992 Archive. Smithsonian Center for Folklife and Cultural Studies.

Lamadrid, Enrique R., and Jack Loeffler. 1989. *Tesoros del espíritu / Treasures of the Spirit: A Sound Portrait of Hispanic New Mexico*. Santa Fe: Museum of International Folk Art.

Lamadrid, Enrique R., Jerome J. Martínez y Alire, and Jack Loeffler. 1991. *Del cielo y la tierra / Of Heaven and Earth: Alabados, oraciones y reflexiones sobre la Hermandad Piadosa de Nuestro Padre Jesús Nazareno*. Sound track exhibit in "Images of Penance,

Images of Mercy" exhibit on the Penitente Brotherhood. Colorado Springs, Taylor Museum.

Levernier, James, and Hennig Cohen, eds. 1977. *The Indians and Their Captives*. Westport, Conn.: Greenwood Press.

Limón, José E. 1987. "Aurelio M. Espinosa's Romantic View of Folklore." Paper presented at the annual meeting of the American Folklore Society, Albuquerque, New Mexico, October 21–25.

Loeffler, Jack. 1990. *Collection of Hispanic New Mexican Folk Music*. Albuquerque: University of New Mexico Fine Arts Library, John D. Robb Archive of Southwestern Music.

Lucero White Lea, Aurora. 1953. *Literary Folklore of the Hispanic Southwest*. San Antonio: Naylor.

Mendoza, Vicente T., and Virginia R. R. de Mendoza. 1986. *Estudio y clasificación de la música tradicional de Nuevo México*. Mexico City: Universidad Nacional Autónoma de México.

Ortega y Medina, Juan A. 1987. *Imagología del bueno y del mal salvaje*. Mexico City: Universidad Nacional Autónoma de México.

Ortiz, Alfonso. 1981. Introduction to *A Ceremony of Brotherhood*. Ed. Rudolfo Anaya and Simon Ortiz. Albuquerque: Academia, 8–17.

Pérez de Villagrá, Gaspar. 1610. *Historia de la Nueva México*. Alcalá: Luis Martínez Grande.

———. 1933. *History of New Mexico*. Trans. Gilberto Espinosa. Los Angeles: The Quivira Society.

Pino, Pedro Bautista. 1812. In *Noticias históricas y estadísticas de la antigua provincia del Nuevo México, presentadas por su diputado en cortes, Don Pedro Bautista Pino en Cádiz el año de 1812*. Ed. Don José Agustín De Escudero and Don Antonio Barreiro. Mexico City: Comisión de Estadística Militar, Imprenta de Lara, 1849.

Said, Edward. 1979. *Orientalism*. New York: Random House.

Spicer, Edward H. 1969. "Political Incorporation and Cultural Change in New Spain: A Study in Spanish-Indian Relations." In *Attitudes of Colonial Powers Toward the American Indian*. Ed. Howard Peckham and Charles Gibson. Salt Lake City: University of Utah Press, 107–35.

Steele, Thomas J., and Rowena Rivera. 1985. *Penitente Self-Government: Brotherhoods and Councils, 1797–1947*. Santa Fe: Ancient City Press.

Thomas, Alfred Barnaby. 1932. *Forgotten Frontiers: A Study of the Spanish Indian Policy of Don Juan Bautista de Anza, Governor of New Mexico, 1777–1787*. Norman: University of Oklahoma Press.

Todorov, Tzvetan. 1984. *The Conquest of America: The Question of the Other*. Trans. Richard Howard. New York: Harper and Row.

Index